WASSAILING

Reawakening an
Ancient Folk Custom

by
COLIN CATER

Edited, with additional material,
illustrations and design by

Karen Cater

edingham
Fair

www.hedinghamfair.co.uk

Published in Great Britain
by Hedingham Fair 2013

ISBN: 978-0-9556475-5-0

Printed in Great Britain by
The Five Castles Press
Ipswich

www.hedinghamfair.co.uk

To
all Wassailers
everywhere

ACKNOWLEDGEMENTS

*I would like to express gratitude to each of the people and or organisations named below
for their support in the development of this Project at all stages.
Each group is presented in alphabetical order*

The Head Teacher and pupils at Branscombe School, Devon; Jim Causley; Ned Clamp;
Sue Cubbin; Gail Duff; Valmai Goodyear; Sian Hayward and Andy McDuffie;
Vaughn Hully; Jenny Jingles; Kathy Wallis for contributing their experiences, songs &
poems and recipes that have helped to give the book much of its personal character.

Mary Humphreys and Anahata for setting the music for the songs.

Ian Horsley of Brandy Wharf Cider Centre and Grimsby Morris Men;
Emma Lile, Curator at St Fagans National History Museum, Cardiff;
The Lions Part Theatre Company; Jon MacNamara of Beerfordbury Barrel Tappers
and Wine Tipplers; Damon the Landlord of Barton Inn, Barton St David, Somerset;
Malcolm Taylor of EFDSS; Jameson Wooders for sharing their expertise,
materials and joys during the formative stages of the project.

Colin Dick; Dunster First School; Fran and Geoff Doel; Mark Lawson; Frazer McRae;
Taffy Thomas for permission to use original artwork and or writing.

St Fagans National History Museum, Cardiff; Ewenny Pottery, Bridgend
for permission to photograph Wassail Bowls in their collections.

Aelfgythe Border Morris; Barlaston Wassail; Elephant up a Pole Morris; Rachael Miller;
Peter Symonds; Widders Morris (Chepstow Wassail Bowl) for use of images.

Chiswick House; Headless Cross, Redditch, Worcs; Lamb Inn Sandford, Devon;
The Lions Part Theatre Company; Lower Uppacott Farm Tedburn, Devon;
Raglan Cider Mill, Monmouthshire for use of wassail event posters.

Common Ground; EFDSS; the Transition Network for use of logos.

Alara Foods of Kings Cross, London; Chanctonbury Ring Morris Men;
Alistair Waugh and Headless Cross Wassailers; Plum Jerkum Morris
for welcoming us into their 2013 celebrations.

Above all to my wife, Karen Cater for her indefatigable labours without which
this Project would probably never have become a book:
specifically her written contributions, photography, illustrations, editing,
typesetting, proof reading and soothing the grumpy old beast.

Contents

Italics denote diary entries, personal accounts and poems

Introduction

Setting the Scene

Wassail, wassail all over the town
Our toast it is white and our ale it is brown

The word 'Wassail', sometimes 'Waes Hael' or 'Waes bu Hael' is a salutation of Scandinavian and medieval origin, meaning 'Be of good health', and frequently used as a drinking toast or to generally wish people well. This account tells how this 'pledge' developed over centuries into customs connected with preparation for and celebration of the Twelve Day Festival of Christmas. Several different types of wassailing customs became widespread, then later contracted or became modified in response to changing social conditions. By the mid twentieth century wassailing had all but stopped, not quite the Sword of Damocles suspended above, but continuous tradition hanging by very few threads indeed.

"Wassail!" - a drinking toast

Then in the mid C20, something remarkable happened – the 'Folk Song Club Movement' unearthed a very rich vein of Wassail songs. This movement also unleashed a wave of interest in (local) English heritage, sending people scurrying into Museums, Libraries and newspaper offices in search of old songs, Mummers Plays and to discover what old customs including wassailing were really like. Wassailing had already restarted at Dunkeswell, Devon in 1953; then in 1967, Chanctonbury Ring Morris Men got it going again (they call it 'Howling' in Sussex). In 1974 Taunton Cider Company started their wassail again at Norton Fitzwarren, Somerset. Follow up to this was initially slow, gathering pace in the 1980s and 1990s before a great whoosh since the Millennium. Now folk enthusiasts, commercial cider orchards, visitor attractions, villages, pubs, schools and 'community orchards' have all taken up the old custom, often developing the event into a compelling extended entertainment, and in 2013 Wassailing has been well and truly re-awakened.

Karen and I are both keen folk enthusiasts, active since we were young, initially in folk clubs, then as performers and musicians; since 1997 through Hedingham Fair designing and selling folk images. We've been part of ceremonial events, including 'Hunting the Earl of Rone' at Combe Martin, North Devon, with the Good Easter Molly Gang and the annual Morris weekend at Thaxted, Essex, as well as countless folk festivals. Our practical interest in wassailing goes back to 1998, holding our first wassail in our newly planted orchard at home. In 1997, we had produced the 'Joy come to our Jolly Wassail' image based on another recently reawakened wassail event. Since then more images have come and we've featured Wassailing several times in the Calendar of Traditional Customs.

Hedingham Fair's first Wassail design; 'Joy come to our Jolly Wassail', 1997

We regard Wassailing as a folk activity, but it's difficult to locate it within many of the ideologies that pervade folk thinking, in particular those associated with Cecil Sharp's English Folk Songs: Some Conclusions (1907). Its notions of 'The Folk', an 'ideal type', miraculously isolated in the countryside, untainted by contemporary fashion and communications media, carrying 'pure' musical / cultural heritage orally to be transmitted when the 'collector' arrives, doesn't square up with real life either now or in times past. What about travelling theatre or with print material such as Almanacks, Chapbooks, Broadside Ballads all circulating freely in the countryside during C19 and before?

What about radio in C20? Whatever the genius of the country environment may be in transforming songs, dances, tunes and ceremonies into the high art recovered by collectors, oral transmission alone is not the whole story. Neither does it explain folk transmission as population has both grown and become more urbanised, or in the age of electronic and digital media.

During the early stages of the 'Folk Song Club Movement' it was fashionable to regard folk activity as socially exclusive, the purview of working class people only. In relation to wassailing this also doesn't stand close analysis, either then or now! Then farm based wassailing likely involved the whole farm community: if several farms were involved (Mrs Leather, 1912) this extended to an entire area. House visiting included both visiting parties and those who received them, often the well-to-do, who were well aware of their (giving) role in the ceremonial. Whilst respecting radical ideologies, evidence argues against approaches seeking to divide communities antagonistically along either social class or religious (see below) lines. We are all 'The Folk'.

Largely for these reasons, we have decided not to use the term 'Revival' when examining what's happened to Wassailing in the last fifty years. We will instead describe this as 'Reawakening'. The term 'Revival' will be used, but will principally be confined to two periods of intense activity in C20 when folk culture was systematically got going again: between 1900 and the early 1920s, then again between the late 1950s and the mid 1970s. At other times during C20 - 21, 'folk' has been an established movement, albeit a minority popular interest, but with significant numbers of active participants. Both C20 folk revivals drew on 'field performers', some of whom (Bampton Morris for example) continue into modern times. As far as Wassailing is concerned, continuously surviving ceremonies have been much less available as a model. During the Reawakening, as an alternative, Wassail organisers have drawn on a substantial archive of songs

Programme and song sheet for our first Wassailing Party, 17th January 1998.

Wassailing Party

· JANUARY 17ᵀᴴ 1998 – being Old Twelfth Night

Wassailing is an ancient (mainly West Country) custom which happens on Old Twelfth Night, and whose principal purpose is to ensure the safe and abundant growth of next year's fruit (cider apple) crop. Last year we planted several fruit trees and as we wish to encourage their rapid development without (much) resort to chemical assistance, what better than to give them as much wassailing as possible!!!

and written records. Latterly this has been supplemented by practical hands-on experience. A major part of both C20 folk revivals has seen collected material transformed through books, new song writing and choreography, orchestral music and by many other means. Wassailing too has changed as it has reinvigorated – whilst retaining a strong core of purpose and ceremonial, it has diversified as it has spread. Many modern wassail events have new sponsors, including types of organisations which simply didn't exist in times past.

The old custom lives again but in a Re-awakened form.

Approaching the task

So how might we approach our task? At the outset we had little idea of its scale but we knew we wanted to make use of actual human experience, both our own and other people's, as this had enriched both Karen's earlier books. We also wanted a recognisable basis in social theory that would reflect our world view. Colin brought his social science background into play, particularly mapping exercises undertaken by Burrell and Morgan (1979). These identified four schools of thought distinguishing between subjective and objective views of the world, and rival sociological approaches between understanding the world as it is observed (the sociology of regulation) and those seeking understanding through a Marxist framework (the sociology of radical change). We are drawn towards the Interpretative school, combining a subjective approach with an understanding of the world as it is, examining the fundamental nature of the social world at the level of personal experience. We are happy to see the social world (of wassailing) as an emergent social process created by the individuals involved. We are also comfortable with a view of the world as problematical, subject to regular re-appraisal and change, whilst assuming that human affairs are cohesive, ordered and integrated. The Interpretative approach, first developed by Kant in C18, seeks to evaluate social activity by concentrating more on its spiritual aspects than on how it is ordered or on economic materialism. Our aim was to understand the realities of organising and / or participating in wassails, within the stream of consciousness of those taking part, following the theoretical lead of Alfred Schutz (1967). It would however be grandiose to describe this work as sociology.

Because of the almost total disconnect between times past and the wassail reawakening, we decided quite early on to separate the previous era from more recent events, and to limit the scope of enquiry to solely British experience. The book divides into two parts, with the first three chapters examining Wassailing in tradition: Christmas festivities involving extensive use of the Wassail Bowl; house visiting peregrinations; agricultural blessings especially of apple trees. All information for these chapters has been obtained from a literature search in 2012, with information widely scattered in books and journals. This also yielded a cornucopia of songs, rhymes, incantations and recipes. Part Two looks at modern times, separating events according to a selection based on who their organisers were. Separate chapters will review wassails organised by Morris and Folk organisations; commercial cider orchards and visitor attractions; wassails taking place within local communities; wassails in 'Community Orchards'. On several occasions individual wassails seemed to overlap more than one category: with each individual event where this happened we were guided by who the principal organiser seemed to be. In some cases the allocations were very marginal. Though we are aware that the majority of wassails that have survived in unbroken tradition from times past into the present are house visiting ceremonies (see Ch 7), the vast majority of modern wassails involve the blessing of apple trees. For this reason we have decided to treat

The Wassail Bowl.

the Apple Tree Wassailing ceremony at Carhampton, Somerset as the pivot between past and present – we hope this will not cause offence in Bodmin or elsewhere.

Much of the information for Part Two has come from an internet search to locate wassails currently happening in the UK: in 2012, we'd expected to find between fifty and sixty but ended in a state of dizzy delight at nearly three times that number. From each find, we copied as much website information as possible, sorting this initially by County. This has enabled us to provide much detail on individual wassails either in the words of participants or from press reports. Interpretation of evidence avoids approaches matching wassails against any pre-determined ceremony structure or by a set of rules to be 'proved' by a research programme. We thought it better to see things from the standpoint of participants who know their events best, and talked to as many people as we could who were involved in Wassailing. We became aware of several issues that would need thoughtful comment, including timings of ceremonies and the influence or otherwise of religion. Both of these issues will be discussed in the main text. Then rude commerce intervened: we had to get into Hedingham Fair marketing and selling mode, so for six months until early 2013 the work stopped.

Apple Howling, Bolney, West Sussex, 5th January 2013

By the time we resumed, some issues had crystallized, so our break had been advantageous. From early 2013, we have visited a number of wassails though there would have been more, particularly from the West Country had not snowstorms intervened. Our visits will appear as Diary entries, and are supported with exchanges of e-mails, informal conversations, written contributions from friends and our own personal involvement as wassail organisers. Apart from the 'Diary Entries', in order to prevent too much repetition, we will try to avoid narrative descriptions of individual ceremonies and events, preferring to concentrate on salient points that make events individual, original and in many cases unique. Towards the end of the book we will include a repertoire of Wassail songs and chants and a selection of recipes. The whole Project is copiously illustrated, principally by Karen's images and photographs as she has typeset the book. All contributions from people other than ourselves will be acknowledged as they appear.

Folklore, Religion and Magic

Prior to the advent of 'folklore', a word coined in 1846 by William J. Thoms, most writings on Wassailing are contained in publications best described as "Popular Antiquities". These include C17 diaries (Samuel Pepys, John Aubrey etc) and Almanacks such as Poor Robin's Almanac. The first elaborate commentary on annual customs was Henry Bourne's 'Antiquitates Vulgares' (1725) subsequently incorporated into John Brand's Observations on Popular Antiquities (1777), followed by William Hone's Every Day Book (1825 and 1827), and Robert Chambers' Book of Days (1869). Apart from Bourne (Puritan) all adopt a value free, non sectarian approach.

'Folklore' brought changes in both method and concept, adopting a narrower view, "of the common people, usually country people, whose culture was handed down orally". At the same time, search for English national identity fostered interest amongst the colonial classes in folk pursuits outside England. Contemporary theories of cultural evolution (of folk myths etc.) from hypothetical 'Aryan' origins led to customs being described as 'survivals', often from primitive, i.e. pre-Christian religions (E. B. Tylor, 1871). James Frazer's 'The Golden Bough' (1890) promoted country ceremonies as 'fertility rituals'. Gentlemen, clerics and others took to the lanes and villages, enquiring about country ways: stories, beliefs, herbal remedies etc, later written up in (so called) learned journals. They often adopted a condescending attitude, with ordinary English people often called 'peasants' – unlettered, uncultured and uncivilized. Prior to the late C19, in sharp contrast to this view, Wassailing had frequently involved interaction between all social groups, sometimes with social inversions such as the Lord of Misrule or King Bean and Queen Pea as a social safety valve.

Following Tylor and Frazer, paganism became fashionable. Contemporary folklore reports of 'County Associations', are crammed with 'witchcraft', 'magic' 'charms and spells', and 'herbal lore', creating the impression of a magical or pagan rural culture, possibly antithetical to and in competition with Church and social establishment. This helped to fuel the possibly mistaken view surviving into current times of wassailing having 'Pagan Origins'. When in 1906 Cecil Sharp felt able to assert positively "Wassailing songs and carols associated with the May Day festival are 'Pagan survivals' ..." (Some Conclusions, [1906], P.125), this was adopted enthusiastically, so that on many, many occasions Morris Dances have been introduced to modern audiences with words like "This dance is an ancient Pagan fertility rite......"

But did Wassailing have 'Pagan origins?' Was it a 'Pagan Survival'? In The Pagan Religions of the Ancient British Isles (1991), Ron Hutton substantially plays down notions of major parts of Medieval Christianity being based on pagan survivals. He also draws clear distinction between religion and magic: country people practiced both, religion on Sundays to request a

Magic; forget conjuring tricks, this is real.
Magic is the manipulation of events in the physical realm by the application of one's will.
In practical terms, it is the focusing and directing of spiritual power by means of intention, or the altering of one's state of mind to achieve the desired change.
Doctors call it the 'placebo effect', Christians would call it 'the answer to a prayer'

from the Ogham Sketchbook (2007) by Karen Cater

better life after death from God; magic at all other times to improve the here and now through their own efforts (to heal illness, recover stolen property, invoke good luck in a building or increase the yield of land or crops – day to day things well beneath the concern of the almighty). At times Christian monotheism did its level best to ban magic, invoking dread terms like 'Satan', 'The Devil' and 'Witchcraft', but this failed utterly and evidence suggests that by C18 & 19, many in the Church were able to accept country low magic and ceremony with some facility. As Wassailing ceremonies, particularly those connected with crops or animals or fruit trees are undoubtedly magical in both intent and nature, does this necessarily make them 'pagan'? Whereas Frazer (1890) argues that for many peoples, the tree was animated by the tree spirit, Hutton (1991) comments that beyond the concept of 'sacred groves' which were nowhere near as commonplace as sacred wells or springs, ancient pagan religions were not overly concerned with trees. Academic literature seems to provide comfort both for arguments in favour of 'Pagan origins / survivals' and for the opposite viewpoint. Apart from asserting that wassailing is both spiritual and magical we are content to comment on matters of religion only insofar as they impinge directly on individual wassail ceremonies.

Social, Cultural and Political Background

In this book, Wassailing has been examined over a period lasting nearly a millennium, but with stronger focus on the last two hundred and fifty years, roughly from 1770 to the present time. At the beginning of that period social conditions were stable, though the agrarian and industrial revolutions were in their formative stages. Wassailing in both house visiting and agricultural blessing versions was thriving almost everywhere, a situation held in common with going a-Maying, harvest customs, Morris Dancing, Mumming and a host of other activities now regarded as 'traditional' or part of England's heritage. This was also true of country song and music, all over the British Isles as it gradually evolved through an interactive process encompassing both town and countryside. Arguably the basis of social order: the Manor, the Parish; the County and national institutions all had a stake in maintaining the stability of the social system. Rich and poor were all involved together, and evidence suggests they were each aware of their respective roles in ensuring its continuance.

As changes to social and economic structure began to take effect during early C19, seed corn was sown for cultural changes that would follow in their wake, not always immediately as the pattern of customs gradually broke down. An early change was the reduction of the Twelve Days festival of Christmas as Epiphany; 6th January, became detached. Breakdown of Elizabethan Poor Relief through the Parishes and its replacement after the 1834 Poor Law Amendment Act with Victorian workhouses, probably contributed to better off people gradually losing both their role and involvement in local money raising customs. Issues connected with management of towns (sewerage, public health) gave rise to greater regulation that later spilled over into the countryside, so that social inversions as safety valves were no longer understood and became condemned as excesses. Also contributory to the changes was the development of a new urban culture, particularly Music Hall songs, that was unlike what had gone before and been shared between town and countryside. These new songs passed out into the countryside after 1850, so that reports by early C20 folk song collectors say that at some point between 1840 and 1870, the old songs (and perhaps dances and customs as well) had not passed down from the elder to the upcoming generation (Cecil Sharp, 1907). Not that the death of the old ways was immediate, in some areas they live on into current time, but disconnection had developed between town and country, that by the mid C20 had placed obstacles in the way of social and cultural understanding between town and country.

The success of the Wassail Reawakening, particularly since 2000 suggests that some of the forces of disconnect may have become ameliorated by C21. Much of the turbulence of C20 (two World Wars, the Cold War and the ideological struggle between right and left) has given way to a period of greater calm. Struggles for minority rights have led to legislation outlawing much antagonistic behaviour; and to recognition of the need to involve as many people and organisations as possible if change is to be managed successfully. Excessive centralisation has unleashed counterbalancing forces: supermarkets counterbalanced with organic and sustainable food production; monopolistic media counterbalanced by the internet. These phenomena, and probably others as well, have heralded conditions in which individualism can flourish. Wassailing has been one of the beneficiaries.

Making use of this book

We initially approached the preparatory work for this book with a fair amount of certainty as to what we might find. This evaporated almost as soon as reading began to yield substantive information. Over time information began to meld, sublimated intellectually so that some 'realities' presented here may seem to have developed effortlessly for us, like pennies dropping in the learning of childhood.

pre-Christmas collecting customs included wassailing.

This is an illusion. We marvelled at the differences in orchard ceremonies based in different places – more at the common elements of blessing that cemented them all together. We were surprised at the manner in which preferred dates for Wassailing shifted and are still shifting. We have still to unravel the full story behind all the pre-Christmas collecting customs, although a direction for further enquiry is beginning to emerge. All of this was taking place before we saw the flexibility and variation in modern Wassail interpretations and marvelled again.

Anyone starting a Wassail may well feel that the world is their oyster – that they can configure their Wassail in whatever way may seem most appropriate. To a considerable extent this may be true provided that it is done in a spirit which blesses and honours what is being wassailed –trees, or people or animals or even buildings. Tradition also has a central core of both practice and belief. We are unsure about the place of religion both now and in times past – Wassailing seems to belong to no religion in particular and yet to be capable of being part of any of them. If anyone approaches this book with fixed beliefs, either faith based or secular we would urge that they examine these in a spirit of finding accommodation. This may involve a need to reflect on views and other matters held dear – we have had to do this.

The text is offered in a linear scheme, but each part of it also exists discretely in its own right, so that the reader can choose whether to approach things cover to cover, or whether to dip specifically into a particular section. However you approach what we've offered we hope the experience is an enjoyable one.

Karen and Colin Cater

April 2013

Part 1

Chapter 1

The Wassail Bowl

Early origins

Among the customs and ceremonies that characterise the English calendar, Wassail or Wassailing is one able to lay claim to great antiquity. Although formal records suggest its first emergence during medieval times, shadowy literary references indicate the possibility of much earlier origins.

The salutation 'Wassail' probably derives from the Anglo Saxon "Waes bu hael" meaning "Be of good health" and consists of two Old English components, 'waes' and 'hael'. Its oldest legend involves Rowena, daughter of Hengist, a Saxon mercenary, who presents the future King Vortigern with a bowl of mulled wine and the cheer "Waes Hael!", to which Vortigern replies "Drinc Hael", now recognised as the traditional reply. This is recorded in Geoffrey of Monmouth's History of the Kings of Britain (c.1140), written in the langauge of C12 but refering to events in C5.

One of the earliest representation of a toasting scene from Bayeaux Tapestry made around 1070

Other early litarary references suggest existence of the word Wassail prior to medieval times and its use both as a salutation and to describe drinking festivities.

A greeting in the epic poem 'Beowulf' written between the 8th and 11th centuries;

"Waes thu hal"
The rider sleepeth,
the hero, far-hidden; no harp resounds,
in the courts no wassail, as once was heard.

Rejoice and wassail! - a Saxon toasting cry before the Battle of Hastings in 1066

Recording similar usage, an anonymous Anglo-Norman Poet witnesses a Saxon toasting cry before the Battle of Hastings in 1066, and writes:

"Rejoice and wassail!
Pass the bottle and drink healthy
Drink backwards and drink to me
Drink half and drink empty."

An alternative window on ancient times is suggested by the possible linguistic origin of the drink 'Lambswool', very much associated with Wassailing and Wassail Bowls in both late Medieval times and subsequently. The Gentlemen's Magazine for May, 1784 quotes Charles Vallancey, an expert on Irish antiquities, who suggests derivation from the Irish 'La Mas Ubhal' - the day of the apple fruit. This was the first day of November, dedicated to the angel presiding over fruits, seeds, etc. According to The Gentleman's Magazine, the angel referred to is the Roman Goddess Pomona. Vallancey identifies the pronunciation of 'La Mas Ubhal' as Lamasool, from which comes 'Lambs-wool'.

Pomona was the Roman goddess of fruit trees, gardens, and orchards, watching over and protecting the fruit, a wood nymph and guardian spirit associated with the flourishing of the fruit trees themselves. There is a grove sacred to her called the Pomonal, located not far from Ostia, an ancient port of Rome. Even allowing for C18 romanticism, this offers the possibility of very ancient lineage for aspects of Wassail ceremonial, if not for the actual word itself. Celebration of La Mas Ubhal, Nov 1st, also represents an interesting precursor, both to modern Pagan Samhain, and to the recent launch of 'Apple Day' by the environmental charity Common Ground - a celebration of the apple harvest, often the second weekend in October.

While the word 'Wassail' is of Northern European derivation, Steve Roud's (2006) view is that its use as anything other than a (drinking) salutation; is probably Medieval English. It was firmly embedded in the English language by the mid C13, not only as a personal drinking salutation, but a festive occasion with much drinking and pledging of healths; a carouse especially around Christmas or

Pomona, Roman goddess of fruit trees, gardens, and orchards, watching over and protecting the fruitfulness of the trees.

the New Year, with the liquor used likely to be a form of spiced ale or Lambswool, (see Recipes Appendix) or mead spiced with sweet herbs. Songs would be sung. Entertainment, sometimes very elaborate would be provided. On many occasions the social order would be inverted for the duration of the festivity and copious amounts of drink would be passed round in a sometimes enormous wassail bowl decked with ribbons and evergreens.

The Wassail Bowl

The 'Wassail Bowl or cup' has been described as a 'High medieval invention' – mentioned by Matthew Paris in C13, in which cakes and fine bread were communally dipped. In the great families it was made of precious metal – silver for the Earl of March d. 1382. (Ron Hutton, 1994) It was not always used for benign purposes. In Caxton's Chronicle [c.1480] the account of the death of King John describes a poisoned wassail cup filled with supposedly good ale; the monk bearing it, knelt down, saying, "Syr, wassayll for euer the dayes so all lyf dronke ye of so good a cuppe.", the Monk being all too well aware that his sovereign's days would indeed be short, and he would never get to drink of such a cup again.

Sandys (1852) reports a payment of a hundred shillings made, in the reign of Edward II (1284-1327), to Isabelle del Holde and Alisoun Conand, damsels of the queen, for crying Noël and Wessel. Wassailing was carried out at court in the reign of Henry VII (1485 - 1509), recorded in the Collection of Ordinances of the Royal Household (Thistleton Dyer, 1876). The Wassail Bowl would be accompanied into the King's presence by the chief officers of the household, bearing staves. Peter de Langtoft recounts a C14 custom involving the Wassail Bowl, in which each person in turn took the bowl and cried "Wassail". He was answered "Drinkhail!" before drinking from the bowl and passing it to another person with a kiss. (Ron Hutton: 1994)

Generally, medieval wassailing took place during the Twelve Days of Christmas; a time of extensive merrymaking in which

17th century, turned wooden wassail bowls with lids may have finials in the shape of miniature cups and covers in the form of a lidded box. These were used to contain valuable spices for the flavouring of the hot wassail drink.

feasting, pageants, drinking, carousing and entertainment were commonplace amongst the well to do. Although Christmas Day itself was a highly significant day in the Calendar, so too was the New Year, and Twelfth Day/Night or Epiphany when the visit of the Three Kings to adore the Christ Child was celebrated robustly as a distinct occasion. Never mind the religion – it was another opportunity for a good beano! Why should there be any attempt to telescope the whole Christmas saga into one or two days, as happens nowadays?

One of the oldest carols known, "Seignors Ore Entendez À Nus", translation from Sandys (1847). Although this is Anglo-Norman, it embodies the Saxon pledging phrases.

Wassail, Wassail out of the milk pail,
Wassail, Wassail as white as my nail
Wassail, Wassail in snow frost and hail
Wassail, Wassail that much does avail
Wassail, Wassail that never will fail

This song was first recorded in 1550 – quoted in John Brand (1813) and W. Sandys: Festive Songs and Carols (1847)

Wassailing at New Year was kept up in the monasteries as well. In front of the Abbot, at the upper end of the refectory table, was placed the mighty bowl styled in Church Latin *Poculum Caritatis*, and from it the superior drank to all, and all drank in succession to each other (Chambers, 1864). Jesus College, in Oxford University, still has a Wassail bowl that could hold 10 gallons of drink and is covered in silver!

Many festivities in which the Wassail Bowl featured also involved 'turning the world upside down'. During Twelfth Night celebrations, sometimes called the Festival of Kings (Hone, 1825) the Wassail Bowl was always passed around. It was a time for Masques and fancy dress. 'Three Kings Cake'; usually a plum cake was eaten in honour of the Three Kings, with one slice being set aside "for God." Immortalized by Robert Herrick in his poem 'Twelfth Night' recipes for the cake may vary but they almost always include a dried bean hidden inside (see Recipes appendix). The person getting the dried bean became King or Queen for the Day and got to choose a consort. An alternative method was to bake two cakes, one for the men with a bean for the King, the other for the women, with a dried pea for the Queen. Once chosen, all normal social conventions were set aside and the King and Queen treated as royalty for the duration. When they drink, the company might cry out "The King (or Queen) drinks!" and take a sip of their own beverages. The idea of Queene of the Bean is traceable back at least as far as a letter of 1563 from Thomas Randolph to Robert Dudley, Earl of Leicester. Sometimes a clove was hidden in the cake as well and whoever received the piece containing it became the Fool. (Chambers, 1864) During the nineteenth century, Twelfth night cakes became more and more magnificent. This was the last swing of revelry before Distaff Day and Plough Monday when work was taken up again after the long holiday (Katherine Briggs, 1974).

Herrick in his poem Twelfth Night (C17):

Next crowne the bowle full with gentle Lamb's Wool;
Add sugar, nutmeg, and ginger
With store of ale too and thus ye must doe
To make the Wassaile a swinger.

C17 Wassail bowls from the collection of St Fagans National History Museum, Cardiff. It is not certain whether any of these bowls would originally have been lidded.
1. Mid C17 dark (possibly lignum vitae) wooden bowl Approx 4.5 inches high. Turned, with straight and wavy edged bands of incised decoration.
2.& 3. late C17 – early C18 turned wooden bowls with pedestal and foot Approx 10 ins high. Raised decorative bands around rim, middle and lower bowl. Decorative turned ridges on foot. 2 has large chip in rim extending to upper raised band.
4. late C18 – early C19 wooden bowl with pedestal and foot Approx 7 inches high. Turned, with raised decorative bands on lower bowl. Decorative turned ridges on foot.

2   3   4

1

This method and the social inversions of Twelfth Night or Old Christmas Eve celebration, i.e. 5th January, coming just at the end of the midwinter period, may echo a much older spiritual belief – this is the night when the Wild Hunt rides and chaos traditionally rules as the otherworldly horde break through into human realms.

Within many private houses, at New Year, the head of the house might gather his family around a bowl of spiced ale, in which ale or dark beer was whipped to form a surface froth in which floated roasted crab apples. The hissing pulp bursting from them resembled wool, one of the recognized derivations of the name 'Lambswool'. From the Bowl the Master drank the health of the entire company; then passed the Bowl to everyone else in turn as a form of loving cup, that they might drink too, using the ancient Saxon phrase, Wass Hael (Chambers, 1864).

Shakespeare alludes to Lamb's Wool in Love's Labour's Lost (1595):

When all aloud the wind doth blow
And coughing drowns the parson's saw
And birds sit brooding in the snow
And Marian's nose looks red and raw,
When roasted crabs hiss in the bowl,
Then nightly sings the staring owl,
Tu-whit, Tu-who—a merry note,
While greasy Joan doth keel the pot.

Shakespeare, also in Love's Labours Lost, writes:

'*He is wit's peddler, and retails his ware*
At wakes and wassels, meetings, markets, fairs.'

While Hamlet says:

'*The King doth wake to-night, and takes his rouse,*
Keeps Wassel.'

The expense book of Sir John Francklyn (1625) contains the notation: "Paid for the cup 1s 6d." Hone (1832) explained this as payment for drink from the wassail-cup. Near Snodland, in Kent, is the C16 mansion of Groves, once belonging to the Hawks family, part of which was pulled down in the late C18. During the demolition, an antique oak beam was found supporting the chimney, on which was a carving of a Wassail Bowl with on either side the words 'Wass hell' and 'Drinc hello'. The two birds on the bowl are hawks—the name of the family who originally owned the mansion.

The Gentleman's Magazine (1784) describes a Yorkshire variant of Wassail Bowl festivities. A family might invite friends to play cards and to have supper in which mince pies were an essential part. After supper the Wassail cup was passed round. Each person in turn would take a roasted apple out of the ale with a spoon, eat the apple and then drinking the health of everyone present, wishing each a Merry Christmas and Happy New Year.

In some houses Christmas could last for up to twenty days or even go on till Candlemas (February 2nd).

The American Washington Irving (1783-1859) describes a C19 English "Christmas Dinner," When the cloth was removed, the butler brought in a huge silver vessel of rare and curious workmanship, which he placed before the squire. ... The Wassail Bowl, so renowned in Christmas festivity. The contents had been prepared by the squire himself; for it was a beverage in the skilful mixture of which he particularly prided himself: alleging that it was too abstruse and complex for the comprehension of an ordinary servant. It was a potation, indeed, that might well make the heart of a toper leap within him; being

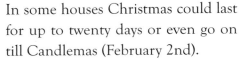

composed of the richest and raciest wines, highly spiced and sweetened, with roasted apples bobbing about the surface."

Perhaps the wassail bowl and country house Christmas is best celebrated in the nineteenth century Cornish song 'Carol for Twelfth Day', from a MS of Cornish Carols compiled for Davies Gilbert, the MP for Truro in about 1826, when the carols were already considered to be old. The song is a cornucopia of conviviality, with the suggestion in the refrain line that each member of the company had brought at least one dish to the party – final verse given here: full text and tune in the back of the book (p215)

Therefore you are to be commended if in this you will not fail,
Now our song is almost ended fill our bowl with nappy ale;
And we'll drink a full carouse to the master of this house,
Aye and to our mistress dear, wishing both a happy year
With peace and love without control who liquored well our wassail bowl.
Let every loyal, honest soul contribute to our wassail bowl.

The wassail bowl was an essential part of Victorian family Christmas celebrations.

To this day, many of the Corporation feasts of London still preserve the well-known ceremony of the Loving Cup that has almost certainly evolved from the Wassail Bowl. The custom is said to have originated in the precaution to keep the right, or 'dagger' hand, employed so that the person who drinks may be assured of no treachery A double-handled flagon full of sweetened and spiced wine (usually called Sack) is handed to the person presiding. Standing up he drinks to the general health, as announced by the toastmaster; then passes it to his neighbour on the left hand, who stands and drinks, then to the next person who also stands, and so on it goes, till all have drunk.

History of Wassail bowl Design

During the 17th century, lidded wassail bowls on stemmed feet were traditionally turned from the exotic and precious Lignum Vitae, a durable, hard, dense oily wood which will sink in water, imported from the West Indies. Lignum Vitae was used for wassail bowls as its high oil content makes it resistant to hot liquids, its density allows it to take incised decoration well and it was widely believed that the wood contained medicinal properties which would cure disease.

Finials in the shape of acorns often adorn the tops of wassail bowls, or miniature cups and covers in the form of a lidded box. Traditionally these were used to contain the (then) extremely valuable spices for the flavouring of the hot wassail.

Wassail bowl designs varied with locality and fashion, as well as the status of the user. Some wooden bowls were decorated with turned or carved designs, or mounted with silver rims and perhaps its owner's coat of arms, whether a family, guild, or corporation.

While many wassail bowls were wooden, ceramic bowls were also made by local potters. However the breakable nature of pottery has resulted in fewer of these surviving down the years.

In South Wales, at the beginning of C19 a highly ornate style of lidded wassail bowl with many handles and loops, richly decorated with figures and chickens, was developed by the Jenkins family at Ewenny pottery, several examples of which can be seen at St Fagans National History Museum, Cardiff, and they are still being made to this day. There were usually 18 handles, to which ribbons were tied, before being paraded as the centrepiece of the customary New Year visiting.

1. 1611 silver mounted, incised decoration of lion and unicorn flanking, the rose of England, Gloucester Folk Museum

2. 1640-1680 Lignum Vitae & Ivory, V&A

3. Charles II (1660-1685) Lignum Vitae

4. 1680-90 yew

5. 1675-1700 earthenware, Wiltshire V&A

6. 1682 earthenware, Wiltshire V&A

7. William & Mary (1689-1702)

8. 1702 earthenware, Wiltshire V&A

9. C17 Lignum Vitae, Silver-mounted, with coat-of-arms of Grocer's Company, Birmingham museum

10. C17 Lignum Vitae, decorated with painted Bacchus, Ceredigion museum.

11. George II (midC18) Lignum Vitae, Silver mounted

12. C19 Lignum Vitae, Silver band.

13. C18 & C19 Wassail bowl Dipper cups, various

all photographs posted on the world wide web.

14

Ewenny Pottery Wassail Bowls;

14. 1890's Earthenware, yellow glaze over white slip, sgraffito decoration* From the collection of St Fagans National Museum.

15. 1910 - Earthenware, green glaze over white slip, sgraffito decoration*. Highly ornate bowl with 18 handles (said to represent the many people taking part in the ceremony). Domed lid decorated with looped handles and moulded chickens, male and female figures and animals between handles, topped with a moulded cockrel. Designed by Rev J H Crossley, precentor of Ely Cathedral.
This is a particularly unusual bowl, being green; most Ewenny bowls are yellow glaze over white slip. From the collection of St Fagans National Museum. (Information from Emma Lile, curator.)

*white clay is mixed with water to form a liquid ('slip') the consistency of cream, into which the pot is dipped, covering it with a thin white coating. This allows decoration to be scratched through, revealing the underlying red earthenware clay, a technique called 'sgraffito'. The pot may then be glazed with a transparent colour, usually yellow at Ewenny.

16. 2010, by Caitlin Jenkins. Asymetrical handles were often used on items from Ewenny since late C19. From Ewenny Pottery, Ewenny, nr Bridgend, Vale of Glamorgan, S. Wales.

15

16

photo - Widders Border Morris

photo by kind permission of Kathy Wallis

Modern Wassail Bowls

17. *Chepstow Wassail Bowl Red earthenware bowl with honey coloured slip decoration; "WASSAIL WASSAIL ALL AROUND THE TOWN", made in 2006 for the 'Wassail and Mari Lwyd' organised by Widders Border Morris.*

18. *Rillaton Wassail bowl, oiled beech, c.2005, turned by a local craftswoman. Rillaton, Cornwall.*

19 & 20. *Turned by Mick Duff from a huge apple tree from Blean near Canterbury that was blown down in the 1987 hurricane. Decorated by a local silversmith and paid for by South East Arts. Used at wassails in Kent at Badlesmere, near Faversham; Waldron, in the Wealden District; Doddington & Mersham. (information from Gail Duff, folk animateur and organiser of Rabble Folk Theatre)*

photos by kind permission of Gail Duff

Wassail Bowls from our own collection;

21 & 22. Three handled Wassail bowls commissioned from Frazer McRae (Steeple Bumpstead, Essex), decorated with apples, apple trees and wassail rhymes.
23 & 24. Three handled Whimple Wassail bowl & Hedingham Fair's Wassail bowl (both by Ark Pottery, Wiggaton, S.Devon)
25. Three handled Wassail bowl by Paul Jessop (Barrington Court, Somerset)

Chapter 2

Here we come a-wassailing

We are not daily beggars that beg from door to door
We are neighbours children that you have seen before

Among the leaves so green

do were fathoming their several gallon
uerading with their Beans and Peas, what
ry of England doing: the farm labourers,
e weavers and spinners, the miners, the
acks of all trades, the children and young
s it should come as no surprise that they
nstead of passing the Wassail Bowl around
carried one around from house to house,

*The Wassail Bowl
was carried around
from house to house.*

offering drink and salutation, sometimes with other small gifts as well, in return for money, or food and drink likely worth much more than the offerings they carried themselves (John Brand, 1813). House visiting customs with a wassail bowl had become established by 1600 (Ron Hutton, 1994) and were located all over the country. The bowl adorned with ribbons and greenery was carried around the neighbourhood. In some places a tree bough would be carried, but the intention was to collect money so that poorer people too might enjoy winter festivities. To entertain their hosts, wassailers had songs, dances, plays, anything the skills of the wassailing party could turn a hand to.

Wassailers offered drink and salutation, sometimes with other small gifts, in return for money, food or drink likely worth much more than the offerings they carried themselves.

But what might they be celebrating? It's not always simple to determine this, particularly as many regional variations abound. Maybe it didn't always matter. Wassailing might begin as early as Hollantide (Hallowe'en; early November - Trefor M. Owen), or just after Harvest (Grampound Wassail Song, Cornwall) and is specifically recorded at Christmas Eve, New Year, Jan 5th (Twelfth Eve or Wassail Eve) and January 6th Twelfth Night. Leaving the different agricultural blessings (apples, oxen, bees etc.) to Chapter 3, the overall impression created by Wassailing songs that have survived is of a society largely at peace with itself at the beginning of C18, able to co-exist across social divisions - a situation described by Bob Bushaway (1982) as 'social cohesion'. This was gradually to break down with increasing agricultural mechanisation during C18 and C19, as Wassailing ceremonies themselves also slowly declined.

Not surprisingly, there are plenty of references to Christmas and New Year, although far fewer to 'God' or 'The Lord' or 'Christ' apart from commonplace usage like 'God bless...' which suggests that the spirit of wassailing was as much secular as religious, thus distinguishable from 'Carolling'. Songs toast 'the Master' and 'The Mistress', occasionally the monarch. Many salute 'this ancient old house' and wish abundance and prosperity in the twelve months to come and long life thereafter. They ask for the 'pretty maid to pull back the pin' in the full expectation that this would happen before the wassailers got too cold after 'wandering through the mire'. Food, sometimes 'mouldy cheese and Christmas loaf'; sometimes something much more elaborate from 'The Butler' is requested in confident expectation. Money also is freely sought, without any hole in the corner attitude suggesting this might be looked down on by the giver.

Other songs refer to keeping the old traditions alive. 'Popular Antiquities' authors (before 1850) seem comfortable with at least the language of England's Saxon / Norse past, and many probably remembered C17 Puritan strictures against enjoyment with some horror. While 'Yule' is not specifically mentioned in many songs or rhymes, there is a strong sense of need for celebration to get everyone through the period of intense cold until the Sun and the light and warmth return in the Spring. Some writers (Philip Stubbes, 1583; Henry Bourne, 1725) describe this as 'Pagan' but they are writing from a Puritan (Christian Protestant fundamentalist) standpoint, and make no attempt to determine whether pagan orientation might be Classical, Norse or otherwise. In some regional traditions Hollantide coincides with the (then) annual slaughter of beasts, before hunkering down for the winter – there may have been more 'plenty' around than is sometimes recognized – stocks of meat, wheat, barley and apples with which to make bread, cakes, cider and beer in time for the annual winter celebration.

Neither was wassailing alone, as a means by which poorer people might collect money and victuals to assist them in celebration. In parts of the country, people went Souling in early November. They went Clementing on November 23rd, St Clement's Day, and Catterning on St Catherine's Day, November 25th. While the best known Clementing celebration is probably that by blacksmith's apprentices at Woolwich Dockyard (G. F. Northall, 1892), these two celebration days became conflated in some places. There is also just a hint in Northall's writing that prior to the Poor Law Amendment Act 1834 some pre Christmas collecting celebrations may have had (quasi) official status as fund raisers for Parishes, legally charged with the onerous task of providing relief to their poor people. As this rhyme from Sussex shows

Cattern' and Clemen', be here, be here,
Give us your apples and give us your beer
One for Peter, Two for Paul, Three for him that made us all
Clement was a good man
Cattern was his mother
For his sake give us some
Give us your best and not your worst
And God will give your soul good rest

December 21st is St Thomas's Day when either children or young women might go Thomassing (particularly in Cheshire or parts of Staffordshire) or Gooding or Mumping (Herefordshire) or Corning (Warwickshire) – all of which ceremonies resemble Wassailing, people collecting to finance their own Christmas celebrations. It seemed as if there were recognizable occasions when seeking charity within one's own neighbourhood was a legitimate activity that would not attract censure or punishment.

Please I've come a-gooding
To buy m'mother a Christmas pudding

A similar though longer 'Pudding' rhyme, part of Thomassing celebrations was found at Bretforton, Worcestershire:

Whistle or wassail about the town
Got any apples, throw 'em down
Cups white, ale brown, barrels made of ivy tree
Come all you lads and drink with me
Up the ladder and down the wall
Half a peck will serve us all
If you buy eggs, we'll buy flour
We'll have a pudding as big as the Tower

English Folk Rhymes, G. F. Northall (1892)

Alternative versions of this custom are more charitable, with money collected given to the clergy or churchwardens who distribute it at the vestry on the Sunday afterwards as St Thomas's Dole.

Well a day, well a day
St Thomas goes to soon away
Then your gooding we do pray
For the good time will not stay
St Thomas Grey, St Thomas Grey
The longest night and the shortest day
Please to remember St Thomas's Day

House visiting wassails were not always carried out by small random groups acting semi independently. At Minchinhampton, Gloucestershire the Wassail Bowl with its small wooden dolls was kept by a man known as the King of the Wassailers. Robert Malcolmson's (1973) researches suggest that Christmas festivities in large houses involving payment to itinerant groups in return for Carolling, Mumming, musicians and Morris Dancing were widespread at New Year particularly in Southern and Midland counties of England. Musicians might be hired, sometimes from a considerable distance away, but many entertainers were the local poor, seeking largess. Wassailers might visit at any time between late November and mid February, as there did not appear to be a set time. There are not many references linking Wassailing and Morris Dancing though this is shown in the

Christmas festivities in large houses involving payment to itinerant groups in return for Carolling, Mumming, musicians and Morris Dancing were widespread at New Year

payment records of the Throckmorton Family of Weston Underwood, Buckinghamshire in 1704 and 1705*. Two centuries later, in Herefordshire (Mrs Leather, 1912), Christmas festivities were enlivened by companies of Wassailers, Morris Dancers and Mummers – particularly near Bromyard and on the Worcester side of Herefordshire. There was a Captain who kept the Punch-bowl or wassail bowl – made of beech wood, able to hold up to two gallons of punch made of hot cider, gin, nutmeg and sugar: they had toast with it and money was given as well.

At Duncton, Sussex, much depended on Richard 'Spratty' Knight, the captain of Wassailers, to co-ordinate the travelling band (Fran and Geoff Doel, 1992). 'Folk' customs are often seen as happening spontaneously, but where organisation is removed as happened with St George's Day celebrations in C16 (Ron Hutton, 1994), customs can soon fall into decline. This almost certainly happened with Wassailing too, as the social cement provided by organisers and sponsors (Farmers, the Church, the well-to-do) gradually eroded as C19 progressed. In the modern Reawakening of Wassailing, the role of key individuals as movers and shapers is again abundantly evident.

Writing from a Marxian standpoint, eminent folklorist Bert Lloyd (1967) presented Wassailing as a survival from an earlier Pagan age, as a means of combating the dread of hunger, as the winter solstice heralded the advent of the season of seed-sowing. Apart from the derivation of the word itself, evidence in support of this view derives mainly from folklore (i.e. late C19) writings. However there is an uncertainty between Wassail songs couched in Christian terms and some of the customs that contain elements appearing to derive from outside Christian tradition. Lucy Broadwood (1893) describes how in Yorkshire 'Children carry green boughs and wave them over their heads asking for a New Year's gift' – the similarity with carrying May Garlands is impossible to disregard. Peter Kennedy (1975) describes how in

---

* private communication with Jameson Wooders

Camborne, Cornwall local carol parties were accompanied by a child dressed in evergreens, who was known as Lucy Green.

Here we come a-wassailing 'long with our Lucy Green
And here we come a wandering as fair to be seen.

This might not seem unusual, were it not that Baltic in countries St Lucy's Day (Dec. 13th) is widely celebrated. Though many of the Scandinavian celebrations were restarted during C20, the symbolism of a young girl dressed in white wearing a crown of candles on her head can be readily interpreted as being concerned with the triumph of light over darkness that embodies most Winter Solstice celebrations. A young girl in white symbolises the purity through which that triumph is achieved. St Lucy's Day is December 13th, a date capable of being regarded as the Winter Solstice depending on how relationships between Julian and Gregorian calendars are interpreted. In Camborne, Lucy Green was firmly embedded with a carolling party, as in Scandinavia, where modern Lucy is also celebrated within Christian tradition.

In Cornwall, some local carol parties were accompanied by a young girl dressed in evergreens, who was known as Lucy Green.

How much does this matter? Christianity is the UK state religion, but increasing numbers of people are secular or atheist, Others, perceiving the corrupting influence of organised Christianity, turn to alternative spiritual pathways including some pre-dating Christianity. The modern era is tolerant, recognising all religions and none. Establishment of direct linkage between folk songs and ceremonies and the distant past (before 1500, say) is almost impossible, but vestiges of the distant past are everywhere. On that basis there is no reason why a modern wassail event should not be Pagan or secular or even Christian in character. These labels are surely not what it's about – it's the spirit of the ceremony that really matters.

All over the town

Wassail, Wassail to our town, the cup is white, the ale is brown.

So they sung in the Isle of Wight, and in Wassail songs found in many other places.

The cup is made of the ashen tree,
And the ale is made of the best barley.

- Langport, Somersetshire collected by C L Eastlake, Jan 1893

Or 'Our bowl it is made of the white maple tree' in Gloucestershire or an elderberry bough on the Gower in West Wales, or a mulberry tree in Staffordshire, or Beech in Herefordshire.

Our Wassail is made of the good ale and cake,
Some nutmeg and ginger, the best we could get.

- Gower Wassail, from the singing of Phil Tanner

Wassailing was a means by which poorer people might collect money and victuals to assist them in the celebration of Christmas.

Neither would the Wassail Bowl be plain but decorated with ribbons and evergreens

Sometimes crowned with laurel and sometimes with bay,
According to custom we'll keep the old way.

- Cornish wassail (Fowey)

from an engraving by John Gilbert 1860

In 1912, the journal 'Folklore' reported Wassailers still going round several Gloucestershire villages: at Minchinhampton, Woodchester, Randwick and Avening – with a large wooden Maple bowl decorated with evergreens, coloured paper and small dolls (Katherine Briggs, 1974). It isn't clear exactly when they went out – perhaps at any time in December. Neither is there any absolute separation between wassailing that visited houses of the well to do and that concerned with agricultural blessings. Lots of well off people were farmers, and it would only be proper to wish prosperity and abundance to their beasts and crops as well as to the 'Master' and 'Mistress'. Many of the house visiting songs do just this, and it happens in reverse when agricultural blessing songs like Gloucestershire Wassail finish with requests like *"Come Butler, come fill us a bowl of the best..."*.

Roy Palmer (1994) describes wassailing as taking place mainly in December, from Maisemore and Shurdington in the north of Gloucestershire south to Little Sodbury and Badminton. In several places in the south of Gloucestershire an imitation bull known as 'Broad' was taken round with the wassail. At Tytherington "they used to have a big swede, hollowed out

Wassailers in about 1930, with 'Broad' - from Tetbury, Gloucestershire.

with eyes, nose, mouth and ears, wi' a candle inside, decked in ribbons and set on a pole". At Uley, 'Broad' is described as having a sad face and large horns. 'Old Broad' is mentioned in the Minchinhampton version of Gloucestershire Wassail noted by James Carpenter in the 1930s, with Robert Wilkins, the singer, telling Carpenter the song had come down in his family for 150 years. In 1970 (Gwilym Davies, 2011), there is a report of the 'Horton Bull' at Little Sodbury Manor, several decades earlier, very similar to Old Broad, but with two men under a papier maché head. The Bull would roar, chase the girls and make them scream. The remainder of the party of six or seven made plenty of noise with tambourine, Jew's harp and mouth organ. They also carried a white wood wassail bowl garlanded with evergreens and ribbons.

So here is to Broad Mary and to her broad horn,
May God send our master a good crop of corn,
And a good crop of corn that may we all see,
With the wassailing bowl, we'll drink to thee.

At Newark Park, men sang in the servants' hall, where there was a great wassail bowl with iron hoops and also decorations of evergreens and ribbons. Not all wassail bowls were so refined: the bowl carried around the farms and big houses in a wicker basket in the Woodchester / Kingscourt area was really a chamber pot decorated with holly (Gwilym Davies, 2011). The three lads who carried it round dressed in women's clothes and blackened their faces, and they were well paid in money and cider, on a good night as much as £3 each

Three lads carried round a chamber pot for a wassail bowl dressed in women's clothes and blackened faces. They were well paid in money and cider.

In the Forest of Dean area, commonly in 1900, recorded in St Braivels in the 1950s and still being kept up at Devauden in the Wye Valley as recently as 1987, wassailing parties would call at larger houses with a pyramid made of leaves, apples, nuts etc.,

usually mounted on a wooden tripod decorated with sprigs of box and hazel nuts. These tripods were called Montys in Chepstow, pre 1914. Members of the party might call out

"Monty, Monty, Happy New Year.
A pocket full of money and a cellar full of beer"
(Jacqueline Simpson 1976)

Much earlier, a similar ceremony on New Year's Day, called 'The Quaaltagh' rather than wassailing, used to take place on the Isle of Man (Joseph Train, 1845). In almost every parish on the Island, a company of young men would go from house to house, singing, before being invited into the house to partake of the best the family can afford.

Again we assemble a merry New Year
To wish each one of the family here
Whether man, woman, girl or boy
That long life and happiness may enjoy
May they of potatoes and herrings have plenty
With butter and cheese and each other dainty
And may their sleep never, by night or by day
Disturbed by even the tooth of a flea
Until at the Quaaltagh again we appear
To wish you, as now all a Happy New Year

Train compared this ceremony to First Footing, though the usual First Footing presents are not mentioned, neither is the word Wassail. The wish of plenty is couched in terms of the local diet staples, comparable with pledging the wellbeing of animals or cornfields during ceremonies in England

In Wales Wassailing took place either at New Year or on Twelfth Night. Cakes and baked apples were layered with sugar in a special wassail bowl with 18 handles most likely made at Ewenny Pottery, near Bridgend; then warm, spiced beer was poured over them. It was passed around the company then the wassail (the cakes and apples) were shared out. A wassail might be taken to newly wed couples or people who had recently moved house by the young men and women of the neighbourhood with sung verses outside the door. In Carmarthenshire, the wassailing ceremony included an object called a 'perllan' a small rectangular board with a circle marked upon it and four ribs of wood running out to the four corners with an apple fixed in each corner. In the circle was a miniature tree with a bird on it. It was taken around on New Year's Day, while another carried the wassail bowl.

"And with us we have a perllan with a little wren flying in it;
he is the ruler of all birds"

This suggests a link in Welsh traditions between the Hunting of the Wren, traditionally in West Wales at New Year or on Twelfth Night and wassailing. Wren hunting involves a wren being caught and paraded around the community in a specially designed wren house during the twelve days of Christmas, often on St Stephen's Day (26th Dec.). Although the wren is now most likely a wooden replica, ceremonies still take place in Carmarthenshire, elsewhere in South Wales at Dingle, Co Kerry, on the Isle of Man and at Middleton near Yoxford, Suffolk.

Neighbours' children / women / money and good victuals

The purpose of most house visiting was to collect money, usually by children or young women. In Nottinghamshire (J. H. Dixon, 1846) young village women went from door to door with a bowl richly decorated, filled with a compound of ale, roasted apples and toast, seasoned with nutmeg and ginger. They sung verses:

Good master at your door, our wassail we begin,
We are maidens poor so we pray you let us in,
And drink our wassail,
All hail, wassail,
Wassail, wassail,
And drink our wassail.

'Cutty Wren' ceremonies still take place at Middleton near Yoxford, Suffolk

On Christmas Eve, in the West Riding of Yorkshire, (W. Henderson, 1879) children carried round figures of the Virgin and child in what they called Milly-boxes (possibly a corruption of 'My Lady'), and filled with spices, oranges and sugar. They sang

For it's Christmas time and we travel far and near,
So God bless you and send you a Happy New Year.

More recent research (Rauridh Greig, 1988) has identified house visiting Wassail customs ('wosslin' or 'wesslin') across a large area immediately north of Sheffield, a mixture of towns and villages with farming and (deep) mining their principal industries. Depending on location each Wassail might take place at any time between Christmas Eve and New Year, always with young girls touring houses singing a version of 'Here we come a Wassailing'. This area is rich in visiting customs with Mummers Plays, Old Tup Plays, Jolly Minering, Carol Singing and Sword Dancing also recorded. Greig identifies two versions of the Wassail custom: one in which a large decorated branch of holly or fir is shaped to look like a Christmas Tree – the Wassail Bough or 'Wossel Boo' was carried; the other a doll carried in a decorated box with an orange next to it. Almost everywhere, children sang 'Here we come a-wassailing', a song widely recorded throughout England, with twenty seven versions listed in the Roud Folksong Index. If children were lucky they might be given a silver threepenny bit in addition to the Christmas cake or cheese or mince pie that was almost certain. The custom met with popular approval: children were always welcome and Greig's informants suggest that it survived at least until 1945.

Further north around Cleveland it was similar but the name was different – they called it a 'Bessel cup', probably a local rendering of 'Wassail cup', with figures of the Virgin and Child, placed in a box and surrounded with such ornaments as they could find. In Holderness, East Yorkshire and elsewhere, wassail was corrupted into vessel, so that the 'Vessel-cup' was carried around at Christmas (John Brand, 1813), accompanied by an image of Christ and roasted apples. Carols were sung and money collected.

A Gloucestershire custom (Roy Palmer, 1994) describes children going from house to house with baskets on their arm, rewarded with apples and cakes, in a ceremony called 'bud-welling,' possibly linked to the wassailing of apple trees still carried out on Jan 5th in some places.

It was not always so gentle. An early C19 Cornish custom (M. A. Courtney 1890) reports parties of 4 – 6 lads going out house visiting on New Year's Eve, with a small bowl, begging money (by implication with some degree of threat or menace). Arriving at a house, they opened the doors without knocking calling 'Wassail' and sang

Three poor jolly wassail boys
Come travelling through the mire.

Courtney doesn't report what might have happened to anyone who was stingy or refused to give, but it's not difficult to see how late Victorian sensibilities might be offended by coming into a house without knocking, and how the view gradually gathered momentum that Christmas (in its broader, longer sense) should be got off the streets and into people's houses

Gaining entry / Riddling / 'The Butler' / The Maid pulling back the pin / Let us in because it's cold

The idea of a competition to gain entry into a house, though not universal is reported in several locations, particularly in Wales. In Herefordshire, also in Devon, at the end of the evening when the health of all the beasts in the beast house has been pledged in cider, both farmers and workers return to the farm house. In some traditions the women would have bolted the door, resisting all entreaties to open it irrespective of the weather, until someone correctly guessed what was on the spit awaiting them all for supper. The person guessing correctly might get a special reward, but the game didn't take long and then the party could begin. An alternative and deeper explanation is offered by Bob Stewart (1990) as "a fine example of a challenge session undertaken to win the right to cross a threshold, where the door threshold may be seen as representing the boundary between this world and the Otherworld and where the women are playing the role of the Guardian whose permission to cross must be sought and won".

Much more commonplace was the straightforward request for the maid to pull back the pin, from Yarmouth, Isle of Wight

Little maid, little maid turn the pin,
Open the door and let us come in.

Sometimes the entreaty is a bit racier as this version of the Somerset Wassail, noted down from Mr Eastlake in 1893 suggests (two verses with a chorus separating)

O maid, fair maid in Holland smock,
Come open the door and turn the lock.

O maid, fair maid with golden (tag),
Come open the door, and show a pretty leg.

A longer example of series of persuading verses was recorded by a Mr Rann of Dudley in 1819 and published (William Hone, 1825) as "The Carroll for a Wassell Bowl" (se p214), and said to be popular in Staffordshire and Warwickshire at the time. As with other regional customs, the participants were female, perhaps as a form of social inversion or 'The World Turned Upside Down'

"O maid, fair maid
in Holland smock,
Come open the door
and turn the lock."

1998 Wassail maid,
our daughter Aly

Good Dame, here at your door
Our Wassel we begin,
We are all maidens pure,
We pray now let us in - With our good Wassel.

Our Wassel we do fill
With apples and with spice,
They kindly will agree,
To take a good carouse - Of our Wassel.

But here they let us stand,
All freezing in the cold,
Good Master give command,
To enter and be bold - With our Wassel.

In modern times, the best known example of 'Riddling' to gain entry to a private or public house is the 'Pwnco', part of the Mari Lwyd (Grey Mare) ceremony in South Wales, sometimes thought of as similar to 'first footing' at New Year. Once commonplace throughout Wales, the Mari appeared in an area as diverse as Carmarthenshire, Glamorgan, North Wales and the Forest of Dean (Violet Alford, 1978). The Mari is usually a horse's skull, set on a pole, carried upright by a man, completely hidden by a white cloth, and profusely decorated with ribbons. Who was in the party probably depended on availability, but Punch and Judy may have accompanied the Mari and performed a step dance with her immediately on gaining entry. In Mumbles, one member would play the part of Ostler and whip the horse until it slowly died, though more often the Ostler looked after the Mari. Before the revelling party could gain entry to the pub or house they engaged in a riddling battle of wits, 'The Pwnco', exchanging challenges and insults in rhyme with those inside, possibly for some time. The Mari has survived in unbroken tradition at Llangynwyd, near Maesteg and now visits the Old House pub, Upper Llangynwyd at about 2p.m. on New Year's Day. In addition a party tour from St Fagans Museum every winter and Llantrisant Folk Club takes its own Mari out all through the dark months of the year. Both Trefor M. Owen (1991) and Violet Alford recognize linkage between Wassailing and the Mari Lwyd; indeed Alford reports that in Carmarthenshire and other southern Welsh counties outside Glamorgan the custom is known as Y Warsel.

The Mari Lwyd; in Carmarthenshire and other southern Welsh counties outside Glamorgan the custom is known as Y Warsel

Here, the Mari is a genuine horse's skull prepared and mounted in the traditional fashion by Ian Jones of Pencoed and donated to Llantrisant Folk Club, who revived the visiting custom nearly four decades ago.

below; Ned Clamp and Llantrisant Mari Lwyd

photo by kind permission of Ned Clamp

Under the Mari Lwyd.

What is the correct term? Do you: put on the Mari? climb into the Mari? dress up as the Mari?

Anyone who has had the privilege to don this remarkable guise would certainly agree that you **become** the Mari. When she's sitting, apparently lifeless, on the settee or in the back of the car, she's still referred to as "her". She is an independent being, someone else who's there with you.

First you put on the white skirt, and you feel like a man in a skirt, and if you are in company, you bear it with a proud dignity - "this is all perfectly normal". Then as you are helped on with the head the transformation begins, and you **become** the Mari.

Initially, as you approach the pub door, it will be dark, you have a restricted view through the jaws, and you are relying on the Ostler to guide you - a whispered "two steps up" or "pillar to the left", you are a passive part of the company. Once the Pwnco has been sung and you have gained entry, the "Lord of Misrule" takes over, and you become an undisciplined animal, charging round the room with the Ostler in tow, stealing hats, scarves, drinks, anything moveable. Eventually insinuating yourself behind the bar before being led out after the final Washael.

At the end of the evening you are hot (even in a frost), weary (the head is very heavy), and remarkably sober – you've either sweated it off, or you haven't had much time to drink.

Ned Clamp

Master and Mistress / Blessings

References to the 'Master' and 'Missus' abound in the house visiting songs, many with requests for charity

Good master and good mistress if you would be willing,
Come send us out your eldest son, with a sixpence or a shilling

Or for drink

Oh Master and Missus will let us all walk in,
And for to fill our wassail bowl and sail away again,

- Curry Rivel, Somerset

Or for food

Oh Master and Mistress if you are so well please
To set all on your table your white loaf and your cheese
With your roast beef, your porrops* and your peas - Curry Rivel again

Having been served with plenty of food and drink, wassailers were usually free in their thanks, blessings and good wishes, as with this Cornish Wassail from Grampound, which has a similar lyric structure to the more modern song 'Soldier and the Sailor'.

We hope that your barley will prosper and grow,
That you may have barley and beer to bestow,
And where you have one bushel we hope you'll have ten,
That you may have beer against we come again.

Other Cornish Wassails make the time honoured salute both to the master and 'Mistress' and to everyone in the House

This ancient old house we'll kindly salute,
It is our old custom you need not dispute.

I wish you a blessing and a long time to live,
Since you've been so free and willing to give.

*young leeks or onions

House visiting customs in decline

By the early to mid C19, in both Britain and the USA, concern was growing that pre-Christmas celebrations on the streets were too loud and drunken, with even the threat of riots. A desire developed amongst those in authority to transfer Christmas off the streets and into people's homes. For the next century and a half modern Christmas practices gradually evolved. Ceremonies like wassailing and the Kentish 'Hoodening' gradually gave way to "carolling". Propagandist novels like Charles Dickens' 'A Christmas Carol' edited out street based celebrations in favour of 'the family'. Publication of Hymns Ancient and Modern, (several versions between 1861 and 1906) established much of the standard carol repertoire lasting till current times. Fat jolly red suited Santa was popularised in a Coca Cola advertising campaign in the 1930s, but first created by American caricaturist Thomas Nast fifty years earlier.

As early as 1825 William Hone was lamenting that Twelfth Eve celebrations and ceremonies, along with other country customs such as sheep shearing suppers (Bushaway, 1982) "have declined since our forefathers' times". Katherine Briggs (1974) reports that in Gloucestershire by 1912, in some villages, the number of wassailers declined from 20 to 4 or 5. Other reports (Jacqueline Simpson, 1976) suggest that elsewhere on the Welsh Borders, wassailing customs died out about 1910. However Wassail songs were collected in Cornwall as late as 1956 (Peter Kennedy, 1975) and Roy Palmer (1974) reports Wassailing survivals in the Forest of Dean well into modern times.

The effects of Victorian social change on traditional customs are well documented elsewhere (Roy Judge, 1979; Elaine Bradtke, 1999; Cecil Sharp, 1907). This affected most country social pursuits and some urban ones as well. What happened to wassailing is mirrored in any examination of country songs, Morris Dancing, Going a-Maying, Whitsun Ales, Jack in the Green, Plough Monday, Harvest Home etc, so that once powerful landmark ceremonies, rites of passage of the agricultural year had all but disappeared well before the ravages of the 1914 – 18 war. Bushaway (1982) argues that a combination of economic and political factors led to withdrawal of consent by the well-to-do, with consequent demonisation of the old ways. Crusades against perceived licentiousness and drunkenness (by an uneasy alliance of clergymen, politicians and newspapers) had combined to drive seasonal gaiety, social inversions and safety valves largely out of existence.

Perhaps the social pursuits of the countryside simply didn't translate into the environment of the new Victorian towns. Communications media were also changing rapidly. The old style 'Broadside Ballad' with its frequent tales of ghoulish murders and executions had by the end of C19 largely given way to popular songs from the Music Halls, presented as sheet music, with a picture of the 'star' on the front cover of a four page leaflet – the singer was becoming more important than the song. By the end of the 1920s most families owned a radio feeding a constant diet of current dance music and singers like Al Bowlly into every home – if wassailing songs got a look in, it was likely to be as songs from a bygone age in programmes like 'As I Roved Out' or 'Have a Go' or 'Down your Way'. As the twentieth century progressed both songs and star singers became increasingly American rather than British

Christmas too was changing. Comparison between Popular Antiquities sources and early C20 writers reveals that by 1910 Christmas had become condensed from three major festivities within a twelve day period to two - Christmas and New Year. The decline of Twelfth Night reported by Hone (1825) had continued to the point that Epiphany is now seen as an independent event, completely separated from the Christmas holiday, no longer the Twelfth (and final) Day, and greatly reduced in significance. In addition to Coca Cola's Red Coated Santa, songs like 'White Christmas', 'Jingle Bells', Winter

Wonderland' and 'Rudolf the Red Nosed Reindeer' established an American led repertoire of secular songs to stand alongside the popular carols. Although challenged by the likes of Noddy Holder (Slade) in the 1970s and subsequently by others, this repertoire remains central to Christmas celebrations right up into current time. The English Father Christmas or Old Christmas or King Christmas, had become largely replaced by Santa Claus as English Christmas celebrations including wassailing became distilled through American experience into an Anglo-European cocktail.

Other house visiting ceremonies include 'Tutti Day' at Hungerford, Berkshire when an orange is presented to the lady of the house in return for a kiss.

Perhaps it would be understandable if house visiting and collecting customs should have had their time and that they simply faded away but it just didn't happen like that. More than anything described above, the 1914 – 18 war nearly put a stop to all sorts of traditional celebrations, and it took another forty years and another world war before establishment bumbledom relaxed its clodpoll grip on popular street celebrations. Now a number of ceremonies have a House Visiting component: the Abbots Bromley Horn Dance, Staffordshire (early September) with its continuous tradition; the Earl of Rone at Combe Martin, North Devon which was restarted in the 1970s (late May) has one processional day in a four day festival where house visiting is a major part. Other house visiting ceremonies include Tutti Day at Hungerford, Berkshire.

Charity has changed too: individuals or groups collecting for their own benefit have been frowned on since late Victorian times. Though it's not strictly illegal touring groups need to be careful when collecting for themselves. Any attempt to do this in a town centre will almost certainly need a local council license and possibly be regulated by the Police. Collecting (either entirely or in part) for a (needy) third party is likely to be more favourably viewed, particularly if the third party is itself a charity to whom proceeds can be donated.

Despite all of this, House Visiting as a form of wassailing has survived in continuous unbroken tradition into modern times in at least four places: Bodmin, Cornwall, and Drayton and Curry Rivel, Somerset and Llangynwyd in South Wales. Dunkeswell in Devon is approaching sixty years continuity since its wassailing was reawakened. Other ceremonies are being re-created: adopting the pub visiting model used by Mummers groups, a number of Wassailing parties have emerged mainly collecting money for charity in local pubs. These include the Beerfordbury group in Bishops Stortford, Hertfordshire (touring since 1989), and Plum Jerkum Morris in Long Itchington, Warwickshire. Among the 200+ wassails discovered during this project, a number have house visiting elements as part of ceremonies concerned more with blessing fruit trees, including those at Hastings, East Sussex, Whimple, Devon and Porlock, Somerset. Amongst private wassails not posted on the net, several visit houses during an evening's or day's celebrating -

Beerfordbury Beer Tappers and Wine Tipplers Association Wassailers in Bishops Stortford, Hertfordshire who have been touring since 1989

Who says the old traditions are dead?

photo - Beerfordbury Wassailers

Inscription adapted from Robert Herrick's 17th century poem.
This three handled Wassail Bowl was made for our own Wassail
in 1998 and holds about a gallon of spiced cider

Chapter 3

We Wassail Bees and Apple Trees

(and fields and cattle too)

Background

Wassail the trees, that they may bear you many a plum, and many a pear:
For more or less fruits they will bring as you do give them wassailing.

- Robert Herrick (1591-1674)

Written during the Puritan religious turmoil of C17, this invocation to merriment, extolling the Christmas season did not endear Herrick to many of the powers of the day. Yet the poem does little more than give expression to a tree wassailing custom already widespread in Elizabethan and Stuart times (Ron Hutton, 1994). Agricultural and orchard Wassailing might take place at any time between Christmas and Twelfth Night; most likely just before the return to work, but varying depending where it was happening.

So what was agricultural wassailing like, indeed what was England like in 1800? Originating as a salutation "Waes Hael", during the 'Middle Ages', these customs and ceremonies celebrated the turn of the year, looking forward, after Christmas. Often the social order was suspended in agricultural communities offering social togetherness, between farmer and worker, man and beast, everyone within a village at the start of the working year (Bushaway, 1982). Many earlier descriptions speak of men 'pledging' to each other and to the trees or animals - toasting them in ale or cider to wish good luck and a bountiful crop. Within these customs resides a clearly magical element invoking the tree to 'prosper and bear', sometimes even calling on God to assist the processes of nature. Ceremonies seek to awaken and cleanse the land and its produce. They overtly seek to dispatch malign influences or spirits and propitiate those that are benign.

Blow well and bud well and bear well,
God send you fare well,
Every sprig and every spray,
A bushel of apples to be given away
On New Year's Day in the morning.
        - 'Bud welling' at Upton St Leonard's, and Gotherington and Woolstone - all Gloucestershire

Blow well
and bud well
and bear well!

Sometimes the invocation was not entirely benign as the implied threat in this C19 rhyme from Devon, quoted in the Gentleman's Magazine (1791) shows:

Apple-tree, apple-tree, bear good fruit,
Or down with your top and up with your root.

Other ceremonies call upon the land itself to generate fertility of trees or crops, visualizing the Earth as Mother:

Apples and pears with right good corn,
Come in plenty to every one,
Eat and drink good cake and hot ale,
Give Earth to drink and she'll not fail.

-The Christmas Book: author anonymous, 1859

There is more than the suggestion here of Mother Earth able to provide bounty for her children, its people, if she is honoured appropriately. Concepts of the Earth as Mother or Goddess are Indo European in origin and several thousand years old and recorded in many societies as peoples migrated westwards and north, including into England.

Apple-tree,
apple-tree,
bear good fruit!

Following the end of C17 Puritan upheaval, the C18 & 19 had become a more tolerant age, in which the Church could turn a blind eye, or even overtly support the conjuring of apple trees, beasts and fields in search of a fertile crop and village wellbeing. If agricultural wassailing is viewed alongside May Games, Whitsun Ales, Harvest Home and other village celebrations, this interpretation becomes easier to support. These celebrations were major rites of passage during both farming and social calendar, taking place in full public view, in some cases for the financial benefit of Parish Churches, also charged with responsibility for secular local government. Bushaway (1982) suggests that because country customs were so commonplace in the early C18 they were not often reported in contemporary media, simply because they were not newsworthy. An early C19 Cornish account by Rev Richard Polwhele describes a tree blessing ceremony in easily recognizable terms, without the slightest hint of censure or disapproval. Between 1700 and mid Victorian times, there is little evidence of country customs and celebrations coming under attack, except from some Protestant writings (Henry Bourne, 1775). This is in sharp contrast to the Witch Persecutions of C16 and 17, and to what would happen later in C19. For the moment, country celebrations, the brewing of simples and herbal medicine was allowed to become a much more private matter.

Earliest references to agricultural wassailing come from south east England. Wassailing fruit trees was recorded in St Albans in 1486 and at Fordwich, Kent in 1585 where groups of young men would go between orchards performing wassailing rites or ceremonies in return for money, a practice known as "youling" in Kent or "howling" in Sussex, where at Horsted Keynes in 1665 Giles Moore the rector recorded giving the 'howling boys' 4d on 26th December (Sean Goddard, 2001). The C17 diarist John Aubrey wrote of toast being placed in trees during a Wassailing ceremony and of professional wassailers travelling from farm to farm, often paid in food and cider. In Exmoor dialect (William

Wassailing fruit trees was recorded in St Albans in 1486 and at Fordwich, Kent in 1585

Hone, 1825) the ceremony was called 'Watsail'. It took place on Jan 6th: and involved a drinking song and throwing toast to the apple trees in order for them to have a fruitful year. In Norfolk there are records of spiced-ale being sprinkled on both orchards and meadows; on the borders of the New Forest in Hampshire, a large group of people had been observed sprinkling spiced ale and apples on the fields, singing very heartily as they went. On this evidence, agricultural wassailing was still widespread in England at the beginning of C19, particularly south of a line between Bristol and Hull, but possibly further north as well, though it was probably not as widely dispersed as Christmas house visiting Wassailing customs.

But what was England like? Under what social conditions did these customs flourish? Steve Roud believes that it is essential for the folklorist to have a well developed sense of history. Gregory King (1696) estimated the population of England to be 5.5 million; by the first census in 1801 it had risen to 8.9 million and it was to multiply five times during C19. Outside London in 1696, the most populous areas were in the South and Midlands with the majority of working people in agriculture. Although Enclosure of medieval strip fields had begun in the C16, it was a piecemeal process before C19, so that some wassailing may have taken place under medieval conditions particularly where crops were being wassailed. (i.e. villages bordered on three large communal fields. In each field every family had rights to a strip of land to grow crops and be self sufficient),

Industry was in the early stages of its development: coal mining was widespread based largely in villages, as was hand loom weaving, though the latter came under threat early in C19. Factories were being set up from 1720; initially powered by water, then later steam power. By 1800 England had a network of canals, shifting produce from village to town more quickly than by road, superseded by 1850 by a much faster network of railways. It is safe to assume that agricultural wassailing

"As I walked o'er the stubble field, below it runs the seam"

- from The Recruited Collier (traditional)

flourished under agrarian conditions throughout C18 but came increasingly under threat as industrialisation and population growth progressed in C19.

The success of the Gentleman's Magazine illustrates growing interest in antiquities amongst the lettered classes in C18 & 19. Reporting Popular Antiquities was more descriptive and factual than later "folklore" writings of C19 and afterwards. There was curiosity about origins, coupled with a willingness to accept that some customs might in part have pre-Christian ancestry. Folklore (c. 1870 onwards) gave rise to different interpretations. While collectors harvested stories, songs, customs from the poor, many of their interpretations varied substantially from source informants' knowledge. Many accounts simply didn't understand country lore, but instead were highly romantic, sometimes bordering on the prurient and sensational, creating an imaginary England rather than one grounded in observation.

"Sun through the apple trees on Christmas Day means a fine crop is on the way"

- traditional weather lore

In particular, while persecution of witches may have subsided, tales of their exploits still abounded in folklore. Where country customs were not overtly Christian in character, they were not seen as complementary to Church activities, as many of the charitable visiting wassailing customs had been (see Ch 2); but as antagonistic. In many places harvest customs had been suppressed, replaced by church Harvest Festivals. Gradually the view hardened that somehow wassailing and Christianity were in opposition to one another: the Christian ceremony was acceptable while the country custom was a salacious relic of a long defeated primitive religion, sometimes called 'Paganism'. Evidence suggests the exact opposite: in the countryside the wassailing custom, a magical rite intended to increase yields by blessing and awakening trees, co-existed very comfortably within an overall Christian social village framework. The only deity in earlier Popular Antiquities literature is Pomona, the Roman Goddess of fruit trees and she only appears infrequently. As C20 has progressed into C21, romanticism in folklore has morphed into a tendency to regard customs from times past as somehow 'weird' or 'oddball' or 'eccentric'. Perhaps old customs seem unusual in the digital age but two centuries ago they were nothing of the sort, and they are central to understanding the popular history of England - to fail to understand them is akin to denying an important part of English history.

Gloucestershire, Herefordshire and Worcestershire

As part of the celebrations for New Year, Ella Leather (1912) describes a custom at Brinsop, Herefordshire, when on New Year's Day morning; men would stand in a circle by a bonfire in the orchard, chanting three times the words *"Old Ci-der"*. On each of the three syllables they would bow as low as possible into the circle as each note is sung, making nine bows in all. The first two notes were sung at a normal pitch but the last, the *"-der"*, dropped to a low growl a full octave below the other notes. The result was a "weird, dirge-like effect" which one might expect to be profoundly hypnotic, almost like a mantra, and a really good invocation of the spirit of cider and the apple tree!

Several days later, on Twelfth Eve, in many places in Herefordshire, thirteen bonfires would be lit on top of a hillside, in a place as conspicuous as possible, burning in a field where wheat would later be growing - one fire would be in the centre

Old Ci-der,
Old Ci-der,
Old Ci -der!

of a circle made by the other twelve - it might be quite a lot larger. According to John Brand (1813) the farmer and his workers stood around the central fire, the master pledges (salutes) the company in cider, then each pledges the others with much shouting and holloaing. Answering shouts and cries would come from other groups of men and fires within hearing distance; as many as sixty fires might be seen

by anyone high up. Similar occurrences were reported from Gloucestershire, at Newent (1884) and in C19 Pauntley, though there were only twelve fires here (Roy Palmer, 1994), where the workers and farm servants drank to the master's health and to the success of the harvest.

But why thirteen fires? - Here reportage shifts into interpretation. Perhaps the most popular view is that thirteen fires represent Christ and the Apostles. Certainly this was believed in Pauntley and other places where the fire representing Judas Iscariot would be quickly scuffed out (perhaps this explains why twelve only), and the behaviour of the other fires used to divine the crop and harvest. Other explanations have the central fire as larger and female, sometimes called the Virgin Mary or Old Meg or the Old Witch. Hone (1827) describes the ceremony as "Burning the old Witch" - who he suggests might be the Druidic God of Death (whoever that is supposed to be! - ed.) with people singing, drinking and dancing around the fire It's also possible that this is one of many 'turn of the year' ceremonies concerned with the death of the Old Year, and the prospect of light and heat with the New Year. Whatever the explanation, the description of thirteen fires has great lineage, the version quoted by Jacqueline Simpson (2003) having changed little from the version in the Gentleman's Magazine (1791)

Bonfires in the field would not be the end of the Wassailing evening. Everyone would return to the farmhouse for supper, more drink and cakes often made with caraway seeds and soaked in cider, which they claimed as reward for sowing the grain. This form of cake at New Year seems to have been very widespread, recorded as far north as Scotland. Supper would also include a large cake with a hole in the middle, though this was probably saved for later on when it was taken to the beast house. By tradition the Farmer / Master filled a cup and standing beside the finest ox pledged him in ale or cider. After that the company follow with all the other oxen, sometimes as many as two dozen, pledging each in turn to guarantee a different part of next year's harvest, possibly using an uncollected verse of the Gloucestershire Wassail:

Here's to thy pretty face, and thy white horn,
God send our master a good crop of corn,
Both wheat, rye and barley, and grains of all sort,
And next year, if we lives, we'll drink to thee again.

> *- Bushaway, Bob (1982): By Rite: Custom, Ceremony and Community, 1700 -1880*

When each ox had been pledged everyone would return to the first ox and the cake would be placed on one of his horns, then he would be tickled or cider thrown in his face till he threw it off – if he threw it backwards the mistress claims the prize; if forward it belonged to the bailiff. An alternative explanation suggests that the direction in which the cake is thrown is an omen of the harvest – forward for a good harvest; backwards and the omens are unfavourable:

The Twelfth cake would be placed on one of the ox's horns.

Fill your cups my merry men all,
For here's the best ox in the stall,
Oh, he is the best ox, of that there's no mistake,
And so let's crown him with the twelfth cake.

T. D. Fosbrooke (1807) relates that in some Gloucestershire villages, after the ceremony, the door of the beast house would be fastened and every participant obliged to sing before he was allowed to depart. Upon quitting the beast house which must be done without the assistance of a candle, the maids play tricks on the company setting pails of water for everyone to tumble over. Finally it was back to the house and feasting and drinking till morning.

Overall the impression created by descriptions of these old ceremonies is of a combination of revelry and celebration with a sense of due seriousness and order. Things had to be done properly, in a way that everybody understood because that's the way it had always been done, even the play acting and trickery. Plenty of noise could be made and liquor consumed; it had always been so. Those taking part seem to be people who were directly involved in managing the land and the animals or working hard to ensure a good harvest. There was more than a small element of privacy about the whole thing. Where Wassailing has survived, much of this has changed: many of the celebrations have become in part public entertainment – the purpose may be the same, although there are far fewer reports of wheat fields or animals being wassailed, but the sense that the wassail was part of the programme of annual farm management has receded, and much of the sonorous, ponderous sense of ritual with it.

Say the two words 'Gloucestershire' and 'Wassail' together and it's difficult not to break into song. Published in the Oxford Book of Carols (1928), the Gloucestershire is as well known as any Wassail song. However, Roy Palmer (1994) and others think it's an artificial text drawn from several different village sources, with the tune collected in Pembridge, Herefordshire though from Gloucestershire singers. First noted in 1813 and first published with a tune by William Chappell (1838), it combines many different elements of wassailing, beginning with the Wassail Bowl carried from house to house, before having several verses that relate to oxen in the beast house. The final verse calls for the "maid with the lily white smock" to slip the lock so that everyone can come in for the party after the wassail was over. However it is the penultimate verse which may in modern times have assumed greatest meaning:

Peter Symonds; 'The Butler', of CROW - the Campaign for the Revival of Wassailing.

Come butler, come fill us a bowl of the best,
Then we hope that your soul in heaven may rest,
But if you do draw us a bowl of the small,
Then down shall go butler, bowl and all.

In many modern Wassails, particularly in Gloucestershire, Herefordshire and Worcestershire, 'The Butler' has assumed a central position, as the MC of the evening. In recent years, Peter Symonds has carved a niche for himself as 'The Butler', forming an organisation CROW- the Campaign for the Revival of Wassailing. In full 'Butler' regalia he'll happily lend traditional colour to a wassail, or a wedding or any celebration reflecting the popular heritage of England.

Kent, Sussex and Surrey

Based on dated records (Fordwich in Kent, 1585, and Horsted Keynes in Sussex, 1665), the south east corner of England can claim the longest surviving recorded wassailing traditions, with the style and manner of wassailing remaining remarkably unchanged over an extended period. Groups of young men travelled between orchards performing wassailing ceremonies for money, a practice known in Sussex as "howling". According to T. W. Horsfield (1827), they would likely be led by a trumpeter with a bullock's horn who took everyone to the best bearing tree in the orchard and chanted the rhyme which begins *"Stand fast root, bear well top ...."* After the chant there would be a loud shout and blast on the horn, then they'd go round the orchard and wassail each of the remaining trees. Then they'd go to the farmhouse and sing at the door to be let in for supper. It was all done to a pre-determined formula, as a bad wassail would surely result in a defective crop.

Opinions vary as to how long the custom survived. In 1852, it was called a 'superstition', but it survived near Chailey in an almost unchanged form – a troop of boys visiting the orchard and chanting *"Stand fast root...."* then regaling the trees with cow's horn music and rapping them with sticks. Charlotte Latham (1868) says that groups of men and boys travelled round the orchards to 'worsle' the trees in the time honoured manner, on New Year's Eve and for several days afterwards. In 1883 F.E. Sawyer said it was 'still going strong'. In Camberley, Surrey a group of boys chanted the "*Stand fast root...*" chant, quietly in a low voice, gradually in crescendo until they were shouting. Finally there'd be a loud blast on the cow-horn. They went round to every tree in the garden, substituting the names of appropriate fruits.

The most elaborate set of records concerns the Knight Family of Duncton, Sussex. Wassailers continued to go out on Twelfth Night right up into the 1920s. A photograph shows Richard 'Spratty' Knight wearing a brightly coloured costume with a string of apples round his neck and a large decorated straw hat with apples on it - with a copper and brass hunting horn, holding a jug of cider and a cake. They met at the Cricketers, Duncton, and then went round several orchards, first to Mill Farm, where they would blow on the cow's horn before the finest tree in the orchard was hit with sticks and sprinkled with ale or cider. Afterwards everyone went to the farmer's door to be greeted with drink or good victuals sometimes money. A number of other calls followed before finally returning to the Cricketer's. Forty years later, in 1967, these events were recalled by Mr Turner in a remarkable article published in the Sussex Gazette in which he describes his excitement as a child waiting for the wassailers;

"At last we would hear them, faintly at first then gradually getting louder. It sounded as though they split into two parties, one coming down the lane past the millpond and the second through the orchard. What we heard was something like this:

Wassailers at the Gate Inn, Marshside, nr Canterbury, Kent. 2010

photos by kind permission of Gail Duff

ALL TOGETHER: *Here stands a good old apple tree*

FIRST PARTY: *Stand fast root*   SECOND PARTY: *Bear well top*

FIRSTPARTY: *Every little bough* SECOND PARTY: *Bear apples enow*

FIRST PARTY: *Every little twig* SECOND PARTY: *Bear apples big*

FIRST PARTY: *Hat fulls*   SECOND PARTY: *Capsfull*

FIRST PARTY: *Three score sackfulls*

CAPTAIN: *Holler, boys, Holler!*

Then there'd be shouting, horn blowing and one heck of a racket. If someone trod in a hole in the ground, you'd hear it. Gradually they would go back to the house and sing – always "Three Jolly Fishermen", usually 'Two little girls in blue', 'Here's adieu to old England', 'The Farmer's Boy', 'If I were a Blackbird'. When they left, we used to go outside to hear more wassailing, the voices getting fainter and fainter as they went through the orchard on to the next stopping place"

Every little twig
Bear apples big

> - *Extract courtesy of Geoff and Fran Doel, Mumming, Howling and Hoodening (1992).*

In Hampshire (Wendy Boase, 1976) wassailing was more associated with New Year than Twelfth Night. Sometimes the wassail bowl would come out as well as the tree ceremonies. At Yarmouth Isle of Wight, children sang this song:

Wassail, wassail to our town, the cup is white, the ale is brown,
The cup is made of ashen tree, and so is the ale of good barley,
Little maid, little maid, turn the pin, open the door and let me in,
Joy be there and joy be here. We wish you all a Happy New Year.

In Kent, wassailing records contain elements of uncertainty. Ceremonies took place at Keston and Wickham, (Edward Hasted, 1797). Young men encircled each tree in turn to chant a variant of "*Stand fast root......*" chant, with much noise. In Kent the 'Howling' name of Sussex has become 'Yowling' or even 'Yuling'. Two curiosities exist in Hasted's account: the event is timed as taking place during Rogation week, but this is surely unlikely as Rogation week is immediately prior to Ascension Day (usually in May), and moves annually with the Easter calendar cycle. It can take place anything up to mid June when Wassailing would coincide with trees dropping surplus fruit, rather than with waking trees from their winter slumber. This seems unlikely. Hasted also identifies the name "Yowling" as derived from Eolus, an obscure Greek God of the Winds. Again this seems unlikely as 'Yule' actually derives from the Norse "Jul", not from classical sources. Not that this has prevented Hasted's account being copied many times since.

Much more realistic is the Blean Hoodening Song, though how much it had to do with orchards is a slightly open question, as Hoodening was more a pre-Christmas visiting activity:

Three jolly Hoodening boys, lately come from town,
Apples or for money, we search the country round,
Hats full, bags full, Half bushel baskets full,
What you please to give us happy we shall be,
God bless every poor man that's got an apple tree.

Hoodening, like some forms of wassailing, was a pre-Christmas visiting activity.

Possibly separately from apple tree wassailing ceremonies, there are also reports that bee hives were wassailed in different parts of Sussex, T. D. Horsfield (1827). Although little is known the logic is perfect – as wassailing is part of the system of farm and orchard management, and as bees pollinate the apple trees, what better than keeping bee hives as well and pledging to the bees in exactly the same manner as to the beasts and trees. The Sussex Wassail Song, collected by John Broadwood in 1843, one of the very earliest folk song collections, has the following lines:

For we've wassail'd all this day long and nothing could we find,
Except an owl in an ivy bush and her we left behind,
We'll cut a toast all around the loaf and sit it beside the fire,
We'll wassail bees and apple trees until your heart's desire.

From Amberley, Sussex comes this lovely bee wassailing song for Twelfth Night, collected by Rev. G. A. Clarkson, who was vicar of Amberley between 1840 and 1897:

Bees, oh bees of paradise, does the work of Jesus Christ,
Does the work which no man can,
God made bees and bees made honey,
God made man and man made money,
God made great men to plough and to sow,
God made little boys to tend the rooks and crows,
God made women to brew and to bake,
And God made little girls to eat up all the cake,
Then blow the horn!.

Devon and Somerset

By the end of the C18, a veritable torrent of references to tree wassailing filled the pages of county newspapers and journals, also the Gentleman's Magazine (1790s), John Brand (1813) and William Hone (1825). In Devonshire many of these describe how after supper the farmer, farm workers and possibly farm servants went to the orchard with a large milk pan full of cider, with roasted apples pressed into it. This differs slightly from the ale based festivities of many large houses and house visiting ceremonies. It is probably in these accounts that many modern understandings of apple tree wassailing have their origins. Despite local variations it is difficult not to be surprised by similarities in the ordering of ceremonies and in the chants, rhymes and incantations passed down.

"God made bees and bees made honey"

Brand (1813) describes how from the communal milk pail each person would take a cup-full of cider in a 'clayen' or earthenware cup brought for the purpose. Standing under each of the more fruitful trees in turn, words similar to those following might be spoken:

Health to thee, good apple tree,
Well to bear, pocket fulls, hat fulls,
Peck fulls, bushel bag fulls.

Each person would then drink from their 'clayen cup', throwing any cider and fragments of roasted apples left at the tree, while the whole company set up a shout.

Groups of young men would go between orchards performing wassailing rites or ceremonies in return for money.

Illustration from the Gentleman's Magazine 1791

William Hone (1825) relates how on Jan 5th, one of the best bearing trees would be encircled by the entire company, and this incantation would be chanted three times

Here's to thee, old apple tree,
Whence thou mayst bud and whence thou mayst blow!
And whence thou mayst bear apples enow!
Hats full! Caps full!
Bushel—bushel—sacks full,
And my pockets full too! Huzza!

T. F. Thistleton Dyer (1876) reports wassailing in Devon on Jan 5th separately at Kingsbridge and Salcombe - the farmer and men going to the orchard with a pitcher of cider, to one of the best trees. Guns are fired over the trees before everyone goes back to the house only to find the door can only be opened after a brief riddling contest with those inside. An earlier reference to the use of guns comes from the Illustrated London News of January 11, 1851, saying how on Twelfth Day Eve, Devon farmers used to rally out with guns and blunderbusses, and fire with powder only at the apple-trees in the orchards, with a chant and a song to ensure a bountiful harvest. Chambers Book of Days (1864) modifies the account slightly with the party going down to the orchard on Christmas Eve bearing hot cake (that has been dipped in cider) and cider as an offering to the principal apple-tree. The cake is formally deposited on the fork of the tree, and the cider thrown over the tree with the men firing off guns and pistols while the women and girls shout:

Bear blue, apples and pears enow,
Barn fulls, bag fulls, sack fulls.
Hurrah! hurrah! hurrah!

Blessing the Apple Trees at Tormohoun is recorded in Devonshire Folklore (1876). This ceremony is not as obviously private as some others, but more of a village celebration. The orchard owner has provided a good supper in advance before men; women and children go to the orchard with bread cheese and cider. A little boy was hoisted up into the apple tree as a personification of 'The Robin', the guardian spirit of the tree and he sat on a branch, where he cried out *"Tit, tit, I want more to eat"* and some of the bread, cheese and cider was handed up to him. While he was sitting in the tree, each member of the party had a cup and stood around the tree singing out the following toast

Hatfuls, capfuls,
Three bushel bagfuls,
Little heaps under
the stairs,
Hip, Hip, Hooray!

Here's to thee, good apple Tree,
To bear and blow, apples enow,
This year, next year and the year after too,
Hatsful, capsful, three bushel bagsful,
And pay the farmer well.

They then drank and fired a fusillade into the trees, making much noise with pistols, guns and any other firearms they could collect, or gunpowder placed in holes bored in pieces of wood - cheering and firing. After more cider they sang

To your wassail, and my wassail,
And joy be to our jolly wassail.

It was the end of winter, with more than a hint of symbolism in many accounts:

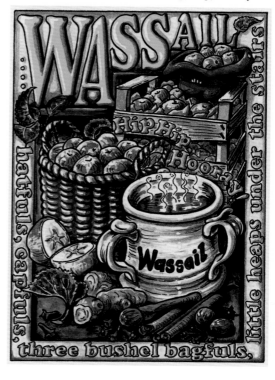

did the spirit of the orchard reside with the largest and most fecund tree, the 'Old Apple Man'? Or did all the trees themselves have spirits or were they attended by spirits both good and evil. For cider makers, the first and most important function of apple wassailing was to ensure a good apple harvest, proportionate to the amount of wassailing carried out. The Wassail was also important when part of a labourer's wage on a farm was paid in cider (finally outlawed in 1884). Noise making in the Wassail scared off insect pests, regarded as 'evil' spirits and attracted the 'good' spirit embodied by the Robin. In a slightly different interpretation it may have been believed in parts of the West Country that the spirits of trees were incarnated in robins and other small birds. One Wassail Song from Jacobstow in Cornwall has several verses in praise of the Robin.

Little robin redbreast has a fine head,
Give us a cup of cider and we'll go to bed,
With our wassail! Our jolly wassail,
And joy come to our jolly wassail.

Little Robin Redbreast has a fine wing,
Give us of good zider and we'll begin to sing,
With our wassail! Our jolly wassail,
And joy come to our jolly wassail.

Little robin redbreast, who was said to have scorched his breast by flying to the sun in order to bring the gift of fire to the world.
- traditional

From all the available evidence it would be mistaken to assume that there was only one best way to wassail. As an alternative, Kingley Palmer and Bob Patten (1971) show that in many places Apple Tree wassailing was a visiting custom involving several orchards during an evening. At Wootton Courtney, Exmoor a woman wassailed her apple trees on her own, pre 1914: singing an abbreviated version of an Apple Tree wassailing song as she put toast in the tree. At Sea, near Ilminster, cider was poured around the tree roots but only the most fecund tree was wassailed. Similarly at Crowcombe, only the oldest and the best tree was wassailed, and a boy was lifted into the tree to place toast, while remainder of the cider was poured around the tree roots. At Wiveliscombe, Cecil Sharp (1909) noted that wassailers danced in a circle round the tree. After firing the guns and making noise they stooped down and raised themselves three times, very similar to wassailing in Herefordshire (see p59). Christina Hole (1976) suggests that in Sussex, it was also not uncommon for all present to bow to the trees.

So even though wassailing took place within an social framework that was Christian, it was demonstrably magical in that it sought to conjure a beneficial outcome through intercession with the trees themselves. That outcome is increased fertility, fecundity that will produce a higher yield of crops. There may be a problem with semantics here - word meanings. Magical or miraculous, is there any difference? It's not so long ago that many diseases were thought to be caused by evil spirits. Thankfully, in those days, women who knew better could cure or ameliorate many ills by using herbal remedies handed down through their families.

Cecil Sharp's (1909) view is that the wassailing ritual is meant to propitiate the earth spirit and thus ensure a good crop of apples in the next season. W. O. Beaumont (1920) comments that warm cider thrown upon the tree or poured over the roots with much noise has symbolic significance in that the blood of the apple tree - cider made from the juice of the apples - is returned to the tree at the dead of winter to revive it for the coming year so that it will "once more blossom and bear fruit". Others invest significance in orchard parasites as evil spirits or in the Robins as guardians. In contemporary times, many wassailers are in no doubt of the spiritual significance of what they are doing: others see it as part of their overall tree management: others simply have fun.

On another matter Sharp and Beaumont are at variance. Both have connection with wassailing at

The blood of the apple tree - cider, made from the juice of the apples - is returned to the tree at the dead of winter to revive it for the coming year so that it will "once more blossom and bear fruit".

Bratton, near Minehead, Somerset. Sharp didn't see the wassailing ceremony at Bratton (Maud Karpeles, 1973, p.61) when it took place on Jan 5th 1905 but it was later reported to Sharp by the Wassailer from whom he collected the song "Wassailers meet in the orchard about seven or eight in the morning, join hands and dance in a ring around and apple tree singing....At the conclusion of the song they stamped on the ground, fired off their guns and ...shouted in unison Hatfulls etc. They then placed some toast soaked in cider on one of the trees and progressed to another tree where the ceremony was repeated." When Sharp asked the singer what happened to the toast, he replied *"All gone in the morning; some say the blackbirds eat it, but...."* Sharp (English Folk Songs, 1920, notes Vol. 2 No 42) was clear that January 5th was when wassailing ceremonies were performed. Paradoxically, Beaumont did see the Bratton ceremony, but in 1920 by which time it took place in the evening and on 17th January ('Old Twelfth Night').

When Cecil Sharp asked the singer what happened to the toast, he replied "All gone in the morning; some say the blackbirds eat it, but...."

Exactly when January 17th became the preferred date to hold Wassail ceremonies in parts of South West England is unclear. In 1752 the (old) Julian calendar had been replaced by the Gregorian calendar in Britain, a readjustment removing eleven days 'at a stroke'. This brought dates back into line with astronomical events but caused 'Calendar Riots' at the time because people thought they'd lost eleven days of their lives. Modern literary 'Calendars' recognise this event making reference to dates events such as Old May Day (May 12th), eleven days after their 'new' counterparts, justifying this as reclaiming the days lost.

References in relation to Wassailing of 'Old Twelfth Night', 'Old Twelvey Night' or 'Old Twelfy Night' meaning 17th January, as opposed to Twelfth Night (January 6th), appear to be both regional and fairly recent. We have found no mention of this title or its related date before about 1920, nearly 200 years after the calendar change. In Devon and Somerset many Wassailing dates did change to January 17th; by 1930 in Whimple, Devon and by 1935 at Carhampton, Somerset. Conversely in Sussex and in Herefordshire / Gloucestershire the celebration date remained January 5th, (though there have been some changes more recently). Some Herefordshire references also now call January 6th 'Old Christmas Day' rather than Epiphany.

Wassailing on 17th Jan 2007 at Whimple, Devon - 'Old Twelfth Night'

In many ways, the modern view of traditional Wassailing owes much to the continuousness of the ceremony at Carhampton, right through the twentieth century. Decline of wassailing in Devon and Somerset can be attributed to several factors (Ellen Taylor, 2003): mechanisation in agriculture and declining wages forcing workers off the land, many into the Welsh coalfields. Improvements in education, revival in formal religion, particularly Sunday Schools, law enforcement and attacks on rowdy drunkenness, changes in popular music taste all helped create the impression that somehow wassailing was 'old hat'. Like other aspects of country culture it somehow failed to pass on to the upcoming generation, some time between 1860 and 1914, varying in different places.

Edwin and Mona Radford (1949) describe Carhampton as surviving until just before 1939 with separate wassail parties going to different orchards, where they were joined in celebration by the farmer and his men, before all later converged on the Butchers Arms pub to end the evening. Gradual decline was arrested in the 1930s when Taunton Cider Company offered help, and wassailing at Carhampton survived World War II. In the 1950s a link was established with Yakima, Washington State, USA, a major centre of apple farming in the USA, some of whose foundation apple stock came from Carhampton. Trees from Yakima were sent over to England in 1958, and then in 1960, a large wassail bowl was presented to be used in alternate years in Carhampton and Yakima, though it is not clear that exchange visits now take place with this degree of regularity.

In the early 1970s, the ceremony suffered what might have been a body blow. The (then) landlord of the Butchers Arms, centre of the Wassail, took the chance to buy a lot of the land behind the pub, grubbing up several trees to build a number of houses, so that only a single tree is now left behind the pub. Apple tree wassailing had been going on continuously in Carhampton for over a hundred and fifty years, and by 1970 was probably one of the few continuing survivors of ceremonies with lineage of several hundred years. In 1972, as a consequence, Homer Sykes, the journalist and photographer specialising in English customs wrote about Carhampton "'Progress' has now put a stop to the custom.... Although there are still a couple of apple trees left, the ceremony has not continued because it was costing more money than it was bringing in".

Despite this, apple tree wassailing at Carhampton did continue and does so to this day. If it had stopped in 1972 would that have been the end of matters? Not a bit of it, as it had already started up again at Dunkeswell in Devon and in Sussex, and has since been re-awakened all over the place in a manner nobody would have foreseen in the 1970s. The English are a resilient and resourceful lot!

"Wassailing the Apple Trees" by Karen Cater. *This design is loosely based on a photograph from Carhampton taken in 1936, together with the words of the song traditionally sung at Carhampton's Wassail.*

Wassailing at the Butcher's Arms, Carhampton, Somerset.

No review of Wassailing ceremonies would be properly balanced without offering pride of place to the traditional wassail held at the Butcher's Arms, Carhampton, in Somerset continuously for over a hundred and fifty years, arguably the seed from which much of the modern reawakening has been able to blossom and bear fruit. Carhampton orchards are now much reduced, with a single tree, the 'King Tree' behind the pub, and a small community orchard not far away in the village, where Old Twelfth Night festivities begin with a Mini Wassail.

Though some people gather in the pub and the bonfire is lit early on, the Butchers Arms Wassail doesn't begin until the procession from the community orchard arrives. Then everyone gathers in a circle round the tree with the light and warmth of the fire and the warmth of the cider to succour the spirit. There's plenty of cider, mulled using a secret recipe handed down from landlord to landlord, and served in plastic cups from a large bucket.

The atmosphere seems informal, very much Somerset as she is now, with songs like "Bread and Cheese and Cider" and "for 'tis now our Wassail Day" alongside any that might be a bit older. There don't seem to be any song sheets — obviously there's no need.

Centre point of the ceremony is the Carhampton Song and Chant, usually led by the Landlord with everyone standing round the trees joining in.

A great cheer goes up and a volley of shotguns rings out, probably not for the only time during the evening. Part of everyone's cider is poured on the roots of the tree, both reward for the past and encouragement for the next harvest. Toast is placed in the tree – the traditional ofering for the Robins – guardian spirits of the orchard. Afterwards there is song and music in the pub.

Successive Landlords, among them Eric Tarr, Martin Tarr, Kevin Nicholls and now David MacCarthy have kept the tradition going into modern times. The Carhampton Song and Chant has been adopted in many wassails all over the West of England and beyond. Above all, the resilience of Carhampton has created the belief in many places that Old Twelfth Night – 17th January – **is** Wassail Night.

The centre point of Carhampton's Wassail; the song and chant and the firing of shotguns into the tree.

Carhampton has survived continuously for over a hundred and fifty years, and has become the model for many wassails across the country.

Wassail - Prosper and bear;
lino cut by Karen Cater based on words from the 'Truro Wassail' song

Part 2

Chapter 4

The Reawakening - Wassailing in 2013

Introductory

Chapters 1 – 3 reviewed the history of wassailing from the origins of the word Wassail until the mid C20. From a spoken salutation between two or more people, pledging Good Health and wellbeing, the word Wassail became attached to specific drinks like 'Lambswool', then to the celebration of Christmas (the full Twelve Days) amongst the well to do, using an elaborate Wassail Bowl. Subsequently it spread both as a pre Christmas fund raising custom amongst poorer people, before being demonised as cadging by the Victorians. In a parallel development, by the end of C16, it had also been extended to cornfields, farm animals and above all, to fruit trees, particularly apple trees.

Around these customs grew a substantial literature. Descriptions of ceremonies, songs, chants and incantations appeared in contemporary publications such as the Gentleman's Magazine, in newspapers, in books and journals, particularly of the Folklore Society. By the time Wassailing customs went into decline a significant if slightly hidden archive existed for anyone who might wish to reawaken them in the future. Much of the archive is now digitised and readily available.

This chapter examines how different groups have made use of this archive over the last forty years to re-awaken the old custom. It will also assess the influence of the remaining 'old' wassailing

Taffy Thomas' recipe for hot spiced cider Wassail drink. A memento of the Christmas party at Essex Singers Club, December 1996, which was to inspire our lasting interest in Wassailing.

ceremonies, particularly the one at Carhampton, and the growing wealth of practical hands-on experience gained as knowledge of reawakened ceremonies has circulated. Our interest (Karen's and mine) in Wassail ceremonies dates back at least to December 1996, when Taffy Thomas was the guest at the Essex Singers Club we then ran, bringing with him a flask of mulled cider and a beautifully decorated Wassail bowl with which to share a Christmas toast. In 1997 Karen produced the first Hedingham Fair greetings card image of a Wassail, followed by other Wassail images and we have written about wassailing several times in the Calendar of Traditional Customs. In 1998, we held our first private Wassail at home to bless the newly planted apple trees in our garden.

When this current project was mooted we decided on an internet search of current ceremonies to assess how widely the custom is now distributed, supplemented with secondary book research. We also visited as many current ceremonies as we could, to find out how and why their organisers had developed them as they had, and we asked several people to contribute their personal Wassailing experiences.

We anticipated finding about fifty active ceremonies in 2012 and were both surprised and delighted to find printed evidence of over 170 wassails in the UK, mainly in England, increasing to over 200 in 2013. Reports came from local newspapers, from sponsoring organisations and from supporting bodies like Orchard Groups and Cider blogs. Some accounts were factual - where and when wassails happened, who organisers were, names of the Wassail Queen or King. Other accounts ventured into history. Wassailing was frequently described as 'Ancient', 'English', and 'Pagan', designed to produce a bumper crop for the following harvest. Ideas were offered about what happened in ceremonies and activities taking place either before or afterwards.

We soon began to see patterns, both similarities and differences. With the possible exception of some wassails organised as social activities for a specific locality, sponsors and organizers of 'Reawakened' Wassails are new entrants. In all but a few cases, wassailing is not a continuous tradition, so the need to do things 'as they have always been done' whilst evident is not always compelling. Whereas in past times, most wassails involved people, nearly all of whom knew each other (this includes people giving to house visiting parties), the modern world is more open and many wassails are designed and advertised to the general public to draw people in, either for a single night's entertainment, or as customers of a cider farm or orchard, or as potential future members and co-workers in a community orchard.

We have written about wassailing many times in the Hedingham Fair Calendar of Traditional Customs. In 2013 the cover illustration featured Wassailing customs from Somerset, Birmingham, Essex, Devon, Cornwall, Bristol and S. Wales.

Gradually we narrowed the 170 wassails found in 2012 down to four groups, determined by who sponsored each wassail, finally settling into the scheme with each group to be reviewed in a separate chapter.

1. Morris Dancers and other folk enthusiasts organising Wassails. This group had provided much of the original impetus to the Reawakening.

2. Larger organisations for many of whom wassailing was part of their calendar of commercial events. After some soul searching we decided to link Visitor Attractions and Commercial Cider Orchards into the same chapter.

3. Bodies identifiable by location, where wassailing has or will become part of the social cement through which community spirit and identity is developed. Within this chapter schools and pubs have been included as well as 'villages'. Most house visiting events are also included here including those surviving continuously from times past.

4. Community Orchards promoting a 'Green' agenda, interested in the rejuvenation of previously derelict or underused spaces, the reintroduction of English fruit varieties allowed to decline into obscurity, together with sustainability and growing seasonal food. Although there is some overlap with cider orchards, it has generally been possible to make distinction on grounds of size.

This approach has limitations. Not all events sit comfortably in a single category. Where a Morris Dance led event takes place in a local orchard, should it be associated more with the orchard or the team. Where a Visitor Attraction was (re)developing an orchard, replanting with old varieties, but running events as well, should it be counted as a Visitor Attraction or Community Orchard? A similar dilemma existed in some cases between Villages and Community Orchards. As far as possible we tried to place events according to who appeared to us as their main organiser.

Morris Dancers and folk enthusiasts provided much of the original impetus to the Reawakening of Wassailing.

below: Plum Jerkum Morris at their annual Long Itchington Wassail 12th Jan 2013

The C20 Folk Revivals and Wassail songs

It is difficult to think of Wassailing as anything other than a folk activity, popular culture taking place within an environment largely removed from mass communication. In past times, as with Morris Dancing (see John Forrest, 1999), Wassailing had medieval courtly origins, but by the mid C19 its primary location was the countryside. The reawakening of Wassailing in the late C20 and C21 owes much to the so-called 'Folk Revival', a movement possibly spanning the entire C20, but with two periods of intense activity, between 1900 and the early 1920s, then later between the late 1950s and the mid 1970s. Both these eruptions took place against the background of searching for true English identity: the first in the face of the industrialisation, urbanisation and population explosion of the C19; the second during a period both of British withdrawal from being an Imperial power and experiencing American post-war cultural dominance encompassing film, television and most forms of popular music.

Almost by its nature, the 'folk' process is transformative: taking songs, tunes, dances and customs from the countryside into a more formalised setting: through collection and selection of repertoire, editing collected material by rewriting songs etc., dissemination through publication and broadcasting, creation of entirely new artistic forms based on 'country' material (e.g. early C20 orchestral compositions of Vaughan Williams, Grainger etc), and not least, performance. The first folk revival (1900 – 1920) and much of the decline of wassailing occurred within the same time period, prompting the question 'How might this first revival have contributed to the Reawakening'? The answer probably lies in collection of songs and customs, with many published in books and journals, which while they didn't circulate widely at the time, they certainly contributed to the archive. Wassail songs had been collected since the early C19, with little distinction between print and oral sources. Individual

Wassailing Apple Trees at Carhampton, Somerset 1936

Books of customs photographs published in the early C20 provided an archive upon which Wassail reawakening could later be based.

wassail songs tended to be attributed generally to counties rather than villages and / or singers. Then in the Oxford Book of Carols (1928), Vaughan Williams included 'Somerset Wassail' and (two versions of) 'Here we come a-Wassailing', both house visiting songs together with 'Gloucestershire Wassail' – an agricultural blessing song.

And here is to Colly and to her long tail
Pray God send our master he never may fail
A bowl of strong beer! I pray you draw near
And our jolly wassail it's then you shall hear

After the first folk revival subsided, collection continued. The second folk revival, with its left wing orientation and emphasis on work, was much earthier than its precursor. Its origins in Skiffle and Blues led to Anglo-American cultural tension running through its early core and eventually produced fracture. English society had also changed since the early C20. Radio and recording had developed means of dissemination much further reaching and more immediate than the printed word. Creation of free Grammar Schools by the 1944 Education Act, for selective intellectual elite, helped produce an enquiring creative younger generation, many of whom seized upon folk songs, dances, plays and customs as true expression of English identity. Some went on to become part of Morris Dance teams, village communities and cider orchard managers whose interest may have stimulated the Reawakening of wassailing. The role of the leaders of the second folk revival should also not be understated: Ewan MacColl and perhaps most significantly A.L. (Bert) Lloyd.

For anyone just starting in folk music in the early 1960s, it was songs that were the first attraction. At my first regular folk club, an 'English songs only' policy existed, readily embraced. One night the 'Cornish Wassail' was sung. What's wassailing? – A question without an immediate answer.

Now Christmas is comen and New Year begin
Pray open your doors And let us come in.

CHORUS:

With our wassail, wassail,
Wassail, wassail,
And joy come with our jolly wassail.

Colin Cater, singing at folk clubs since the 1960s. One night the 'Cornish Wassail' was sung. "What's wassailing?" we asked.

At about the same time the Home Service (Radio 4) ran a series called 'The Song Carriers' hosted by Ewan MacColl - just three or four songs in fifteen or twenty minutes recorded from 'field' singers. The ceremonial songs programme included a group from Cornwall singing the 'Malpas Wassail', same song structure as above but with deep sonorous harmonies and absolutely wonderful intervals on repetitions of the word 'Wassail'. Seeds were being sown and these were added to as folk club guest singers included Wassail songs in their sets. New books were being published and above all LP records produced. By this time, 'Topic Records', set up by the Workers Educational Association, and under the artistic direction of Bert Lloyd was both scouring the country for outstanding young singers and helping them with some of the material featured on their LPs. In 1965, Topic released 'Frost and Fire' by the Watersons –voices, and harmonies, including 'Here we come a-wassailing' and

Phil Tanner's wonderful 'Gower Wassail' (see p208):

We know by the moon that we are not too soon
We know by the sky that we are not too high
We know by the stars that we are not too far
And we know by the ground that we are within sound

CHORUS

Fol the dol, fol the doldy dol, fol the doldy dol,, fol the doldy dee,
Fol the dairol, fol the daddy, sing tooral-aye-do!

Ten years later, in 1975 The Watersons were to revisit ceremonial songs in the equally iconic compilation 'For Pence and Spicy Ale' which included the 'Malpas Wassail' and one they called the 'Apple Tree Wassailing Song'

Lily white lily white lily white pin
Please to come down and let us come in.
Lily white lily white lily white smock.
Please to come down and pull back the lock.

Joy, health, love and peace,
Be all here in this place,
By your leave we will sing
Concerning our King.

from 'Please to see the King' by Steeleye Span 1971

CHORUS

For it's our wassail, jolly wassail; joy come to our jolly wassail.
How well they may bloom, how well they may bear,
That we may have apples and cider next year

Hat fulls cap fulls, three bushel bags full
And little heaps under the stairs
Hip hip hooray

Between these two albums, in 1971, 'Please to see the King' was released by Steeleye Span. It would be years before either Karen or I found out that the King was actually the Wren, King of the Birds, able in legend to fly perched on the back of an eagle to the highest altitude possible. Its sacrifice at New Year, is maintained in Wren Hunting customs celebrated in a few coastal communities including in Wales, and has long been symbolic. A captured wren (now a wooden replica) is paraded in an elaborately decorated cage on top of a pole. Among participants, the wren's capture and death symbolises the death of the old year and the promise of return of the light. In Wales (this based on a conversation with Emma Lile, Curator at St Fagans National History Museum, Cardiff in March 2011), Wren processions are considered to be a form of (house visiting) wassailing. As such in Wales it has much in common with the Mari Lwyd (Grey Mare), also a house visiting custom mainly at New Year which the Welsh are also proud to describe as Wassailing. According to Emma Lile, apple tree or orchard wassailing is almost unknown in Wales

Old Christmas is past. Twelfth tide is the last
And we bid you adieu. Much joy to the New

Forty years on from the 1970s it is easy to see a causal relationship between popularisation of Wassailing Songs and the current Reawakening, even if the fuse burned slowly to begin with. When early Wassail pioneers began to set their events up, by their own admission some had little to draw on. The only active 'old' orchard Wassail widely known about was at Carhampton, Somerset, as visiting ceremonies at Curry Rivel and Drayton, Somerset were a well kept secret. Unless you lived in Cornwall, Bodmin was a long way away and until recently the Mari Lwyd at Llangynwyd, South Wales has not been thought of as wassailing outside Wales. As many wassail Re-awakeners were already active folkies what better than to draw on existing song repertoire. It was either that or write your own. In our survey, over 80% of the 200+ wassails included wassail songs. This applies as much amongst Community Orchards and Village ceremonies, showing that they too see wassail songs as part of wassailing heritage. In some places Community Orchards report difficulties learning the songs and teaching them to audiences. But more than 10% of wassails have their own recently written songs or poems, so the repertoire is growing.

It hasn't just been the old songs though. In Somerset (particularly NW Somerset including Bristol) there is a sizeable cluster of Wassail ceremonies. Many of these are only too keen to have The MangledWurzels (tribute band of The Wurzels) as their booked entertainment, suggesting that the Wurzels repertoire, including 'Drink up thee Cider' and 'Where be that Blackbird', touches Somerset culture in ways the older songs can't always manage. Wassails celebrate Cider, the Apple and Apple Trees; wonders that many in Somerset regard as all their own. Let's not forget Carhampton either – for many the Wassailing capital of the entire world. When wassails were in serious decline, many made the pilgrimage to Carhampton, perhaps only once, but that was enough. "Old apple tree, we wassail thee .... Hatfuls, Capfuls, Three bushel bagfuls. And a little heap under the stairs Huzza" - in how many ceremonies do these words figure? Even though they are traceable back to older written sources, much 'hands-on' experience will have come from Carhampton.

Much of the impetus for Wassail Re-awakening has come from Morris Dancers, recognising the need to rediscover English popular traditions, and finding imaginative ways of developing them.
below: Chanctonbury Ring Morris Men at Bolney Wassail 5th Jan 2013

Morris Dancing and wassailing

Much impetus for Wassail Re-awakening has come from Morris Dancers, recognising the need to rediscover English popular traditions, and finding imaginative ways of developing them. Nearly half the Wassails surveyed had Morris Dance involvement, either as organisers or as booked entertainment. How might this be when Morris Dancing had itself only just been saved from near extinction in the early C20? The 'Merrie England' movement of the early C20 occasioned revival of many aspects of British folk culture including Morris. Existing 'traditional' teams were 'discovered': dances collected and books published. For several decades Morris Dancing became enshrined in the school curriculum. Initially there were many female and mixed gender teams, but from the late 1920s the view gained strength that Morris was for 'men only', and a popular Cotswold Morris archetype developed that still remains strong - men in white with bells on their legs dancing with handkerchiefs or sticks. Through its regular Meetings, ties between the Morris Ring (organisation) and the Anglican Church were fostered, but dancers were also encouraged to describe Morris Dances as having 'Pagan origins' – a view now largely discounted. Male dominance was successfully challenged from the 1970s onwards as women reasserted their right to dance Morris, and as dances from other areas of Britain became popularised: Lancashire, Cheshire and Pennine West Yorkshire (North West Morris); Shropshire, Herefordshire and Worcestershire (Border Morris) and East Anglia (Molly Dancing).

It's curious that very little in terms of Wassail re-awakening predates the 1970s. Morris Dancers between 1930 and the 1960s were very aware of locality. Collectors had been careful to ascribe village identity to dances and tunes, calling each village 'A Tradition'. Announcers were encouraged to say things like "This is a dance from Bampton in the Bush". Away from Morris though, dancers primary folk interest was country dancing, an indoor activity in winter. Change came with the advent of folk song clubs in the 1960s, often held in cold dingy pub rooms, often left wing in character; rank with anti Americanism, anxious to rediscover Britain's own culture and/or to create a new one. One of the messages from folk song pioneers Ewan MacColl, Bert Lloyd etc. was that everyone should research their own area, initially to look for songs. Go and seek out local newspapers, museums, the archives at Cecil Sharp House, and be amazed at what you might find. You may even be lucky enough to live close to people who knew the old songs, or who still take part in an active ceremony or custom. There may be a local Morris side close by. If not, then start one up. So a (folk club) movement that began largely sedentary soon became very proactive. Some old ceremonies attracted tourists from far away – Padstow, Bampton, Abbots Bromley – and not just folkies either. Others started up because people teased out there had once been local customs where they lived, including Rochester Sweeps. Hastings Jack in the Green and the Earl of Rone at Combe Martin, North Devon.

Some old ceremonies attracted tourists from far away - Abbots Bromley and Padstow, or local customs were revived - Hastings Jack in the Green and Rochester Sweeps.

Then in the late 1960s and early 1970s Folk Festivals really got going, thanks in no small part to a visionary English Folk Dance and Song Society (EFDSS): Sidmouth, Whitby – both a week long; Chippenham, Fylde, Dartmoor, Loughborough – all owed much to EFDSS. With the Festivals came greater participation. Workshops proliferated. Rediscovered dance forms found an

abbots bromley / horn dance — Padstow / May day — HASTINGS JACK in the green — ROCHESTER SWEEPS

outlet: dances were exciting and spread like wildfire: dancers could wear (Black) face make up and brightly coloured tatter jackets; music was much more rhythmic and could be played by big noisy bands including several drummers. Nobody minded if teams wrote their own dances either! Morris was suddenly liberated from its white archetype. Two decades later in the 1990s things developed further when black make up became matched with black tatters and a darker image of Border Morris emerged. Many of the newer dancers were Pagans, for whom the so called 'Pagan Origins Myth' rather than discrediting the notion of Pagan origins of customs actually justified much of what they did; English traditions were pagan then and are certainly Pagan now! If they could be served up with a bit of culture shock, so much the better! But the new Border Morris dancers shared with their Cotswold cousins a desire to safeguard and develop England's heritage, whatever they believed it to be, so that many current Wassails are either organised by Morris Dancers or feature them as entertainment.

Border Morris with black faces and drummers emerged, and the 'Pagan Origins Myth' actually justified much of what they did.
above: 'Witchmen from the Daarkside'

One further factor to consider is seasonality. From the 1930's onwards, Morris had been a summer season long activity – pubs on weekday evenings and events at the weekend. But what might an active Morris side do to break into their long sequence of winter practices? As remnants of other customs and ceremonial became unearthed, some Morris teams saw that running a Wassail offered one possible solution. So it was that in 1967, on January 6th, Chanctonbury Ring Morris Men held their first Apple Howling, the ancient name for Wassailing in Sussex, a ceremony which has continued unbroken ever since, now held at Old Mill Farm, Bolney. It is based substantially around newspaper reports of the ceremony held at Duncton until the 1920s, and uses the "Stand fast Root, Bear well top..."chant formerly used in Sussex. The Chanctonbury celebration didn't immediately give rise to others. It was to be over a decade before in 1983 Grimsby Morris Men became part of the new Wassail at the Brandy Wharf Cider Centre, Lincolnshire; run by pub landlord Ian Horsley, based on Carhampton. It was held on the Sunday nearest Old Twelfth Night (Jan 17th) but using modern music from The Wurzels and Fairport Convention. In 1984, Leominster Morris began their annual wassail: in keeping with local tradition they celebrated on January 6th – Twelfth Night and incorporated the thirteen bonfires from past Herefordshire celebrations. Then in 1992, a second Apple Howling re-awakening took place in Sussex on Twelfth Night, at the Star, Waldron, involving Long Man Morris but inspired by Rabble Folk Theatre animateur, Gail Duff.

These four early ceremonies illustrate the involvement of Morris Dancers from a very early stage in the Wassail Reawakening, usually working with pubs or cider orchards. They show two separate celebration dates: Twelfth Night (Jan 6th) and Old Twelfth Night (Jan 17th), with preference seeming to depend on location. There is also a clear mixture of parts of celebrations researched from earlier times and newly created or borrowed elements included to make a joyous evening. This has become part of the whole Wassail Re-awakening. Each of these four early ceremonies has borne fruit in the shape of further Wassail events, small apple trees growing into large orchards! Since the 1990s many more Morris teams have started their own wassails.

It clearly works!

Poster for the Waldron Wassail 4th January 1992, the first to be run by Gail Duff and Mark Lawson in E. Sussex

Image by kind permission of Gail Duff and Mark Lawson

WASSAIL!
AT "THE STAR" WALDRON IN EAST SUSSEX
on SATURDAY 4th JANUARY 1992
7.00pm.
WASSAILING CEREMONY.

TRADITIONAL SONGS IN A SING-A-ROUND WITH THE COPPER FAMILY.
8.00pm ONWARDS

TRADITIONAL WASSAIL BOWL AND GAMES.

Wealden leisure
A SERVICE OF WEALDEN DISTRICT COUNCIL

Getting Wassailing going again in Sussex and Kent

I had been thinking about a wassailing revival for a number of years and then in the early 1990s running the Wealden Folk Project gave me the funding and support that I needed. As far as I knew Wassailing, or Apple Howling had completely died out in both East Sussex and Kent, and that before 1992, there had been no revivals. I wasn't aware then but have discovered since that Chanctonbury Ring Morris had started one in 1967 in West Sussex. So in January 1992 I decided to run one at The Star, in the village of Waldron, in the Wealden District. The pub was chosen as it had a big garden with a large apple tree. Long Man Morris was invited to take part as I wanted the custom carried on locally by local people and they're still running it at the same place. I also invited the Copper Family to lead the singing both round the tree and inside the pub afterwards. This was a one-off. Bob Copper shouted the 'Stand fast root' rhyme for us. To make the evening more interesting Mark Lawson of Whitstable Hoodeners researched some traditional games like Snapdragons and Gurning for a Cheshire cheese which he also came along to run.

For the next couple of years, Mark and I went down to Waldron, taking Rabble to dance alongside Long Man and to lend them the bowl turned by my husband Mick from a huge apple tree from Blean near Canterbury that was blown down in the 1987 hurricane. We had it decorated by a local silversmith. It was paid for by South East Arts and we're still using it. When Long Man Morris got their own bowl made, we decided that driving 35 miles across country on a cold January night wasn't a good idea. We started our own at the Red Lion, Badlesmere, near Faversham, Kent. We continued there for some years, moved briefly to Palace Farm in Doddington, but now go out to the Gate at Marshside, Kent. For a while, a party from Sussex including a few Mad Jacks Morris and various bonfire people, came up to Badlesmere, but then they started their own at Whatlington. From there, the whole thing spread like Chinese whispers and Wassails now happen all over the place. We even tried one at Brogdale near Faversham once, home of the National Fruit Collection, but it was too commercial. I also helped start one at a small village on the Marsh called Mersham. Mark Lawson has even been out to Surrey to help start wassails at Oxted and Lingfield.

I think the origins of most of our older customs are Pagan and the reasons that they were carried on was partly because people liked them, partly because they were a covert way of keeping the Old Religion alive, partly because they were just a 'way of life' that people fell easily into and didn't want to get out of and also they were just bigger things that people did 'for luck', like throwing salt over a shoulder or not walking under ladders. They are deep, deep down in our psyche and we need them for that reason, rather than their being overtly religious. In historical, rather than religious terms, they were things that continued organically whoever was in power and whoever the god of the moment might have been. They transcend religion. They are the thread that holds us to the ancestors and to Nature and to the cycle of the year. Different religions can still put on the decoration, whether the trees are blessed by a vicar or whether a Pagan ritual is used. As folk practitioners we are fortunate in that we can still do them and our year does not just consist of Christmas from September to December and a great blank for the rest of the year. And the great bit is that we can use them as we want whilst still keeping the basic theme. Even those who don't claim to be Pagan can still celebrate at the major festival times because there is always a custom or tradition to take part in or re-discover. Those of us who do, get the best of both worlds!

Gail Duff, organiser of the Wealden Folk Project- October 2012

Doddington Wassail,
Mark Lawson and
Gail Duff place toast
in the tree.

photo by kind permission of Gail Duff

Reawakening in the Cider Orchards

In 1974 the Taunton Cider Company held a Wassail on Jan 17th, Old Twelfth Night, at its Norton Fitzwarren factory. It's surprising that commercial cider orchards ever stopped wassailing, although the history of Whiteways Cyder of Whimple during C20 (Eric Whiteway 1990) is insightful. This charts a combination of commercial success, with major technological advances, a series of business mergers and large scale changes in drinking taste. Whiteways became involved with once iconic brands like Sanatogen Tonic Wine and Babycham, eventually becoming part of the Allied Breweries group. All control over the original production base and the spirit that inspired it was lost. Whimple became transformed from a cider making plant to a bottling plant. Contact with orchard suppliers disappeared and by 1989 activities had largely ceased. Perhaps it's not surprising that wassailing apple trees became forgotten. A very similar pattern of events also led to the demise of Taunton Cider in 1995, the closure of Norton Fitzwarren (which is now a housing development) and loss of five hundred jobs.

However the Taunton Cider Company wassail reawakening has left a legacy. They are widely credited with keeping the wassail going at Carhampton in the 1930s, though some wonder if their motives had more to do with publicity than tradition. When they resumed in 1974, they were the first cider company to take up

Major technological advances contributed to the demise of many of the smaller cider producers during the twentieth century.

the old custom again. Their ceremony was an 'invitation only' event primarily intended as a reward for workers. Taunton Cider is also thought to have been the first in modern times to have featured a Wassail Queen in their ceremony (James Russell, 2011), an idea since widely followed.

It would be a decade or so before other cider producers followed Taunton Cider, during which time both the industry and public taste had begun to change again. Mergers and marketing that made household names of Whiteways, Bulmers, and others had also left independent orchards and craft producers with viable if smaller businesses. Here wassailing offered not only spiritual transformation and the promise of a larger crop but the chance for a large crowd to enjoy a thunderingly good evening; coverage in local and regional media, and possibly to make a substantial donation to charity. In 1987, wassailing started up at West Croft Cider, makers of Janet's Jungle Juice, Brent Knoll, Somerset: in 1988, it was also begun at Westons Cider of Much Marcle, Herefordshire, in conjunction with Leominster Morris, who had wassailed since 1984 and who ensured a sound basis in Herefordshire traditions. Roger Wilkins of Wedmore, Somerset, a cider enthusiast as well as producer started his wassail in 1999, followed by Rich's Cider, and many others in Somerset, Devon, Gloucestershire and as far east as Kent. By 2010, public perceptions of both cider and wassailing had changed sufficiently to allow Gaymers Cider, part of an international drinks group with an orchard at Stewley, near Ilminster, Somerset to invite Tom Parker Bowles of the Daily Mail to write up their wassail, which he did in highly favourable terms.

Some independent orchards and craft producers were left with viable if smaller businesses.

Social Cement – the Spirit of Place

Before easy public transport, all wassails were celebrated locally, both their strength and weakness. Wassails surviving continuously long enough to be described as 'traditional' all have their basis in local communities. In three places in England, Bodmin, Drayton and Curry Rivel the wassail is a visiting custom, with a small and usually closed group of wassailers visiting houses in turn to bless their hosts, their trees and sing the wassail song they've carried for generations. At Curry Rivel, the wassail begins at the King William IV and always finishes there (after as many as ten house visits) with the Burning the Ashen Faggot ceremony some time after 10p.m. In South Wales, at Llangynwyd, near Maesteg, the Mari Lwyd party goes out each New Year's Day. At Bodmin, wassailing takes place on Twelfth Night (January 6th). Origins can be traced back to 1624 and the Wassail has become an important part of the town's annual calendar of events. The exception to house visiting as a 'village' wassail is at Carhampton, which is centred on the Butcher's Arms. The Carhampton ceremony has contracted from one involving several orchards as these declined, but its ability to attract both tourists and great affection has ensured its survival. Its long standing reputation and widely copied haunting chant have enabled its influence to spread far and wide – many reawakened wassails use the Carhampton chant, and the belief is now widespread that Old Twelfth Night, January 17th is *the* night to go wassailing.

Roughly a quarter of the modern Wassails discovered in the survey are based in local communities. Of these the majority take place in one or more orchards, often with an event afterwards to end the night. A smaller number involve a series of house or orchard visits, with a similar number held in schools and several in pubs. For the enthusiast distinguishing between continuous and reawakened wassails, the earliest modern wassail is almost certainly that held at Dunkeswell, Devon every year since 1953 on January 17th. A group of wassailers goes from house to house during the early part of the evening with the visit to the orchard not taking place until midnight. In 1993, wassailing was reawakened in Whimple, Devon again on January 17th. Whimple has strong cider traditions and an equally powerful sense of its own history. Mentioned by folklorist Sabine Baring Gould in 1908 and again in the Devon and Exeter Gazette (1931), its wassail lapsed during World War II and has been reawakened by Whimple History Society. Several orchards are visited and as the evening's fame has spread, it now draws in musicians and singers from all over Devon and beyond. In 1992 wassailing began at Stoke Gabriel, Devon. This has become a family child friendly event taking place at twilight with different types of entertainment. Now held on the Saturday closest, to January 17th it shows how traditions evolve to meet modern circumstances. From these beginnings twenty years ago, many other ceremonies have been established, in Cornwall, Devon and Somerset and elsewhere all over the country.

Whiteways Cider memorabilia from the collection of the Whimple History Society

Sustainability, Englishness and Community Orchards

Prior to the Millennium only a few Wassail Re-awakenings had started, mainly in areas where Wassailing had continued well into C20, and any disconnect lasted no more than a few decades. Little evidence existed to show how well wassailing might flourish away from the locality of an old event or among people with no specific interest in Cider or Folk customs. Could it be that wassailing might be just a wee bit esoteric? Reawakened wassails had not always adhered directly to their antecedents' format. They seemed to have a central core both in their spirit and constituent parts, but many ideas consciously borrowed from elsewhere have been incorporated to make them more mainstream. These include torchlight and lantern processions; bonfires; Wassail Kings and Queens; food and drink as part of an evening's jolly; Mummers, storytellers and amplified music (mostly folk based), as entertainment; collections for charities.

To a considerable extent wassailing has taken off since 2000 because of the 'Green' movement, already focussing on the English Apple. Awareness had grown that hundreds of English apple varieties were becoming extinct - a major loss of horticultural heritage. Between 1970 and 1997 orchards had declined by almost 40,000 hectares in the U.K., a 64% reduction in 27 years. Orchards fallen into disuse needed to be rescued, new orchard spaces found; old varieties re-popularised, old skills relearned. In 1990, the environmental charity Common Ground set up Apple Day on the third Saturday in October, as a national orchard harvest celebration – public events to raise consciousness about English Apples, and encourage local groups to research and establish community orchards. By 2000 this had proved so popular that Apple Day events had spread throughout the month of October. In 2006 Common Ground published 'England in Particular' which included an outline description of Wassailing. One year later The Apple Source Book came out, an account of nearly 3,000 varieties of British apples, with distinctive flavours and places of origin, together with apple stories and associated customs. It also included recipes, information about apple identification, and ideas for juice pressing, cider making and wassailing. In 2008, it was followed up with publication of the Community Orchards Handbook. All three publications have been heavily influential, so that many Community Orchards have sought to include a Wassail as a winter activity.

Volunteers meet at Community Orchards to plant trees, prune, and harvest.

So, what is a Community Orchard? This survey has identified nearly 60 ceremonies taking place in community orchards and there seem to be a number of linking factors. First and foremost, they are nearly all run by volunteers; only a few larger ones have paid staff. Volunteers meet several times a year to plant trees, prune them, prepare land for cultivation, build furniture and equipment such as bee hives, harvest the crop and perhaps run one or two other public events as well as the Wassail. In many cases, areas of land managed are quite small: former allotment plots, old orchards revived after a long period of disuse, part of the estate of large houses fallen into disrepair and now run by a local council, urban recreational land saved from development by a local political campaign, land donated by a benefactor to hold off the developers. Some community orchards are larger: part of a nature reserve or city farm, or managed by a nearby ethical restaurant. In some cases they are part of larger farms but heavily dependent on volunteers and not large enough to be called a commercial cider orchard. Many community orchards are situated in heavily urbanised areas, including London, Birmingham, Nottingham and Bristol, as well as in Wales and Scotland, not the sorts of areas normally associated with orchards or wassailing. For many, their principal concern is sustainable food, food with character and taste in marked contrast from what's available from the supermarkets, seasonal food using traditional English varieties. Many are supported through umbrella organisations like the Transition Network,

Incredible Edible or the London Orchards Project, Abundance London or the Avon Organic Group, or the Gloucestershire Orchards group

Many community orchard wassails have a markedly different character from those organised by Morris teams or cider orchards or as village celebrations. Some hold preparatory activities, concerned with tree management or the wassail itself, before the wassail starts. A number include a long walk as part of the event. People are encouraged to bring food and drink 'to share' and there is sometimes considerable ethical reticence about use of shotguns (weapons) or cider (alcohol). Some quite openly recognise that they don't know much about wassailing and are even nervous about singing – it's quite likely that they will create their own songs or poems rather than use the old ones, Many make substantial use of entertainment to expand the event – Morris Dancers, community choirs, storytellers, brass bands, face painters for the kids – the list goes on. It is doubtful whether any of these wassails stretch far back before the Millennium, some run for a couple of years and then lapse, but it's amongst Community Orchards that wassailing is growing most rapidly.

In 2006 Common Ground published 'England in Particular' which included an outline description of Wassailing. One year later The Apple Source Book came out, an account of nearly 3,000 varieties of British apples, with distinctive flavours and places of origin, together with apple stories and associated customs.

Geographical distribution of wassails

Among Wassails found in the survey, thirty six different county areas of England, Scotland and Wales are represented. Of these, the most populous groupings are in Somerset (36) and Devon (19), areas which justifiably lay claim to apple wassailing heritage. Of the 36 Wassails in Somerset, ten are organized by cider producers; sixteen are village celebrations, but only six happen in Community Orchards mainly in the North West of the county. Of nineteen in Devon, three are in commercial orchards, but there are nine village wassails. In Devon, Cornwall and Somerset, visitor attractions have become actively involved in wassailing. All but three of nine wassails in Gloucestershire are held by cider orchards, as are four out of five wassails in Herefordshire. In both these counties it's not easy to distinguish whether orchards or Morris Dance teams are Wassails' principal organizers. In Sussex, Morris Dancing is central to all ceremonies.

Of those situated outside traditional wassailing areas, many locations are urban. There were eight wassails in London, all but one in community orchards. Seven events are held in Bristol and three in Birmingham, again all in community orchards. Elsewhere, wassails are held in places as far flung as Cumbria, Lancashire, Yorkshire, Durham, Lincolnshire, Staffordshire, Warwickshire, Northamptonshire, Oxfordshire, Hertfordshire, Cambridgeshire, Dorset, Cornwall, South Wales, and Scotland. From its traditional heartlands, wassailing has gone national.

The Wassail season

Discussion about what is the most appropriate time to go wassailing occurs in several places in the book. Until early C19 when Christmas was a full twelve day holiday ending on January 6th, all Wassailing seems to have happened during the Twelve Days or leading up to it, particularly on Dec 21st but perhaps as early as November. Although Twelfth Night gradually became separated from Christmas as C19 progressed, there is little reason to think that Wassailing dates altered before early C20 and in Cornwall, in Sussex / Kent and in Gloucestershire / Herefordshire / Worcestershire any departure from the Twelve Days is likely quite recent.

The situation in Devon and Somerset differs markedly, through the emergence of Old Twelfth Night (January 17th) as the preferred night to Wassail. The Ashen Faggot Ceremony at Curry Rivel takes place on January 5th, sometimes called Wassail Eve, or Old Christmas Eve. Bushaway (1982) describes a Herefordshire ceremony with thirteen bonfires as taking place on Old Christmas Eve (i.e. Jan 5th, Twelfth Night). The reasoning for both timing attributions is unclear – both fall within the Twelve Days of Christmas, but it is just possible they have moved from a pre-Christmas timing, out of a local unwillingness to accept the loss of eleven days following the adoption of the Gregorian calendar in 1752 – i.e. that that both events originally happened on Christmas Eve, and moved back eleven days in protest when the new Calendar came in. However it is not known when the Curry Rivel date was set; was it in C20 or earlier? As far as other wassails held on January 17th are concerned, there is little evidence for this date anywhere before

Until early C19 when Christmas was a full twelve day holiday ending on January 6th, all Wassailing seems to have happened during the Twelve Days.

As much as blessing and fellowship, wassailing is about celebrating the turn of the year.

1920, which suggests the change might be cultural, perhaps inspired by Folklore (see Ch 3 p72).

Does this matter? In 2013, approximately 10% of wassails were celebrated on January 17th, mainly village events. Nearly double that number happened on Twelfth Night or the day before. Only 30% of wassails

happened on either of the preferred dates. Of the remaining 70%, a few take place before and during Christmas. Most happen during an extended season, from the second weekend in January (particularly the weekend nearest January 17th) to the second weekend in February. Some others fall outside these times completely. Organisers seem pragmatic when choosing dates. Events happen when people are most likely to come and when entertainment (Wassail MCs, storytellers, Mummers, Morris Dancers, etc) can be booked to appear, with some in high demand. At present there is little or no sign of wassailing following Mumming and Morris Dancing into an all year long folk continuum, and while the primary purpose of Wassailing remains associated with the return of the Sun and Waking the Trees from their Winter Slumber, this is probably unlikely to happen in the future.

What are Reawakened wassails really like?

Points of Difference and Similarity

Looking at a sizeable number of wassails, sharp variations are visible. Who might the MC be? In times past, determination of who might MC a Wassail would often have been automatic – the Farmer, the Master of the House, more likely 'The Butler', who turns up in the 'Gloucestershire Wassail', still an almost universal figure in Gloucestershire, Worcestershire and Monmouthshire, often officiating at ceremonies like weddings as well as Wassails.

A jolly Wassel-Bowl
A Wassel of good ale,
Well fare the butler's sole
That setteth this to sale - Our jolly Wassel

"*The Carroll for a Wassell Bowl*", (William Hone, 1825)

'The Butler' often officiating at ceremonies like weddings as well as at Wassails. During the 2012 Chepstow 'Wassail and Mari Lwyd', the wassail party became part of a wedding celebration. A presentation to the bride and groom was made consisting of three elements each with its own significance: the yew for long life, nuts for fertility and the candle for the light and love the couple bring to each other.

photo - Chepstow Wassail

A different tradition exists in the notion of 'The World Turned Upside Down', once very prevalent as a social safety valve. Anyone might rule for a day or even a week. It might be historical figure like Lord of Misrule, or could be chosen at random by hiding a bean or a pea inside an Apple or Plum cake. Once chosen, the entire company would follow the wishes of 'King Bean' and 'Queen Pea' for the duration, drinking copiously till the revel's end.

Now, now the mirth comes with a cake full of plums
Where Beane's the King of the sport
Besides we must know, the Pea also
Must revel here as Queen of the Court

Which knowne, let us make joy-sops with the cake
And let not a man then be seen here
Who unurg'd will not drink from the base to the brink
A health to the King and the Queene here

Mid C17 – possibly written by Robert Herrick

A second area of considerable variation surrounds activities held either before the Wassail or afterwards. Activities prior to a Wassail tend to happen more in (small) community orchards – perhaps as a magnet to attract new volunteers, letting them sample some of the work they might do as members of the group. As an alternative, where wassail events are aimed at families and particularly children, entertainment including face painters and storytellers is often an added attraction, as are craft workshops making torches or lanterns that will be used later in a procession.

What entertainment might there be after the Wassail? Perhaps everyone will return to a central point for beer / cider and apple cake. Entertainment might consist of Mumming, or Morris Dancing, Belly Dancing or possibly a choir. A Wassail supper might be provided. Alternatively there might be a ceilidh or barn dance, or the chance to dance the night away to the delights of Chicken Shed Zeppelin or the MangledWurzels. Some events are free: others carry an entrance charge. Some organisers make a donation to charity, either from a collection or from ticket sales. These variations will influence the character of an individual Wassail.

Although there are many differences between modern wassail ceremonies and events, it is also manifest that a common philosophical and spiritual core links them together, offering the seed of further growth. Wassails are celebrations in which people come together to share food and drink, and pour blessings upon one another and the trees, fields and animals that surround them. Sometimes they also work or share their lives with them. Nearly all events take place at the darkest time of the year, summoning back light and warmth. It's a chance to enjoy a good jolly, but there's also an underlying belief that it's magical and will conjure a larger crop. Trees are seen as animate beings who will respond to being well treated especially if pests are dislodged and guardian birds encouraged. For many the whole process is spiritual.

Anyone going to an orchard wassail may experience some or all ceremonial elements that have been handed down from times past. They may be asked to bring something to make a noise and to wear wellies if it's muddy. . During the ceremony there may well be:

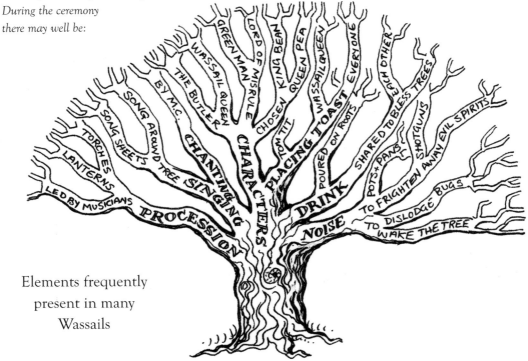

Elements frequently present in many Wassails

Blessings and Fellowship

Origins of the word 'Wassail' lie in fellowship and in giving and receiving blessings. 'Waes Hael', 'Be of good health' – these are words that ring as much around modern wassails as at any time in centuries past. Cider, beer, juice, apple cake, cheese are all brought to ceremonies so that they might be shared and circulated freely around. Sometimes cider will be decanted into a three handled wassail bowl so that whoever is drinking at least one other hand will be on the cup. At other places plastic cups will be handed around so that everyone can dip them into a communal bucket of cider or beer that is itself replenished from time to time. Any liquor remaining may be poured on to the ground or over the tree roots as a gift to the tree – returning its fruits to encourage greater fruitfulness in the year to come, or as homage to the (Roman) Goddess Pomona, guardian deity of fruit trees and fruitfulness, still recognised and regarded in some fruit growing areas. People will probably surround the trees to be wassailed; songs will be sung; Food and blessings will be given, to the trees, the birds as guardian spirits; the company or to buildings, all followed with considerable noise. Kingley Palmer records that in Somerset arable and stock farmers were celebrated with these verses altered to suit.

Good luck to the hoof and horn
Good luck to the flock and fleece
Good luck to the growers of corn
With blessings of plenty and peace

- Folklore of Somerset 1976

At Curry Rivel, Somerset where the Ashen Faggot is burned at the conclusion of the Wassail, there used to be a Wassail Lamp bearing the following inscription. (We enquired about this out of season but the Landlady didn't seem to know anything about it – we hope that it is in safe keeping in the village)

Apple Tree I Light with Glee, While Bell and Candle Wassail thee.

The landing of the Holly Man outside Shakespeare's Globe Theatre, Bankside, London, 6th January 2013

More recently, for the last seventeen years, the players of the Lion's Part Company have held a Wassail beginning outside Shakespeare's Globe Theatre, Bankside, in London. Their ceremony is highly original but also draws heavily on written records. It begins with the landing of the Holly Man outside the Globe, after a half hour boat trip from the northern bank of the Thames. Several blessings are spoken and writ large on banners so that the large audience can join in. Afterwards, the company processes to the George Inn, Borough Market. They choose King Bean and Queen Pea to lead festivities from a bean and pea cunningly concealed in the apple cake. There is Mumming and a celebration with few rules, in the C17 manner of Robert Herrick and John Aubrey – the World turned Upside Down. As part of the festivities a further recently written blessing is declaimed to the George Inn itself

Wassail to this old building
Long may she stand
Every barrel and every brew
Cheer the company bravely
Every drinking day!

The Turn of the Year

As much as blessing and fellowship, wassailing is about celebrating the turn of the year and symbolises the death and regeneration of the Sun. Its positioning within the twelve days of Christmas, particularly where it has been celebrated on Twelfth Day illustrates this.

Now jolly old Christmas, thou welcomest guest
Thou from us are parting which makes us look wisht
For all the twelve days are now come to their end
And this the last day of the season we spend

Cornish Wassail Song from Grampound - from J. Barrett, Truro

Other Wassail songs wish Merry Christmas and Happy New Year: other folk customs recognise the dark winter times as ones of renewal. Immediately following Twelfth Day was the agricultural return to work, celebrated widely as Plough Monday in eastern counties. Nearly all Mummers Plays, whose real season is deep winter, include scenes of combat between a hero and an assailant in which one or both is killed before being revived by the magical 'Quack Doctor'. These scenes have been frequently thought symbolic of death of the old year and return of the New. Particularly in Herefordshire and Worcestershire, wassails may include a thorn cage stuffed with straw and carried on top of a pole. After toast has been placed in the apple tree and cider sprinkled on its roots, this thorn cage, the 'Herefordshire Lantern' is ignited: for the wassailers this represents the sun reborn. The Herefordshire thorn cage bears an uncanny similarity to the (Welsh) decorated Wren house – itself symbolic of the return of the light and the defeat of darkness. At the midwinter, the coldest and darkest part of the year, people encourage the return of light and warmth taking part in ceremonies of sympathetic magic to affirm their faith that it will be so.

Chiddingfold Tipteers Play (Mummers) 27th December 2010 The Quack Doctor prepares to bring the slain back to life. Symbolic of the death of the Old Year and the birth of the New.

Spirituality

As the Herefordshire Lantern shows, the way in which modern wassails are both put together and written up suggests that many people participating see them as spiritual. Tree blessing ceremonies are intended to be transformational, to increase the yield at harvest time as this old rhyme from Painswick Gloucestershire says. Without wassailing this might not, probably would not happen. It's magical

Blowe, blowe, bear well, spring well in April,
Every sprig and every spray bear a bushel of apples against
Next New Year's Day

But it's not just the ceremony as a whole that is spiritual, but several of its component parts. In many places, people invest the trees themselves with spirituality. It may be that one particular tree is wassailed, the King Tree (as at Carhampton), or the Old Apple Man another name sometimes given to the largest tree, where for many the spirit of the orchard was thought to reside. At Colwall, Worcestershire, the Butler, the Wassail MC walks clockwise ceremonially three times around the tree celebrating the orchard spirits, before pouring cider on the roots of that tree. In other ceremonies, a significant number of trees are selected - three trees at Torbryan, Devon; thirteen in the Hunter's Moon, Sussex Wassail. A major part of almost all tree wassails is that the tree should be woken from its winter slumbers, with noise of horns, shotguns, drums, saucepan lids, musical instruments, anything, in the belief that evil spirits can be chased away and the trees flourish. Even where science has reduced evil spirits to the temporal status of bugs and parasites as reports of the Wassail at Fairfield orchard, Lancaster suggest, the process of waking up the tree is seen to be valuable. At Dunkeswell, Devon, evil spirits are portrayed in human form, as young lads dressed up as Witches in white dresses, who lurk in the boughs of the trees, only to be chased out of the orchard with shotguns fired at midnight to the ringing accompaniment of church bells. Not only do evil spirits need to be chased away from the orchard, the place is blessed with guardian spirits as well. Amongst tree wassails it is almost universal that toast is placed into the trees 'for the Robins', the guardian spirits. Often this is done by young girls – Wassail Queens, sometimes dressed in white symbolising purity. In some places, blue tits are seen as guardian spirits and as with the Dunkeswell witches, the old practice locating young lads as Tom Tit up in the trees waiting for toast to be passed up to them has been revived. 'Tit, tit, I want something to eat' they cry at Peterstow, near Ross on Wye, Herefordshire. At Colwall, Tom Tit's role is more conventional; placing toast in the tree as the Wassail Queens do.

Young boys up in the branches represent 'Tom Tit', the guardian spirit of the Apple Trees. "Tit, tit, I want something to eat" they cry at Peterstow, near Ross on Wye, Herefordshire.

Discussion of spirituality almost inevitably raises the parallel issue of organised religion. During the last four hundred years or so, while the religious history of England has passed through several eras the official established religion has always been Anglican Christianity. The degree to which other traditions have been tolerated has varied. Much of the language of old wassail songs and chants indicates a Christian context in which wassailing took place, though the spiritual nature of ceremonies might suggest other root sources. Much depends of the view of the interpreter. Past writers (Stubbes, 1583, Bourne, 1776) have been Christian zealots anxious to suppress anything that didn't conform to their narrow world view. They tended not to be fond of wassailing – words like 'grotesque' seem to crop up frequently.

TIT, TIT, I WANT SOMETHING TO EAT!!

By contrast, much modern wassailing commentary, particularly in local newspapers takes pleasure in describing it as derived from England's 'Pagan past', an approach perhaps intended to show wassails as somehow different from other forms of modern popular enjoyment – a counter culture. The world view of this book seeks to escape from overuse of labels, either religious or secular. Wassailing is part of the lore of the English countryside, able to be practiced by anyone. Ceremonies held at Blagdon, Little Hereford and elsewhere are presided over by Christian ministers confident that increased yields of apples are evidence of the grace of God, an explanation that would probably not even occur to many wassailers. Others (Stretham, Cambridgeshire; Torbryan, Devon) are overtly Pagan. Most lie somewhere in between: they are undeniably spiritual without being attached to any single organised religion. Kenninghall Wassail in Norfolk in 2008 was described thus "I felt caught up rapturously in a timeless, wintry, shared warmth" In 2009, Tom Parker Bowles wrote about the wassail at Gaymers Cider Orchard, Stewley, Somerset, "Although the ceremony might seem anachronistic in this digital age, it's as much about community togetherness as it is a piece of English pagan history. .... It made perfect sense to chase off the evil spirits, and toast the cider god with the golden fruit of his own trees....... Far from the mess of outdated clichés and over-romanticised tradition I had imagined the night to be, I feel rather moved. The whole ceremony makes perfect sense"

Chapter 5

Morris and Folk Wassails

Wassail Reawakening owes much to folkies and Morris Dancers, but it's been very much a bottom up affair with groups developing their own methods of blessing trees and involving participants. Knowledge is freely available now, particularly through the internet but this hasn't always been so. In 1967 and for a long time afterwards wassailers struggled for information on which to base ceremonies. The diversity amongst twenty six groups on which this chapter draws thus bears testament to considerable ingenuity and ability to ferret things out. In the interests of sensible ordering we have distinguished between wassails held in orchards, those based around pubs, and those which involve visiting several venues, either private or public houses. There are certainly other Morris teams and folk clubs who Wassail differently, good on them and we'd love to hear from them.

Chanctonbury Ring Morris Men served cider and cakes after wassailing the oldest tree in Bolney orchard.

Orchard wassails

Old Mill Farm, Bolney, where Chanctonbury Ring Morris Men hold their wassail is an apple farm. Its aroma is pervasive and its produce is available for sale at the farm shop. Yet this doesn't feel commercial, rather there was an overwhelming sense is of generosity and fellowship in the gifts of cider and apple cake after the ceremony. Chancs have a unique place in the wassail reawakening; starting in 1967 they are the first wassail of the folk song club era. Using the "Stand fast root ......" chant they have anchored their ceremony firmly in their Sussex heritage, and in the General Hullabaloo they have something truly individual.

Apple Howling, Bolney, West Sussex. 5th January 2013

The evening of the first Saturday in January was mild and muddy. We arrived at Old Mill Farm, Bolney, where Morris men in tatter jackets with tinsel and Christmas lights on their top hats were directing cars to parking spaces on tracks and in yards around this working farm. 'Wobblegate Pure Apple Juice', was advertised as the main crop on the farm sign by the road, and we were going to be given samples after the 'Apple Howling' we had come to witness. The farm shop was well stocked with the usual fruit and veg you would expect to find, but one entire wall was groaning with shelf after shelf of bottles of the farm's own speciality tipple – apple juice from bramley or cox, and 'Real Cider' too, both sweet and dry.

The master of ceremonies called the company, now numbering about three hundred, to order with a megaphone and invited those who wished, to carry a flaming torch, and everyone to follow him in procession to the oldest and largest tree in the orchard, which was about to be 'Howled' or Wassailed. I watched as an ever lengthening torchlit group snaked its way down into a shallow valley and then up again to the trees – an effect both eerie and spectacular

The 'Old Apple Man' was a magnificent mature tree, the representative of the entire orchard for the evening's purpose of scaring away evil spirits and conjuring a better crop for the coming season. We all formed a ring around the tree, with a hundred or so torch carriers creating a ceremonial space. Though the weather was not very cold, the heat from the torches was palpable as I stood sinking gently into the soft mud at the edge of the circle.

First we called out the invocation; Here's to thee old apple tree, Mays't thou bud, mays't thou blow! Hats full, caps full, bushel, bushel bags full, Sacks full, barns full, and our pockets full too! Hurrah!

Next the MC squirted a libation of cider from a plastic squeezy bottle onto the branches and around the roots to encourage good growth, then he placed pieces of spiced wassail cake soaked in cider in the fork of the tree, which we were told was to ensure the goodwill of the robins. Then everybody chanted; Stand fast, root! Bear well, top! God send us a howling crop! Every twig, apples big! Every bough, apples enow! Hurrah!

Eight children were called for to beat the tree with sticks (a task several enjoyed thoroughly!) which was intended to awaken its spirit from winter slumber. Someone shouted to a professional photographer "Oi. Did you know you've got a big lump of mud on the end of your. . . . . lens?" to the amusement of many of the crowd. Then we all sang the wassail song;

"Wassail and wassail all over the town
Our cup it is white and our ale it is brown,
Our cup it is made of a fine ashen tree,
Likewise our malt of the best barley.
And it's your wassail,
And it's our wassail,
And it's joy be to you
And a jolly wassail

It didn't seem to matter that instead of ale in an ashen bowl, the ceremony on this night used cider in an old washing-up bottle!

Chanctonbury Ring Morris Men danced several Cotswold style dances on the lane as it was too soft and slippery this year to dance under the tree, followed by one of the highlights of the event — the general hullabaloo! A shotgun signalled the start for hundreds of pots, pans, tin lids, rattles, horns and anything that could make a noise to be beaten, shaken or blown for a full two minutes of unimaginable din. The signal from the shotgun to end the hullabaloo was almost drowned out!

With all evil spirits well and truly frightened away, we gave three cheers for the apple tree, three more for our host the farmer, and three for the company — ourselves! before we all tramped back to the barn for cider and wassail cakes. I took one sip of the strong dry cider and decided that as I was driving I dared not drink it, so I poured mine into Colin's cup, who was enjoying his own thoroughly! The Morris men danced again, and then invited us to join them in a session of music and songs afterwards at the local pub, which turned out to be a splendid evening of chorus songs and conviviality.

The overwhelming feeling of this event was of generosity; although a collection is always taken to help defray the expense of putting on the Apple Howling, costs are rarely covered, but the men of Chanctonbury Ring continue to celebrate the annual rite as they have done for nearly fifty years, providing entertainment for the local community and an opportunity to promote the business of the farm hosting the event. The life-force of the apple tree is encouraged for the next season's fertile growth, and the people who participate in the apple howling exchange greetings and blessings at the turning of another year.

Karen Cater

In wassail ceremonies in Kent, including that at Keston, hosted by Ravensbourne Morris, people throw salt over their shoulders towards the tree for luck. Elephant up a Pole Morris from Coventry wake the trees up with noise and by beating the ground with sticks. Held at Ryton Organic Gardens over lunchtime on the Sunday before January 17th, they recite poetry before everyone encircles the main tree for the Wassail, after which it's down to the pub for a pint and more dancing.

Elephant up a Pole Morris wake the trees with noise and beating the ground with sticks, then encircle the main tree for their wassail.

photo - Elephant up a Pole Morris

No more than seventy miles away from Coventry, on Twelfth Night (Jan. 6th), Leominster Morris makes its annual homage to the goddess Pomona bringing a blessing on the orchards of the county of Herefordshire. Similarly to Chanctonbury Ring, Leominster Morris Wassail draws strongly on local traditions. Staring in 1984, and after eight years collaboration with Weston's Cider of Much Marcle, between 1988 and 1996, this wassail visits a different orchard each year. From a nearby pub, with flaming torches, a procession of a couple of hundred people sets out for the orchard. Following the gift of toast and cider to the tree chosen to represent the orchard, the Herefordshire Lantern is ignited (see Ch 4, p109), but also in the orchard a circle of twelve bonfires has been created with a thirteenth, sometimes called the Judas Fire in the middle. This is then lit and immediately stamped out before the other twelve bonfires are lit simultaneously. What does this signify? Interpretations differ. Perhaps it is Christ and the apostles, with the traitor instantly obliterated while the others represent light as the eternal renewal: perhaps it is the twelve months of the coming year and the ending of the preceding year (for other explanations see Ch 3 p60)

On the second Saturday in January, in Sussex one of the most successful wassails of recent years has been run by Hunters Moon Morris, with a bonfire, Tipteerers (Mummers) Play, ceilidh and several invited guest Morris teams. For the tree blessing, thirteen trees were decorated with ribbons that shimmered in the torchlight. Thirteen is a magical number – the moons in a year, the numbers in a coven, many traditions regard thirteen as symbolic. Here they represented renewal in a winter orchard and the promise of a larger crop as they were blessed with mulled cider and cider cake. Sadly, this wassail became a victim of its own success and the ever increasing numbers attending both presented a security hazard and undermined the mystical and spiritual purposes that had led to its creation in the first place. In 2012, Hunters Moon decided to relocate, and their wassail in 2013 was a much smaller event in a pub close to their home base. However, at least two previous Hunters Moon guest teams have become involved in new wassails starting up in 2013.

In Cumbria where damsons are the principal fruit crop, Crook Morris has begun wassailing a damson orchard in the Lyth Valley. They celebrate tree blessings and ousting evil spirits with as much noise as possible, together with the renewal of the New Year, marked with a 'Wren' ceremony. 'The King' is sung and a miniature wren in an ornate cage is hung in the branches of the King tree. In 2012, collections raised a goodly sum for the Kirkby Stephen Mountain Rescue team too. In contrast, Uplyme Morris of Lyme Regis, Dorset offered something more formal. Children, with song sheets, took part in the ceremony of 'The Toast' to wake up winter's slumbering orchards, followed by the first performance of "Mummers the Word" - with a cast of ten and a horse called Finley. This new play was performed

With flaming torches, a procession sets out for the orchard.

Bolney Wassail 2013

three times around Lyme, with torchlight processions in between and interspersed with madrigals by Lyme Bay Chorale.

Not everyone takes ceremonial or even Morris Dancing quite so seriously. Wickham Morris, who hold a Wassail at Fruitwise Heritage Orchard, Durley, Hampshire are unsure whether Morris Dancers should be wassailing at all, as there are few records of this from times past. They played, sang and danced in the dark, drank hot spiced cider and enjoyed a nocturnal barbecue, though they left out the guns and placed bags of peanuts and fat balls in the trees for the small birds. They've also added to tradition by putting up bird boxes in some of the larger trees! In short they do it their way and in the process raise a fair bit for charity.

when Morris Dancers go wassailing, they'll go 'in kit' and often 'made up', with their bells on, with sticks, hankies and other clobber and with their musicians.

Pub wassails

When is a Morris Dancer not a Morris Dancer? Silly question really as the answer is "Hardly ever". So it shouldn't be a surprise that when Morris Dancers go wassailing (either organising or as entertainment), they'll still be Morris Dancers. They'll go 'in kit' and often 'made up', with their bells on, with sticks, hankies and other clobber and with their musicians. They may well invite other teams to their events. Sometimes they'll centre on one pub: others wassail 'on tour' visiting several (public) houses either walking or by car. And there will always be ale, lashings of it, unless they're on a cider sabbatical.

On the second Saturday in January,

Isca Morris Men hold a traditional cider Wassail at The Ostrich Inn, Newland, near Monmouth - an evening of joy and conviviality under the watchful eye of 'The Butler'. Lots of songs are sung and a splendid wooden wassail bowl passes freely with wassailers pledging good health to each other and to the whole company. Another well known pub wassail is that held at The Fleece, Bretforton, near Evesham, Worcestershire. This is a large event, hardly surprising as Evesham is in one of England's primary fruit growing areas. Many other Morris teams come, alongside Civil War Re-enactors, with much traditional singing and mulled cider. A torchlight procession leads everyone through to the apple orchard and afterwards back to the pub for a really festive evening.

In similar vein, one of two Wassails celebrated annually by Hook Eagle Morris Men has parts in the Vaughn Millennium (Community) Orchard and then the Waggon & Horses, Hartley Wintney. When the torchlight procession returns to the pub, by tradition the Morris Men enter by the back door, toast the landlord and depart through the front door, pledging good health to everyone. More dancing and merriment follows particularly when the Squire of Hook Eagle appears through the pub door with the Wassail Cup followed by a foaming jug of good ale.

At Bishopsteignton, Devon the wassail is led by the Apple Queen and her entourage, together with Grimspound Morris, a Mummers troupe, musicians and singers. Everyone brings lanterns & torches to the orchard, which has no light, along with pots & pans, buckets & spoons which together with muskets wake the trees. Then a

Grimspound Border Morris

procession follows the musicians to the Bishop John de Grandison Inn, for mulled wine, roast local pork and apples, Border Morris dancing and a mummers play. At nearby Torbryan, situated between Newton Abbot and Totnes, about a week later Beltane Border Morris hold a ceremony that appears similar but with the symbolism strikingly stronger. The Apple Queen is a young girl dressed always in white as a symbol of purity in the belief that a blessing from a pure spirit will be more potent in dismissing evil spirits from the orchard and encouraging growth and the new crop. Toast for the Robins, shotguns and pouring cider on the ground feature in time honoured manner. The Carhampton song and chant is used, but Beltane Border would like to find a tune for the local Cornworthy song, first printed in the Gentleman's Magazine in 1805, over two centuries ago.

The Apple Queen is a young girl dressed in white as a symbol of purity in the belief that a blessing from a pure spirit will be more potent in dismissing evil spirits from the orchard.

Huzza, Huzza, in our good town
The bread shall be white, and the liquor be brown
So here my old fellow I drink to thee
And the very health of each other tree.
Well may ye blow, well may ye bear
Blossom and fruit both apple and pear.
So that every bough and every twig
May bend with a burden both fair and big
May ye bear us and yield us fruit such a store
That the bags and chambers and house run o'er.

OBJ Morris of Wokingham, Berkshire, a mixed Border team formed in 1996 hold an annual wassail at the 'The Boot', Bracknell, to which several neighbouring teams come. They've researched traditions carefully to develop a ceremony combining ideas from different sources. Their wassail cake contains a hidden bean: whoever gets it becomes King of the Bean and presides over the ceremony, appointing a consort to assist. As well as blessing the pub tree with noise, toast and cider, like Crook Morris they incorporate a Wren Hunt. After they've sung 'The King' they bury the wooden wren under the apple tree with much ceremony. For several years OBJ Wassail took place in mid January, but in 2013 it was put back a month to February 17th, to allow the team to lead the ceremony at nearby Warfield Walk 'n' Wassail, held on January 5th at Jeallotts Hill Community Landshare. All the experience OBJ has acquired through their own event was thus able to be planted in another location and amongst new people.

Duton Hill Folk Club Wassail 2011.

Paul Reece as 'Master of the Revels' intones the wassail chant.

Visiting and Folk wassails

Soon after Karen and I moved to Southey Green in 1995, we set about turning the back garden into a small orchard with three apple trees, a damson and a plum. Once the trees were planted we decided to wassail them on January 17th, as we had heard that was the day to do it. We hastily cobbled together a ceremony with songs and incantations including the Herrick poem (see p53) and some of the 'Hatfuls, capfuls ....' chants. We invited several friends and asked each of them to offer a blessing and to pour spiced cider on the trees (being careful to avoid the Leylandii). Afterwards there was supper and a bit of music. This went on for three or four years before it gradually lapsed. Several years later in 2010 when Duton Hill Folk Club started we decided to try again.

Three apple trees, a damson and a plum - the small orchard we planted to wassail in our back garden at Southey Green.

Duton Hill Folk Club Wassail at The Three Horseshoes

We had started a new folk club in the summer of 2010, in the upstairs room of a country pub that was full of character, real ale and collections of random stuff in glass cabinets, with amusing feminist graffiti all over the walls of the ladies' loo. Now Yuletide was approaching and we thought it was beholden upon us to start a few traditions of our own. After a convivial evening over a meal, the organising group decided that a Christmas party absolutely must include a Wassailing!

We bought a young potted apple tree with a single small apple still attached and placed it, still in its pot, in pride of place on a table in the middle of the club room for everyone to see as they arrived. Crackers were pulled, carols were sung, and a quick round the room session of seasonal songs and tunes gave way to the very first Duton Hill Folk Club Wassail! I brought a three handled wassail bowl from which to share the hot spiced cider, passing from hand to hand around the company as Colin sang his own wassail song with everyone joining in the chorus. Then to the tree blessing, Mary as MC recited;

"Wassail your trees that they may bear many an Apple, many a Pear,
for the more or less fruit they will bring as you do give them
Wassailing"

then cider punch was poured onto the tree roots, and toast placed in the branches, after which we all sang;

"Our Wassail, jolly Wassail, joy come to our jolly Wassail.
How well they may bloom, how well they may bear,
so we may have apples and cider next year."

"Hat-fulls, cap-fulls, three bushel bag-fulls,
little heaps under the stairs,
Hip, hip...." "HOORAY!"

with a roll on the drum, and as much noise as we could make to scare away the evil spirits. After this the whole assembly filed down to the bar singing "Here we come a-Wassailing" to bless the pub and the landlord with;

"Now master Derek, thanks to you we'll give,
and for our jolly Wassail as long as we live,
and if we survive for another new year
we'll do this again, and hopefully we'll have a decent apple tree by
then..!"

The party atmosphere continued for the rest of the night as beer, cider and song combined with the warmth of friendship and the roaring fire in the hearth.

Everyone agreed this had been a wonderful evening and that the wassail should become an annual event, but what to do with the little apple tree? We discussed donating it to various places in the locality, perhaps to start a community orchard, but eventually decided it should be planted in the pub garden (which Derek very kindly did for us) to be the permanent 'Wassail Tree' for the folk club.

The following December we wassailed our very own Duton Hill Folk Club apple tree, though this time we performed a specially written topical Mummers Play beforehand. The Wassailing proceeded pretty much as it had the previous year, but first we all had to negotiate the fire escape down to the garden carrying all the paraphernalia for the ceremony while also playing a tune!

By the third year, the tradition had been well and truly established, and it was with a little disappointment we had to abandon our own tree in favour of a 'surrogate' apple tree. It had rained and rained for a fortnight before the Wassail, and it seemed as if the whole country was flooded, Duton Hill was sodden and Derek's garden would have been ruined by tramping feet. So taking our cue from an annual wassail held at The Barton Inn, Barton St David, Somerset, we cut a branch from my own garden's Bramley, 'planted' it in a pot, and again wassailed indoors. This year we used the chant from Sussex, with Paul as 'Master of the Revels' intoning; "Here stands a fine young apple tree, Stand fast root, bear well top...." which caused some amusement. Mary had provided shed loads of toast 'for the Robins', then in the absence of shotguns for evil spirit scaring, we distributed party poppers to everyone who fired them with gusto, releasing a cascade of paper streamers to festoon the 'tree'. After all, traditions have to evolve with the changing times to survive! Then down into the main bar of the pub to toast and bless Derek as Master of the House, with Mary and Anahata singing the Wassail song from Truro in Cornwall. Several weeks later, at Derek's invitation a much smaller party went back to wassail the real tree in the garden when we were joined by some of the lads who happened to be in the pub, and who definitely wouldn't have been at a folk club Christmas party.

Next year – who knows!

Karen Cater

A 'Kissing Spear' - When held over someone's head, it is customary for that person to kiss their neighbour.

In 2004, on the first Tuesday after Boxing Day, members of the folk community in Hastings, East Sussex set up the Hastings Howl, using the Sussex name 'Howling' for Wassailing. Part of their motivation was a sense of dissatisfaction with large, often ticketed, local Wassail events, and the belief that Wassailing had once been more a community based tradition with wassailers moving from house to house. This type of house visiting ceremony also offered better opportunities to sing much loved Wassail songs. Homes were chosen that have at least one fruit tree (of any kind) in the garden. When the Howlers arrive they sing a song while enjoying a glass of spiced ale, mulled cider or wine or Lambswool; whatever treat the host has prepared. After that it's out into the garden armed with toast and cider to bless the tree and the traditional Sussex chant is given "Stand fast Root, Bear well top ...... "

This is followed by the satisfying crack of large Rookies (bird scarers) and the cheers and shots of the assembled Howlers, with drums, saucepans, whistles for even more noise. The Wassail bowl is passed around and the usual toast, "Wassail", "Drink Ale" After that, it's back into the house for more singing and fellowship. Songs the Howlers love best include 'Sussex Sugar Wassail', 'Gower Wassail', 'Here we come a-wassailing', and the 'Boars Head Carol', with lots of others sung as well. Howlers wear a mix of Victorian-esque or rural clothing. Bodices and britches are regularly seen: buxom wenches and tweedy Squire types are a common sight. The 'Bearer of the Toast' wears a hat decorated with apples and carries a basket of toast, apples and song sheets, plus the Kissing Spear. This is a branch of apple tree, decorated with ivy, ribbon and mistletoe. When held over someone's head, it is customary for that person to kiss their neighbour. The final stop is The Stag Inn, in Hastings Old Town, where there is a small orchard at the top of their hillside garden. Here the Howlers gather to perform the rites for the last time, and then join the lively folk session inside the pub.

One of the very earliest re-awakened wassails has taken place every year since the 1980s, just on the Hertfordshire side of the county boundary with Essex, close to Harlow, Hertford and Bishops Stortford. It's organised by the Beerfordbury Barrel Tappers and Wine Tipplers Association, an unlikely name for part of the local Stortfolk Folk Club. Dressed in tatter coats and carrying sticks they usually go out for five evenings, just before Christmas, each one a tour of as many as ten pubs where they sing Carols and Wassail songs and offer street theatre cameos. Collections are taken for a range of local charities, and several hundred pounds are usually donated each evening. Their website states that their December timing isn't traditional. Well, actually it is, because just before Christmas was exactly when wassailers used to go out collecting for charity, even if the charities were a bit more personal then (See Ch 2). They say it's just a cover for all sorts of silly behaviour and in their own words:

"We sing two or three wassail songs per pub and the regulars generally then pay us to go to the next hostelry."

But they're coming up to their thirtieth anniversary.

Cookley Wassail, near Kidderminster takes place on the first Friday in February. Organised by Foxs Morris, a large mixed Border Morris team; it links both Morris and Wassailing with the local community. The team has close connections with Cookley Sebright Primary School whose Head Teacher first got it going. Festivities start at The Anchor in Caunsall, with a

Foxs Morris

display of dancing before the fruit trees are wassailed. It then moves to the Eagle and Spur in Cookley where there is a torchlight procession around the village, finishing at the School

Not far away from Cookley, at Long Itchington in Warwickshire, another wassail is hosted by Plum Jerkum Morris. As their name suggests, their interest is more in Plum than Apple Trees, but this is a walking tour- the small village of Long Itchington is still blessed with five pubs, each to be visited by the teams who join Plum Jerkum for the day's dancing and merriment. Plum Jerkum has a particular interest in the local yellow plum variety, the Warwickshire Drooper, and who can blame them? 2012 was a very poor year for all English fruit and to judge by the quality of the Plum Jerkum spiced plum cider we sampled, it's well worth fighting to preserve.

Wassailers from Warwick university, Mixed Rapper & Sword, Liecester Anstey men (Cotswold style) & hosts Plum Jerkum in Long Itchington. Ink & pastel by Colin Dick

Long Itchington Wassail, Warwickshire 12.01.13

The "Duck on the Pond", a pub with a view of its namesake, saw the gathering of a motley crew of Morris dancers and Mummers for the 'Annual Long Itchington Wassail' on a chilly January lunchtime. As the crowd gathered, the pub became strewn with the paraphernalia of Morris Dancing and Mumming – swords, shields, stick bags costumes painted with the Cross of St George, top hats festooned with pheasant feathers Around the pond, early snowdrops were in bloom, hinting at the possibility of the bitter weather that was to come the following week. We'd come to this event because an elderly artist friend, Colin Dick, had sent me an ink sketch he'd done at the previous year's Wassail, and we were intrigued.

But this was not only a Wassail it was a Morris 'walking tour' in an unspoilt village in the very heart of England, with several pubs still doing good trade in these straightened times. Plum Jerkum dancers wore mostly black, with top hats and each dancer in a different colour tatter jacket. They were a jolly bunch, with guests Coventry Mummers, Bradshaw Mummers and Alvechurch Morris. Bradshaw Mummers performed a traditional combat play where St George fought a Turkish Knight wearing the most fantastic long curly-toed shoes, but instead of swords, the weapons they employed in a capering duel were Morris handkerchiefs! Both heroes eventually lay slain on a mat painted with a crime scene body outline to be revived by the ever present Quack Doctor. Suddenly, a pyrotechnic explosion, and Beelzebub appeared through a cloud of smoke, before the cast ended with a song to make way for Alvechurch Morris, with their more traditional Welsh Border style of dancing, mostly in frock coats and corduroy trousers.

Then it was on to 'The Harvester' for the wassailing of the plum tree. We were told that the wassail had originally happened in the garden of 'Short Scratch Cottage' further down the road, as the newlyweds who lived there were anxious to start a family, and they had heard that wassailing encouraged fertility. Apparently it worked a bit too well, as after a few years they had produced several children and had to move to a bigger house! Now a young plum tree had been planted in a raised triangular bed opposite the pub, outside the old shop, and it was to this tree that the wassailers had turned their attention. Starting with a greeting and the dancers tapping the trunk with their sticks, the Wassail song was sung and a small boy tied toast on the branches with lengths of string threaded through the slices. A starting pistol twice fired shots to scare away the evil spirits. We all cheered and the residents of the old country store brought out trays of hot spiced Plum Jerkum in plastic cups. Breathing in the steam that rose from the scalding liquid and savouring the fruity flavour, we were both struck that there could be no better way to warm the cockles of your heart and your frozen fingers at the same time! Though Plum Jerkum tasted quite similar to hot spiced cider drinks sampled at other wassails around the country, it had a depth and richness that was the unique gift of the plum. We wondered if any of the dancers knew how my artist friend was, as we had not seen him recently, when someone said 'he's sketching in that car over there!' I took a steaming cup and carried it over to Colin Dick, who was bundled up in warm clothes against the chill and drawing on cardboard with pens and pastels. 'Ah, Plum Jerkum!' he said as we shared a toast to the New Year.

Coventry Mummers then performed a Plough Play, sometimes called a Wooing Play, in which a Recruiting Sergeant tries to entice a reluctant Carter 'to take the shilling', but when a 'Fair Maid' (in fact a cross-dressed bloke with a beard!) shows him a child and claims he is the father, he changes his mind and joins the army without delay. A fight between the Recruiting Sergeant and a Farmer culminates with the Doctor enacting his symbolic role with the resurrection of the characters signifying the return of the life force for another year and the renewal of the cycle of the seasons. Alvechurch Morris and Plum Jerkum danced again outside the pub on a wide tarmaced area that made a perfect Morris stage. Sadly we couldn't stay till the end of the wassail and missed its finale at the "Green Man" pub just down the road. We wished our generous hosts adieu and headed back towards the "Duck on the Pond", then eastwards to a land of watery fens and Straw Bears.

Karen Cater

Plum Jerkum Morris at Long Itchington Wassail.
Watercolour and pastel by Colin Dick

Amongst the more unusual Wassails is that held in Chepstow every year in mid January, organised by The Widders Border Morris who call it the 'Wassail and Mari Lwyd'. Chepstow is the first town most people speed past after crossing the Severn Bridge into Wales. Situated on the River Wye, with its ancient Marcher Castle it gazes across into an English enclave, part of Gloucestershire that is itself bordered to the north by the seemingly untamed Forest of Dean. The event reflects the meeting of English and Welsh culture that Chepstow itself symbolizes. In recent years the 'Wassail and Mari Lwyd' has become a large winter festival drawing both dancers and watchers from long distances. The first wassail takes place at the lower Dell, near Three Tuns pub in mid afternoon and then again at the Bandstand near The Bridge Inn in the early evening. Peter Symonds, The Butler, usually conducts proceedings along with The Forest of Dean Morris men and friends. The event includes singing, dancing, blessing an apple tree and hanging pieces of toast soaked in cider on its branches.

Mari Lwyd (the Grey Mare, see p44), the ancient Welsh custom is widely regarded in Wales as a (visiting) Wassail. On this long day there are several Mari Lwyds going out with the Morris tours, all with the chance to visit several houses. However, the unique element to the Chepstow Wassail is the meeting of the Wassailers and the Mari Lwyd Party. One of the bridges linking Chepstow with England is an old iron footbridge across the Wye. In the early evening the (English) Wassail group and the (Welsh) Mari Lwyd group gather on the border, the middle of the old iron bridge, where they greet each other and exchange flags in a gesture of friendship and unity between them. The Welsh then invite the English to join them in Wales in their merrymaking. And great is the merrymaking in the pubs during the evening. Even in 2013 when the event was curtailed by heavy snow, the wonderful Wassail Bowl (see p27) made in 2006 circulated ever more freely.

photo - Aelfgythe Morris

Aelfgythe Border Morris, formed 2008, held their first Wassail on 28th January 2012, at their home pub, the Weighbridge Inn, Alvechurch, Worcestershire. Aelfgythe was a Saxon woman made a saint, recorded by chronicler William of Malmesbury (1095 - 1143).
The team is female, dynamic, very striking in appearance, supported by a large band on a variety of instruments including didjeridoo and djembe.
The wassail was a poignant occasion, marked by the planting of an apple tree a 'Winter Gem' in memory of Robin Walden, who was very special to many people in Alvechurch. A new dance 'Ælf Wassail' was written for the occasion and Jenny Jingles wrote this atmospheric poem.

Aelfgythe Morris Wassail

Hie we all to the orchard wide,
The smallest tree to find
For we have come to wassail thee
That we hope you shall prove kind
Merry met, and merry be, and 'wæs hæl' to us all

Midwinter's past, the old year is dead
The New Year's welcomed in
'Tis time to wake thee from slumber
And beg for thy favour in Spring
Merry met, and merry be, and 'wæs hæl' to us all

Maleferous imps in thy branches
Torment and cause thee blight
With clam'rous din we cast them all out
And banish them away to the night
Merry met, and merry be, and 'wæs hæl' to us all

Good spirits now we call unto thee
Fair robins with scarlet breast
To feast on the bread adorned on thee
With their grace thy shall be blessed
Merry met, and merry be, and 'wæs hæl' to us all

The fruit of last year's labours you see
Sweet cider we pour at your trunk
Thy brethren's gifts were well-received
But that cider's now all been drunk!
Merry met, and merry be, and 'wæs hæl' to us all

So, O Tree, we have come to thee,
We have sung to thee and blessed
So wake your roots and bud your boughs
Bear us sweet apples of the best
Merry met, and merry be, and 'wæs hæl' to us all.

Chapter 6

Cider Orchards and Visitor Attractions

In parts of the West of England, many see wassailing as their own special preserve, part of the unique culture of the region. The association with cider is strong and the claim to an unbroken tradition is powerful in several places. As wassailing was reawakened, commercial cider orchards including Taunton Cider at Norton Fitzwarren, West Croft Cider at Brent Knoll (pre 1990), and Roger Wilkins at Mudgley were amongst the earliest to restart, giving wassails starting later a solid foundation of practice on which to draw. But are there any special circumstances surrounding commercial cider orchards as organisers of Wassails? The issue is complex because wassails organised by Morris teams and others frequently take place in cider orchards and sometimes any distinction can be quite fine. We have tried to locate this distinction around whether Wassail ceremonies are an end in themselves; whether they are part of a longer 'event'; or most persuasively whether they might fit into a continuous annual pattern of business activity.

Wassail Bowl made for Taunton Cider Company, whose cider orchard at Norton Fitzwarren was one of the earliest to restart wassailing.

As our survey yielded increasing information, wassails were found at a significant number of Visitor Attractions, who also have an annual pattern of business activity. Some were National Trust (NT) properties; some were under public authority control and some owned independently. These Visitor Attractions nearly all had orchards, so wassailing had

transformational as well as marketing significance, and wassails might also provide educational opportunities. Slowly we were drawn to the view that purposes underlying wassailing in Visitor Attractions differed only slightly from Cider Orchards, so linking them together seemed logical. Of the forty three wassails examined in this chapter, sixteen are at Visitor Attractions with the remaining twenty seven in Cider Orchards of which all but four are in the West Country: seven in Devon, nine in Somerset; five in Gloucestershire and two in Herefordshire. Of six wassails in the far West in Cornwall, four are held in visitor attractions and only two in cider orchards.

Principal amongst the Cider Companies holding Wassails is Gaymers, who have been wassailing since 2007 at their Stewley Orchard near Ilminster, Somerset. Originally from Norfolk, and with history possibly dating back to C17, Gaymers moved to Somerset through a series of business mergers and acquisitions. Since 2010 they have been part of international drinks conglomerate C & C Group plc, based in Ireland, the second largest cider producer in the world, who also own Bulmers, Magners, and the Blackthorn brand names. Other larger producers who wassail include Weston's of Much Marcle, Herefordshire (since 1988); Thatchers at Sandford, North Somerset; Barnes and Adams, of Wootton under Edge, Gloucestershire and the Kent Cider Co of Faversham. All these companies have brands that can be purchased in most major supermarket chains.

Thatchers, Magners, Weston's and Gaymers Ciders; all brands owned by companies who hold wassails and also sell their cider in major supermarkets.

Newly reawakened wassails in the West Country were able to build on foundations of the continuous celebration at Carhampton, perhaps helped by written archives of traditional ceremonies which had lapsed only within living memory. Chapter 3 showed considerable diversity between different orchard wassailing events in times past, as well as a common ceremonial purpose. By the late C20, because Carhampton alone remained as a working model, its format has been widely followed so that the core of cider orchard Wassail ceremonies has become almost a constant.

However, modern Wassails held in commercial cider orchards or visitor attractions are not just ceremonies: more likely the ceremonies are part of an evening's entertainment with several different parts. A whole range of different offerings is now available for anyone going to several Wassails. Ever since the introduction of the Wassail Queen at Norton Fitzwarren in 1974, organisers have looked for imaginative ways of presenting the old custom in an accessible contemporary format (including that of historical re-enactment). Diversity has ruled. Many ceremonies are now presided over by a Wassail Queen. Others have a King or a King and Queen. At Wilkins Cider, Mudgley the King is crowned by Father Time. At Peterstow in Herefordshire, Tom Tit presides. As for the entertainment - try getting away from Morris Dancers, you'll be lucky! They're at twenty two of the forty three venues. Eight venues report Mummers Plays, including a

Many venues book Mummers as entertainment at Wassails.
below - Langport Mummers - in great demand for Somerset wassails.

continued on P136

Roger Wilkins Cider Farm, Mudgley, Somerset

It was a Sunday lunchtime in late September, driving through a maze of Somerset country lanes, we marvelled at the sheer abundance of apples in every orchard we passed. We were hopelessly lost, until suddenly we saw a jolly painted sign pointing the way to Roger Wilkins cider farm, and we finally arrived at just after the advertised closing time.

Roger was drinking with a few local friends in his cider barn as we sheepishly poked our heads around the door and apologised for turning up late. "O, ho!" cried one, spotting Colin's 'Wassail' T-shirt, "anyone wearing a shirt like that is welcome here! Come in – have a drink!" With that we were ushered in and offered a choice of dry, medium or sweet, served in half pints (which was probably wise for the uninitiated!) from huge ancient barrels standing on a concrete platform. After years of dripping from the taps, the cider had eaten channels into the concrete. This was cider made in the time honoured way by a man who obviously cares passionately about his craft. And excellent it was too; rich and slightly cloudy, no artificial ingredients here, and my head was swimming fairly quickly.

The barn itself was a large building, but quite how old was difficult to guess. One chap told us it was a good job they had the air-conditioning on today (a round hole in the wall, which might have been a window if there had been glass in it), apparently in the winter it is stuffed with a pillow,

then they say they've got the heating on! There was evidence of spiders festooning the walls around the door and in the corners, and we were told how the cobwebs kept the dust from dropping from the roof and caught the vinegar flies that would otherwise become a nuisance. It seems the spiders were doing an excellent job of keeping the place clean.

The conversation flowed from the water levels on the 'moor' (Somerset Levels) and the effects it was having on the breeding birds, through the merits of good butchery on the quality of beef, the various TV personalities who had visited the cider farm and featured Roger in their programmes – Jamie Oliver, the Incredible Spice Men, the Hairy Bikers – and even the settee which had once belonged to Frankie Howerd in the 'lounge', an area rather like a cattle stall, decorated with a strange mural and several plastic chairs, no doubt for the ease of visitors. Asking about the timing of the Wassail here, Roger told us he always went on the Saturday before 17th January, or the Saturday after – it depended when he could get the 'Somerset Levellers' who did the music for the evening!

The Wassailing obviously worked, as the orchard outside was groaning with apples; yellow, pink and red "there's all sorts in there, bitter-sweets and everything". Roger had to return to the farmhouse to see to the gravy for his lunch, so we thought it best to leave him to it, but not before we purchased a two handled cider mug with a picture of the barrels and the legend 'Wilkins Farmhouse Cider'.

Karen Cater

Plough Play at Skidbrooke, Lincolnshire and a Hooden Horse at Wilson's Orchard, Northampton. There are storytellers at Buckland Abbey, Devon and Sulgrave Manor, Oxfordshire, and belly dancers at West Croft Cider. Everywhere there's music, perhaps more folk than anything else, but including a few rock bands, with names to delight like Compost Heap, the Skemmity Hitchers, Somerset Levellers, Fallen Apples and the Mangled Wurzels. This might contrast with a quartet of singers (Freshwater, Isle of Wight), or choral music from the Wiltshire Wailers (Courts Gardens, Holt, Wiltshire) or a full stage production from Blast from the Past Theatre Company (Coughton Court, Alcester, Warwickshire). At Sulgrave Manor, you can even join Wyndbagge the Piper!

At Somerset Rural Life Museum considerable attention is paid to past Wassail traditions. Not only is the Wassail King or Queen is chosen by the 'Bean hidden in a cake' method, the evening includes an Ash Faggot burning, based on nearby Curry Rivel. Away from the West Country the pattern changes, so that at Kent Cider Co., Faversham, the traditional Wassail chant "Stand fast root, Bear well Top..." is used. Also, in keeping with local traditions, they call the ceremony 'Yowling' and throw salt over the tree. At Weston's Cider, Much Marcle, the Herefordshire traditions of the Burning Bush and the twelve Bonfires (Judas Fire) continue strongly: while it's a cider orchard wassail, Silurian Morris Men are firmly in charge. Another Herefordshire peculiarity is the presence of the Roman Goddess Pomona from medieval literature in the Leominster Morris Wassail. She also crops up in accounts of the ceremony at Skidbrooke Cider Company, Louth in Lincolnshire, so could there be a connection? Yes, it all goes back to the 1980s when there was contact between Leominster and Ian Horsley who was then getting Wassailing going at the Brandy Wharf Cider Centre, Gainsborough, Lincs, Ideas were exchanged including the significance of Pomona to apple tree blessings.

Not all the events organised by cider orchards or visitor

Silurian Morris Men are in charge at Weston's Cider Wassail, Much Marcle, Herefordshire

attractions have a primarily commercial purpose. Some are educational: at Manor Farm Country Park, Bursledon in Hampshire, the event is called 'Hampshire Traditions' and also includes blessing the plough, and a Mummers Play. At Sulgrave Manor everyone is invited to "Be entertained with stories of the twelve days of long ago Christmases, and to discover the ancient customs of the Lord of Misrule and Plough Monday". Elsewhere emphasis is placed on fun, oriented towards families. At Cotehele (NT), St Dominick, nr Saltash in Cornwall, visitors are encouraged to "help the team ensure that the orchard provides a healthy crop of both apples and mistletoe by donning brightly coloured hats and playing musical instruments" At Trelissick Gardens, Feock, in Cornwall (NT), the request is to "Dress up in foliage and follow the King and Queen of Wassail into the garden on a torchlight walk". At Dartmoor National Park, the atmosphere is positively wholesome. After singing the Carhampton song to several trees, the party, many wearing Apple head dresses, return to the fire for apple juice and homemade apple cake. Bread is toasted on the fire and taken to the oldest tree, dipped in cider and hung in the branches. One of the park Rangers then pours cider on to the tree roots. Daventry Country Park advertises their wassail held on Twelfth Night as a great way for the whole family to celebrate the New Year. At Wilson's Orchard, Northampton, again on January 6th each tree is

Mistletoe readily grows in apple trees. Wassailing ensures that the orchard provides a healthy crop of both apples and mistletoe at Cothele, Cornwall.

Wassails held at cider orchards and visitor attractions provide a welcome opportunity to thank staff, bring in visitors at an otherwise quiet time, and promote sales. A regular element of the annual commercial cycle, as well as a great outing!

wassailed in turn. "Friends came in family groups, some with their own torch or lantern, gathered around a bonfire. Some brought drums; some brought comfy seats for the older people. They sang wassail songs while spuds wrapped in silver foil and shining apples nestled in the embers, and the Wassail drink, apple juice from the Orchard's own trees, with orchard honey, herbs and spices simmered by the fire. Each person toasted everybody present then the trees as well".

Some cider orchards are motivated as much by the desire to recover and preserve old and endangered local varieties of apple, pear and plum as by any thought of commerce. In Gloucestershire a cluster of at least six wassails exists, that we sourced through Gloucestershire Orchards Group website. Formed in 2001 the group aims to conserve, promote and celebrate traditional Gloucestershire orchards. It has built up a wealth of expertise: orchard management, fruit tree nurseries; juice making, Cider and Perry making; and maintaining local varieties. One member, Wick Court, at Arlingham has been wassailing for fifteen years with assistance from Gloucestershire Folk Museum and CROW, including their own version of the Gloucestershire Wassail song. In 2013, two new wassails, at Stroud and Painswick started up. Approaches in Gloucestershire are flexible, with both afternoon and evening events, often family and children friendly. The Wassail season is also gradually being extended. Significance of both Twelfth Night and Old Twelfth Night is recognised but events happen when it is most convenient, with at least two events in 2013 planned for February. Of two events cancelled on January 19th 2013 because of heavy snowfall, one was reorganised for February, while the other was not rescheduled to take place until blossom time.

At the Eden Project, at Bodelva, Cornwall, the ceremony is private but very different, limited to the gardeners, the orchard workers alone, and held strictly on January 17th. The team toasts bread on a bonfire, steeps it in cider and hangs it on the bare branches of a single tree symbolising the whole orchard, which is planted on the perimeter of the site with many rare Cornish and South West apple varieties, including Pendragon, Cornish Aromatic and Captain Broad. This ceremony bears more than a passing resemblance to Cecil Sharp's collection at Bratton in 1905 (see Ch 3, p72). They make plenty of noise too, though like others elsewhere they avoid using guns for ethical reasons.

Among Wassails organised by commercial cider orchards and visitor attractions are several that make an entrance charge, in some cases limiting numbers by ticket. Of the forty three wassails surveyed, twenty three had entrance charges; six were by invitation only, so that only fourteen, roughly one third were open to the public on a walk in basis. For many venues ticket limitation is necessary to prevent events becoming hazardous, particularly where events attract several hundred visitors. Charges ranged from as little as £1 to £35 for a family of four. £8 seemed to be about average and some visitor attractions charged their normal entrance rates only. So what might anyone get for their money? In all cases, entrance and participation in the ceremony: in most cases entertainment before and during the ceremony (Morris etc) and probably afterwards. A small number of events had a supper afterwards; more held a barn dance or ceilidh; more still created an open dancing area in a barn for their rock band. Sometimes food and drink was free, but bars and farm shops were also open providing the chance to buy food and to get well oiled too. All this and a mysterious

The Wassail Queen at Norton Fitzwarren introduced in the 1970s

atmospheric ceremony make for a really good night out – a chance to warm the cockles of your heart in the depths of winter. It isn't surprising that several of the venues are able to report charitable donations totalling several thousand pounds.

Perhaps taking a lead from the Taunton Cider Company's reawakening of its Wassail in 1974, several of the ceremonies are either private events or by invitation only. The early Taunton wassails were a reward for all the workers, in the offices and the orchards whose efforts had helped the company prosper in the previous year. It was a chance to break down social barriers and also to invite (commercial) customers whose regular orders had contributed to the Company's success. The first Wassail Queen at Taunton was a young woman, probably in her early twenties, with the idea seemingly modelled on Carnival Queen Traditions.

Localiy produced cider for sale in the National Trust shop at Barrington Court, Somerset. The Wassail bowl, used at their annual Wassail, was made by local potter, Paul Jessop. His pottery workshop is located in the outbuildings craft centre there.

In other ways the Taunton Reawakening may have acted as a model to others. Contemporary photographs show wassailers dressed in 'theatrical style' country costumes from a bygone era including bowler hats, waistcoats, neckerchiefs, and typically 1970s Laura Ashley dresses. Cider was carried in a pail that looked like a coopered barrel, with a two handled jug regularly dipped into it. In the background, on a stage were Adge Cutler and the Wurzels, pride of Somerset and Cidershire. Less than ten years later the Taunton ceremony was featured on BBC Points West, so in retrospect it's easy to see how Taunton Wassail became a model for making Wassails into full blown evening events, with all manner of entertainment celebrating the past. It also became a model for promoting cider offering the possibility of all kinds of media spin off. Large invitation only ceremonies now take place at Gaymers Stewley Orchard, Ilminster, Somerset, at Kent Cider Co. at Faversham, at Thatcher's cider at Sandford, near Weston-super-Mare, Somerset, and Thirsty Farmer Cider whose Wassail takes place at Rothley Orchard, Leicestershire.

What common values do this group of wassailing venues share? Clearly they all believe that wassailing works, that it's fun and that doing it restores part of England's heritage. More than this, a wassail provides opportunities for publicity at a time of year when this might otherwise be in short supply. It is often unashamedly part of company and venue marketing. For many visitor attractions, a wassail is an additional winter event when fewer visitors are coming. Though some are deliberately scheduled around the Christmas period, the majority happen in January. Both commercial cider companies and visitor attractions have websites updated regularly both before and after events. Many have a presence on Facebook and Twitter, and make extensive use of local and regional media: newspapers, radio and TV, both before and afterwards, providing

The inclement weather of spring and summer 2012 resulted in a poor apple harvest, but some people blamed insufficient Wassailing!

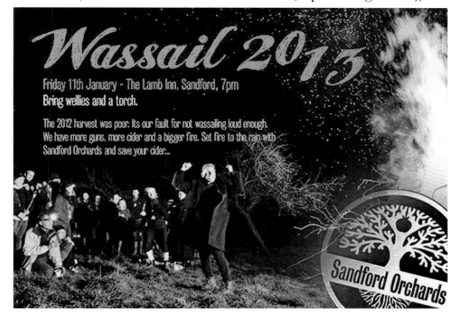

information for likely wassail participants and general interest publicity.

Thatcher's cider wassail is regularly filmed. Wassailing offers an opportunity to get lots of people 'on site' sampling both cider and farm shop produce. More than this, with a large event a company can invite customers, and people of influence perhaps from a long way away to help develop the profile of their brand. After all, cider producers are not just in competition with each other: cider is in competition with beer and lager for the palette of the young and not so young of the whole nation and probably internationally as well. If wassail ceremonies can be surrounded in mystique in the local and national press – dark eerie nights, flickering bonfires, ancient pagan origins, spooky chanting, the roar of shotguns and cheering – so much the better. No harm can come from having Tom Parker Bowles, son of the Duchess of Cornwall extolling the virtues of Wassailing in the Daily Mail. As The Daily Telegraph (Jan 2009) put it "Commercial cider-makers have got in on the act. Wassailing is seen as a valuable tradition but, more cannily, also a unique way of thanking their supporters and customers" As John Thatcher of Thatcher's Cider said in the same article "It's one of the better things that we do in the cider industry to promote traditions,"

Pomona

"I am the ancient Apple Queen,
As once I was so am I now.
For evermore a hope unseen,
Betwixt the blossom and the bough.
Ah, where's the river's hidden Gold?
And where the windy grave of Troy?
Yet come I as I came of old,
From out the heart of summer's joy."

William Morris

Chapter 7
The Spirit of Place

Many previous writers on Wassailing have emphasised it as a celebration of locality as much as a pledge to people or animals, or yet the chance to welcome the turn of the year and the return of light and warmth. Ceremonies are associated with farms or villages: songs are associated with Counties. Though agricultural wassailing might have once been very widespread across the Southern half of England, its incidence gradually narrowed down to three smaller areas (see Ch 3). Analysis of much of the Reawakening (Ch 5, 6 and 8), focuses primarily on event organisers, but this Chapter addresses the question "Where", to explore whether 'places' still contribute to the nature and spirit of Wassails.

As elsewhere, putting events in specific chapters has presented difficulties. A provisional chapter title of 'Villages' was eventually judged unworkable as not all Wassails identified for this Chapter could be identified with recognised notions of 'the Village'. The selection included events happening in the closed community of a school; some in the much more open setting of a pub; also included are visiting customs, some with very long and continuous provenance. Among Wassails based around locality some had a distinctly historical orientation while the remainder offered social cement bringing sometimes quite diverse communities together. It was decided eventually to examine each of the subsets separately, before looking at the grouping as a whole to evaluating the effect wassails might have on the communities where they were located, and the extent to which different locations for wassails might influence their character.

This poem discribes a single event, though similar wassail parties in private houses are known to happen unrecorded all over the country. This one was in January 1997 at Liz Giddings house at High Easter, Essex. (It was Liz who wanted the wassail- she'd have been about 15 then) There were about 20 people there, all friends from the local morris and folk music session community, some with their teenage children.

Written by Sue Cubbin, author of 'That Precious Legacy, Ralph Vaughan Williams and Essex Folk Song', and singer/fiddler in Potiphar's Aprentices.

Liz Giddings plays fiddle and melodeon in The Most Unexpected Band and has performed with Roger Digby, Matt Quinn, Bob Davenport and Jim Bainbridge.

WASSAIL POEM

In the chill evening, in the winter dark
We followed little candles down to where
the fruit trees stood
A little hushed

The long grass,
wet with tiny drops shining in the light
Soaked shoes and trousers
We sang to the trees and toasted them
And laughed at the fun and our foolishness
Then, bolder, threw the cider and
beat the saucepans
And left bread and ribbons
And tramped back into the bright house
For music and more to eat and drink
And in the dark, the foxes and hares
And sleepy birds
Who had stopped and listened
While we sang and reached out for a moment
Turned back to their own business and forgot us

I don't believe in magic
But I remember the smell of the dark
And the feel of something there
And I like the trees in the dark
And apples

House Visiting Customs

Bodmin Wassail in Cornwall happens on 6th January, Twelfth Night, starting at the Shire House on Mount Folly, from 12 noon. Bodmin's tradition is ancient: in 1624 when Town Clerk Nicholas Sprey donated a wassail cup, the custom was already well established. Dressed in "gentlemen's hand me downs" - top hats, Dickie bows, waistcoats and tails, Bodmin's wassailers collect money for charity; visiting private houses, nursing homes, pubs and shops. With their two unique songs: the Bodmin Wassail, and the Old Song, the wassail is a central part of the Town's calendar, supported enthusiastically by the people of the town. Now, with a new Wassail Bowl, to replace one lost before World War II, the Wassailers can offer people a drink at the end of the Christmas holiday in the old fashioned way, as always intended.

Dressed in "gentlemen's hand me downs" - top hats, Dickie bows, waistcoats and tails, Bodmin's wassailers collect money for charity; visiting private houses, nursing homes, pubs and shops.

Since 1953, wassailing at Dunkeswell, Devon has taken place on 17th January, when the custom of 'Old Twelfie' was restarted. Wassailers go from house to house chanting greetings and singing a traditional Wassail Song. Towards the end of the evening, everyone goes back to the Village Hall to sample the local 'Witches' Soup and Pie' washed down by 'Witches' Brew' – both made especially for this day. Just before midnight, they go to the orchard, where with shotguns and great shirkling, young lads dressed up as Witches are chased out of the orchard – a custom peculiar to Dunkeswell. How this part of the custom came into existence is unclear though it may lie in local C19 folklore reports which are liberally laced with references to charms, spells, incantations and witches. Whatever the influences, this Wassail is unique and central to Dunkeswell's annual calendar.

Drayton Wassail, near Langport, Somerset is always on January 5th Old Christmas Eve, sometimes called Wassail Eve and goes back an estimated 250 years (Kingley Palmer and Bob Patten, 1971). It starts at the Crown Inn; and both large houses and smaller ones are visited, most by prior arrangement. At each house, the Drayton wassail song is sung, and the following toast is said

God bless Missus and Master and all the family
Wishing you a Happy Christmas and a bright and prosperous New Year
And many of them

Participation in Drayton Wassail is limited to people born in the village, though an exception was made for local singer Charlie Showers in 1950. Knocking on the door is strictly forbidden – the song is sung and the toast said, and as the last verse of the song shows there is an absolute denial of begging.

We're not come here for to eat or to drink
But to keep up the custom for another year

Nonetheless, money is collected, though now it's for charity rather than for the wassailers

Curry Rivel Wassail, near Langport, Somerset also happens on January 5th; before the Burning the Ashen Faggot ceremony at the King William IV in Curry Rivel. The Faggot was originally made of ash sticks, about 5ft long bound together with willows and tied with a fastening called a 'rose'. Once enormous, able to burn throughout the Twelve Days of Christmas, the ashen faggot is now smaller to fit in modern hearths. G. R. Willey's (1978) description of Curry Rivel wassailing identifies a group of eight people with a designated leader. Bill Richards, the eldest wassailer can trace his family's involvement with the Ashen Faggot for over 150 years. He is now in his mid 80s and has taken

Burning the Ashen Faggot ceremony at King William IV in Curry Rivel near Langport, Somerset

The Faggot is made of ash sticks, bound together with willows and tied with a fastening called a 'rose'

part continuously since 1947. Wassails are made at ten houses across the social spectrum, as addresses as different as 'cottage', 'farm', 'close' and 'house' suggest. Despite the recent short closure and re-opening of the King William IV pub, the Curry Rivel tradition has been continuous since the early 1900s, with its local song collected by Cecil Sharp in 1909, which has a characteristic three line stanza, shared with the song at Drayton.

Oh Master and Mistress, we not done you any harm,
Pray pull fast this door, and let us pass along,
And give us hearty thanks for the singing of our song

The song from nearby Langport has a more unusual verse, suggesting antique origin. It's thought locally that the 'girt dog of Langport' refers to the Danes, who came up the River Parrett to attack Langport, the ancient inland port close by Curry Rivel. Alfred's defeat of the Danish leader Guthrun at Athelney in 878CE came as a relief to the local population, who were still celebrating it a thousand years later. It also circulated widely in southern Somerset, as the same stanza was also collected as part of a Wassail Song from Crowcombe, twenty five miles from Langport by Cecil Sharp in 1908 (Tony Wales, 1968)

The girt dog of Langport he burnt his long tail,
And this is the night we go singing wassail!

More modern visiting wassails include those at Porlock, Somerset and Walthamstow in East London. At Porlock, the party assembles in the early evening at Dovery Manor Museum and parades through the village, wassailing at several private orchards, ending at the Community Orchard. Wassail ceremonies are followed by folk singing and a Mummers Play. Walthamstow is a day event with workshops to learn wassail songs and make lanterns before a lantern parade around Walthamstow village, to include wassailing stops at sheltered accommodation, the Village Square and local apple trees, ending at Wingfield Park. Afterwards everyone assembles at the Nags Head before walking up to Walthamstow Folk Club.

Each of the older visiting Wassails is an established part of the community in which it takes place. Participation in the wassailing group appears to be limited, in some places more so than others, but a much larger cohort is drawn in as recipients of blessings, songs and chants. Very little, apart from the Ash Faggot burning at Curry Rivel seems to draw tourists in, so that the wassail contributes a measure of character and identity to the places in which it's located. It helps to create 'The Spirit of The Place'. It's not easy to extend this view to the more modern ceremonies as yet, though it might well happen with repetition over time.

photo - Dunster Buttercross Community Orchard

Pupils from Dunster First School wrote their own Wassail song and designed a sign for the new Dunster Buttercross Community Orchard (see p149)

Wassailing in Schools

At the time of writing, at least eight schools hold events described as wassails, with most centred on apple trees and orchards. As might be expected in a school, wassails are held in the spirit of discovery, not only customs and traditions but also sustainable and self sufficient food production, and healthy food preparation. Whether the wassail is primarily musical or more concerned with trees and food, it's helping to give young people a sense both of their historical culture and future responsibilities as they grow up. Like the older visiting customs these wassails help to create 'Spirit' within 'The Places', the schools and where they're located, and their influence may also extend outward into their surrounding communities.

At Eltham College, south east London and at Queen Elizabeth Humanities College, Bromyard, Herefordshire the emphasis is on music and performance, similar to an end of term play. QE College has more than one Steel Band, a Barbershop Quartet, a choir and a school band, so that their pre-Christmas Wassail is both multicultural and the highlight of the autumn term. Eltham has its own Morris side, the Morris Minors and their event includes Mummers Plays and Wassailing Songs.

With one exception, all the school orchard based wassails involve collaboration with external bodies. Wassailing has spread north of the English border to Steiner School, Edinburgh, where it includes a lantern walk around the community garden, followed by wassail poems and songs, all arranged in conjunction with Transition Edinburgh. At Child First Moulton Nursery, Northampton, the children are all under five, but their wassail included eating jacket potatoes and salsa made from vegetables they had grown themselves. They made punch and musical instruments before singing to, feeding and blessing the trees. At Holway Park Primary School, Taunton the wassailing ceremony took place around the one remaining tree of the old orchard on whose site the school was built.

Dunster's Buttercross Community Orchard was planted in 2011. On the morning of Jan 17th 2012 pupils from Dunster First School held a mini wassail. Bread soaked in apple juice was hung from some trees, with lots of noise and singing the Dunster wassail song written by pupils, who have also designed a sign for the new orchard. During the evening there were festivities for the village community. On the evening of Jan 17th, Bickleigh-on-Exe Primary School, Devon wassailed the Community Orchard; in a colourful ceremony presided over jointly by the Queen of the Wassail and the Lord of Misrule. As well as a bonfire there was dancing, singing, much apple cake and cheers to remind the trees to wake up after the shortest day on December 22nd.. Also for the evening of Old Twelfth Night, pupils at Branscombe Primary School, East Devon wrote their own wassailing song in collaboration with both Folk South West and the National Trust to help raise awareness of the importance of trees and orchards as wildlife havens and meeting places for the community.

In Branscombe Vale sweet apples grow and robins nest and feed
And we wassail with crusty bread and cider showers the trees
And candles bright gleam through the night and home-made lanterns glow
With shouts and bangs above our heads to make bad spirits go.

Social Cement in the Villages

Eighteen ceremonies are reviewed in this section with the majority happening in the Devon and Somerset wassail heartlands, suggesting a combination of folk memory and awareness that these ceremonies belong here. This is coupled with the outward spread of the Carhampton ceremony, and of established Reawakened wassails run by folk people and the cider orchards. Nobody doubts the antiquity of wassailing, but much modern practice also draws in previously unconnected mythologies and traditions. In the last seventy years the Green Man has evolved from being a foliate head carved in stone in churches and cathedrals, to being a dancer, sometimes with a blackened face and often dressed in a green tatter coat. Such a figure takes the role of 'The Butler' (MC) at the wassail held at Colwall, Worcestershire, where a small boy, known as the 'Tom tit', is lifted into the tree to place toast in the branches to feed the robins in the orchards. Lots of wassailing records exist of 'Tom Tit' and people believe that it is this practice that gives its name to 'toasting' speeches during modern feasts and ceremonies.

In contrast to Tom Tit, nearly half the events had a Wassail Queen placing toast in the trees or in some cases a Wassail King and Queen. At Westbury-sub-Mendip, Somerset where a Green Man is MC, the Wassail King and Queen are selected by a variation on King Bean and Queen Pea involving the drawing of two golden walnuts from an apple cake. Here the traditional ceremonial burning of the Ashen Faggot has also been incorporated into the wassail evening. Topsham in Devon held its first wassail for more than 70 years in 2009. Its organisers believe that a long standing and traditional link with the land was re-established; and a seasonal ritual was celebrated joyously marking the transition from the dead of winter to the fertile rebirth of spring. As with other local ceremonies, Topsham has its own recently written wassail song celebrating both the wassailing rite and the locality

In the orchard dark we muster
North Wind whistles through
the Northwood tree
Gather Topsham, Sing and rattle.
We'll bring cider back to thee.

Topsham Wassail Song by Adrian Wynn

There is much that locality based ceremonies have in common, and they are also distinct from events run on the basis of interest. They tend to be smaller than many Morris or commercial events though the wassails at Outwood Post Mill, Surrey and at Colwall include torchlight

The Green Man, once a carved foliate head, has evolved into a dancer with a painted face and green tatter coat. At some wassails he takes the role of MC

processions and attract nearly three hundred people each. At Sowden House and Stoke Gabriel, both Devon, wassails are conducted in lantern light only. Local folk entertainment is both widespread and very diverse, with Morris Dancers, Mummers Plays, storytellers, or country dancing, and music almost everywhere. In some places the singing was more formalised: Sowden House had a choir; similarly at Colwall, their own recently written Wassail song was led by a choir to make sure that everyone picked it up. At Little Hereford, singing was led by a singing ensemble whilst at Bere Ferrers the services of a well known West Country shanty group were engaged.

At Sowden House, children are described as putting on a "charming little play" then later the Lympstone Mummers play was performed. The Langport Mummers, who feature at a number of Somerset Wassails, are described at Westbury-sub-Mendip as "a highly acclaimed folk drama group, who performed an irreverent and hilariously cutting contemporary play which caused many a titter". The Little Hereford event also included a contribution from hand bell ringers. At Great Gidding, Cambridgeshire included thoughtful and heart rending poems written by two members of the company. Villagers were described as being "Drawn to the Jubilee woods by the light of a bonfire and the waning gibbous moonlight".

Not only are these events smaller in scale then some others, many are more intimate. In some places they are highly articulate, even arty, and many seem to involve the entire social spectrum of village life, making wassailing both a socially inclusive pursuit and one restricted to a defined catchment area. While blessings, fellowship and spirituality are important, success is also judged by the overall quality of the event, and perhaps the extent to which it contributes to bringing the community together. At several events, participants retire for a formal supper when the tree blessing is over: several also collect money and here the charity benefiting is often for the improvement of village facilities themselves.

Wassailing and the Historians

At several events, local experts are asked to set the scene by explaining the origins and purposes of wassailing. At Bere Ferrers and at Yarlington, this is done by a local historian who might also know a bit about cider apples and cider-making. At Rillaton in Cornwall, historian Kathy Wallis, of the Linkinhome Wassailers, based the ceremony on an early C19 account by Rev Richard Polwhele;

"The custom of saluting apple trees is still preserved both in Cornwall and Devonshire. In some places, parishioners walk in procession, visiting the principal orchards in the parish. In each orchard they single out the principal tree, salute it with a certain form of words and sprinkle it with cyder or dash a bowl of cyder against it. In other places, the farmer and his workmen immerse cakes in cyder and place them on the branches of an apple tree and, in due solemnity, sprinkle the tree"

Kathy Wallis pours cider on to the roots of the apple trees in the orchard at Rillaton, Cornwall

Rillaton Wassail, Cornwall. 19th January 2013

The Saturday closest to 17th January

Muffled voices and the sound of laughter echo along very narrow country lanes – no streetlights to guide us, no torches to shine the way, just the stars shining down on a clear winter's night. The local farmers, the villagers and their friends are off to wassail the apple trees as they have done for centuries past in this part of Cornwall.

I've always wassailed my apple trees and have done so since I was a child wherever I happen to have been living at the time. The neighbours either thought I was totally mad or came and joined in, sometimes a bit of both. When I bought this house it came with centuries of history attached as it had been the Dower House for the Manor of Rillaton which dated back to pre-Domesday. You can't live in a place like this without becoming an integral part of it and, sometime after I had planted my new trees in the garden, I found a copy of the tithe map only to discover I had planted my trees where the orchards to the Manor had stood for centuries. It was inevitable then that I should wassail the trees as close to old 12th night as possible. I invited the neighbours. The village came. The following year we were asked to wassail the new orchard at Higher Westcott and the old orchard at Lower Rillaton Farm. Standing under the oldest tree in the old orchard with the great grandson of the woman it was planted for on her wedding day, pouring the cider into the roots and placing the toast in the branches, was something very special. In the past two years we have included yet another orchard in the wassail tour and now do four orchards before returning to the cottage for the wassail feast. Part of this is always apple crumble served with clotted cream, and made from the apples of the wassailed trees brought into the cottage in the autumn.

'In comes I old Father Christmas welcome here or welcome not.' The words ring out around the cottage as the Rillaton Mummers perform the South East Cornwall Mummers Play as part of the evening's celebration. It was a chance entry in an account book for the Manor that led to this. 'three farthings for the mummers.' When these accounts were drawn up in the late 1780s the Manor house had vanished and the main house left standing was mine, so it would have been to my cottage the mummers would have come, all those years ago, to perform the South East Cornwall mummers play on a midwinter's evening. It just seems right to continue with this.

It takes most of the day to prepare the cottage for the evening and I always have Pete Coe's calling on song playing in the background while I work, even though we are privileged to have been given our own Wassail song and our own Mummers calling on song by Mike O'Connor, which are used for the actual ceremony and later for the play. Some years ago I stopped in the middle of the dining room and found I had tears in my eyes as the reality struck. I was doing exactly the same thing as others have been doing in the same place, at same time of the year and for the same reason, for hundreds of years; another tiny piece in the circle of life. It's an uncanny feeling and if you stop to think about it, it gives a tingling feeling down the spine.

So, the muffled voices and the sound of laughter on a dark winter's night will continue in this tiny hamlet on the south-east corner of Bodmin Moor doing what others have done before us for centuries past.

Kathy Wallis

The Dower House, Rillaton Manor, where Mummers were paid three farthings in the late 1780s

Of all the villages that wassail, Whimple probably has the greatest sense of its own history. Not only was it the home of Whiteways Cyder for over a century, it boasts a thriving History Society, whose founder, John Shepherd reawakened the local Wassail in 1993. The Society has funded Whimple's own independent museum. Here the wassail is firmly located on 'Old Twelvey Night', Jan 17th. After a musical warm up at the New Fountain Inn, and a chance for everyone to practice the Whimple Wassail song, the company sets off a few steps up the road to wassail the last remaining 'Whimple Wonder' apple tree.

A-wassail, a-wassail! The Moon she shines down;
The apples are ripe and the nuts they are brown.
Whence thou mayest bud, dear old apple tree,
And whence thou mayest bear, we sing unto thee.

Chorus:- With our wassail, wassail, wassail!
And joy come to our jolly wassail!

Before visiting several orchards, the sizeable procession resplendent with Devon Flag and large band pause outside the house of the last (mock) Mayor of Whimple to remember John Shepherd. Whimple has a fair share of its own folklore too. Roger Smith, MC for the event regaled the crowd with stories of the fame of Whimple cider; "At Whimple two of the Rectors were both cyder makers and cyder drinkers. Their joint tenure of office covered more than a century. One day the Exeter coach set down the bent and crippled Dean at the Rectory door. After three weeks 'cyder cure' at the hospitable Rectory, the Dean had thrown his crutches to the dogs and turned his face homewards, 'upright as a bolt'" When John Shepherd died, the people of Whimple decided to leave the office of Mayor unfilled as a tribute to him. Roger Smith now acts in his stead and together with the Wassail Queen, wearing her crown of Ivy, Lichen and Mistletoe, all produce of the apple tree, and her Princess who carries the toast, lead the musicians and the whole company to the orchards for each of the ceremonies.

Whimple Wassail. Jim Causley with his accordion and the Wassail queen and princess holding the toast which will be placed in the trees after the shotguns have scared away the evil spirits. All surrounded by the words of the Whimple Wassail song.

Details in the corners show clockwise from top left: Henry Whiteway inspecting the apple crop; the Devon flag with cider and apples; items from the Whimple History Society Museum; and the pail of hot spiced cider into which the wassailers dip their cups after each tree blessing.

Over the years Whimple Wassail has become one of the best known of all wassail events. As well as the village history, this is in no small part due to the musicians, in particular to the well known folk singer and local personality Jim Causley. In the early days, music was provided by a single concertina player. Jim took over the music in 2004 with friends from the Dartmoor Pixie Band, so that there is now a large and energetic band. This Wassail has been previously described in the 'Ogham Sketchbook' by Karen Cater and filmed both by the celebrated folklorist Doc Rowe and the BBC for Countryfile.

The Making of the Music at Whimple

I first became involved with Whimple Wassail after it had been revived in the 1980's by Whimple History Society. At that time the music for the Wassail was provided by a local band, that I was a member of. For the procession this band played a selection of Irish tunes walking round the different orchards. I felt there was something not quite right about this and after visiting other fabulous local traditions with a lot of processing such as Padstow, Hunting the Earl of Rone at Combe Martin, Minehead and Exeter Lammas Fair I felt that Whimple too should have its own processional tune to really cement that sense of tradition and ritual.

When I made my first CD I really wanted to record the 'Whimple Wassail song'. I had heard that there might be more than just the two verses that are sung around the apple trees, so I went to David Rastall of the Whimple History Society who lent me a cassette tape from the late John Shepherd (much loved local character and mock Mayor of Whimple) who had sourced the song. On the tape was a lady singing the 'Whimple Wassail Song': I knew the tune already but there were four extra verses with fairly standard wassail song lyrics when compared with the more unusual first verse. Much more interestingly; after the song the lady announced that she was about to play "The Whimple Wassail Processional Tune", a delightful march played on a concertina. I was very excited about this! At the following year's wassail, I tried to reintroduce this tune. It didn't go well; the band showed no interest in the tune or the potential of reviving a lost part of the tradition. As for the idea of playing the same tune continuously throughout the procession... they clearly thought I was some musically inept fool who was completely off his rocker!

Another year later I decided to sneakily slip the Processional Tune in during a break, just to help get it into peoples' subconscious! Something changed that night, I think the presence of my Dartmoor Pixie Band friends brought a lively spontaneity to the celebrations that was greatly enjoyed by everyone there and afterwards a spokesman for the History Society wrote enthusiastically about the success of that years wassail in the village magazine. Next year more local folk musicians came along and we have now gathered a loyal band of musicians every year. The processional tune has become a very recognisable part of the Wassail and many people say how excited they feel hearing it when we first set off to visit the Whimple Wonder Tree at the beginning of each year's Wassail.

Whimple Wassail 2007. Knowle Cross Farm orchard l to r; (musicians only) Paul Snow (fiddle), Jackie Oates (viola), Mark Bazeley (melodeon), James Delarre (fiddle), Matt Norman (drum), Jim Causley (accordion) and Kerry Jo Causley (drum).

In 2012 we were visited by a mysterious concertina player who seemed to know the tune very well, and was delighted it was being played. We got chatting as we processed and it transpired that she was the lady on the cassette, and had written the tune herself back in the 1980's! I thought this was wonderful; a bit disappointed it wasn't ancient but I think that deep down I always knew. She had been involved in the early days of the Wassail and had led the procession alone: later when she moved away the music and singing fell away completely. I asked her if she knew anything about the origins of the song but she didn't and sadly Mr Shepherd took that secret with him to the grave. BUT! She had based her processional tune on that of the wassail song. I felt stupid for not spotting this myself, but equally thrilled to learn that the Processional tune had its foundations in something already present in Whimple. It's also great to have someone else in the village who shares my passion for traditional customs and understands what makes them work; what makes them really become a beloved and essential part of community life.

Whimple Wassail is a living example of how an almost forgotten tradition can once again become a greatly loved community event that brings people together in a very.......... (what's the word I'm looking for here; Ancient? Earthy? Basic? Simple? Essential?) way. It gives everyone the chance to reconnect with Mother Nature that is rare for most modern folk and it makes them proud of their little patch of land in this incomprehensibly massive universe.

Jim Causley

A historical wassail of a much different character has been celebrated every year since 2004 at Barlaston, Staffordshire, drawing on local history and the ancient origins of the word 'Wassail'. It takes the form of a torchlight procession and verse-saying through the village to honour local famous Anglo-Saxons. After walking across two miles of heathland, it culminates in a traditional folk dance around a century-old tree on Barlaston village green. Twelve Saxon-themed banners, one for each month of the year, are carried in the procession and placed at the Duke of York Inn. In 2012, the event celebrated Wulfhere, King of Mercia in the mid seventh century, whose hill fort palace is near Barlaston. Times were more brutal then. Pagan King Wulfhere flirted with Christianity before rejecting it, and went on to murder both his two sons who had converted to Christianity. Now people pledge good health to each other, sing Auld Lang Syne at midnight and collect money for the Riding for the Disabled Association.

Although built within living memory, it is difficult to visit Shakespeare's Globe Theatre at Bankside in Southwark without seeing it as a window on former times, particularly the late Elizabethan and Jacobean eras, when Marlowe, Ben Johnson and Shakespeare himself were writing. These were troubled times with England in the throes of a social and religious revolution lasting more than a century, which would see the execution of Charles I, a brief period of England as a republic, the restoration of monarchy in 1660 and the eventual triumph of Parliament and Anglican Christianity. How does this relate to wassailing? Very closely because the early C17 theatre as one of the main bulwarks against Puritanism, and guardians of entertainment and enjoyment. Herrick's poems of the Wassail and of King Bean and Queen Pea may well have been associated closely with happenings at the Globe.

photo - Barlaston Wassail

A large papier mache model of the Mercian King Wulfhere led the procession at Barlaston Wassail, Staffordshire

Give then to the king and queen wassailing:
And though with ale ye be whet here,
Yet part from hence as free from offence
As when ye innocent met here.

Robert Herrick (1591-1674) "Ceremonies of Christmas Eve"

Nearly twenty years ago, the Lion's Part Theatre Company with help from folk singer Tim Laycock decided to recreate the Wassailing festivities of Twelfth Night in that era, with as much colour and extravagance as they could reasonably assemble. Practically, they decided to position it on the Sunday nearest Twelfth Night and to create the extraordinary spectacle of the Holly Man, the winter guise of the Green Man decked in fantastic green make-up and evergreen foliage arriving by boat at Bankside to be welcomed ashore with full actorly flourish and ceremony, toasting both the people and the River Thames. Following the arrival, everyone processes the short distance from the Globe to the George Inn on Borough High Street where the wassail gets into full swing with the Mummers Play performed by the Bankside Mummers, the selection of the Wassail King and Queen using the time honoured King Bean and Queen Pea method dating back to Shakespeare's time, much storytelling and the ubiquitous presence of the Kissing Wishing Tree.

The Lion's Part
Twelfth Night
celebrations poster

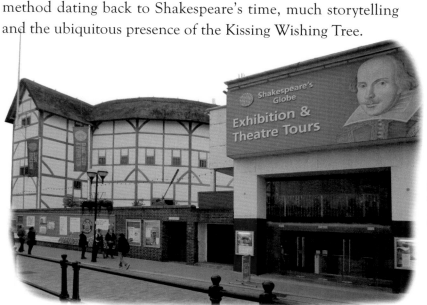

Shakespeare's Globe
Theatre, Bankside,
London

Twelfth Night celebrations, by the Lion's Part, Shakespeare's Globe theatre, Bankside, London.

2.45pm Sunday 6th January 2013

Almost by chance, just as we arrived on Bankside about half an hour before the start of Twelfth Night celebrations we looked across the Thames and saw a small canopied barge rowed by two pairs of oarsmen, like those in Tudor times, leaving the north bank opposite Shakespeare's Globe Theatre A large crowd was gathering, some expressly for the Wassail, some out of spontaneous curiosity. After what seemed an age, a noisy procession of players and musicians led by a town crier with a loud actorly voice and bell, suddenly strode into the assembly and announced the beginning of festivities.

Meanwhile the barge had tacked across the river, back and forth against the tide to take its place at the steps below. Standing on board, decked in evergreens and carrying a decorated staff of greenery was the 'Holly Man', a great festive Green Man, with his exquisitely painted face crowned with shining red berries and variegated leaves of holly. The Holly Man disembarked and mounted the steps up to the embankment, accompanied by bagpiper and flagstaff, as the Town Crier boomed out words of greeting, leading everyone in a chanted blessing of both boat and river, the words of which were painted on a large banner held high for all to read.

I found it impossible to see most of what was going on as the crowd was enormous and tightly packed; I was being jostled and found myself gradually propelled away from the spectacle. There were people holding cameras and mobile phones at arm's length above their heads to catch a sight or take a photo, but the best view to be had was for those sitting in the branches of the trees that lined the pavement! Then a bloke with a huge photography case, bristling with cameras and long zoom lenses pushed through the crowd right in front of me. He obviously knew something, so I followed in his wake and gained a better vantage point.

Now the company of actors – 'The Lion's Part' – strode across the street and arranged themselves on the steps of the Globe theatre, where another banner was unfurled with much pantomime style banter, to show the words of the GLOBE WASSAIL which was declaimed in blessing of the theatre and company:

> "Blowe winde, Globe bear well, Spring well in playing,
> Every Lathe & every Timber Bear the Tongues of Poets,
> Next New Year's Summer!"

This verse was rather familiar, seeming to be an adaptation of the apple tree wassailing verse, with its implication of the bearing of fruit, from the version collected in Painswick, Gloucestershire (see p110)

Standing behind me was a group of four city gents in handmade shoes and cashmere coats, discussing the authenticity of the ceremony in patronising tones, but when it was announced that this was its nineteenth consecutive year, one conceded "in that case I have a little more respect for the thing", his companion in its defence; "Oh, but I think it quite charming".

Afterwards the procession moved away up the street towards Borough Market where there was to be a performance of a Mummers play and the crowning of King Bean and Queen Pea, to be followed by music, dancing and storytelling, then Mince pies and mulled wine at the George Inn, Southwark.

The crowd swept past and I fell behind, unwilling to fight my way through the streets; I felt I was an outsider here, perhaps as a country dweller I found the metropolitan environment to be a claustrophobic barrier. What I did enjoy was the magnificent costumes, especially the Holly Man – his garb, but in particular his make-up were stunning! The ceremony itself was firmly rooted in the historical tradition of the Shakespearian theatre, though obviously adapted for this modern city audience, for most of whom it seemed to work magnificently.

Karen Cater

Wassailing in the pub

The White Lion, Norwich, held its first Wassail in 2013 With Golden Star Morris providing entertainment.

As the wassail Reawakening gathers pace, an increasing number of pubs are picking up on the opportunity for a good night out, particularly when the pubs make cider a speciality. The White Lion in Norwich, voted East Anglia Cider pub of the year by CAMRA (Campaign for Real Ale) in 2012, held its first Wassail event on Jan. 17th 2013, with Golden Star Morris of Norwich providing the entertainment. During the evening a young apple

tree was wassailed which will now be given to one of the pubs fifteen cider producers for the future. On the first Saturday in January, the Carshalton Jack Frost celebration involves visits to four pubs, and includes singing to the apple trees and making loud bangs to wake them to growth for the coming year. At The Royal Oak, Rye Foreign, Peasmarsh, East Sussex people meet in early January to sing around the pub's apple tree, blessing it and toasting it with lots of loud bangs. Afterwards the singing goes on in the pub with lots of squeeze boxes and much drinking of cider and strong ale. Elsewhere the Reawakening is peppered with wassails in pubs organised by Morris teams, or to which people go to relax after the tree blessings have been concluded.

Some of these events are highly original. During summer 2012 Karen and I spent an interesting afternoon looking for and eventually finding the Barton Inn, Barton St David, near Somerton, Somerset. We were intrigued by a brief newspaper cutting asking "Is this the world's only indoor Wassail event? Come and enjoy what could be a unique evening as the apple trees are brought inside the pub for the seasonal celebration".

We turned up just past lunchtime closing and immediately the pub name hanging upside down in large letters announced that this would be unusual. The pub yard was being sluiced down and we looked for the apple trees in tubs that I certainly

was expecting to be the ones carried into the pub to be wassailed. Then Damon, the Landlord came out and explained that it wasn't quite like that and if we came back when he opened up again in the early evening he would tell all. Three or four hours later we duly returned and were welcomed warmly. We were immediately struck by a framed lino cut hanging on the wall "The Cider House" – three blokes sitting round a table, one playing a squeeze box with a bottle and several glasses on the table, all in a pose of intense concentration. Damon did tell all – on the morning of the wassail he and a couple of friends armed with a chainsaw went by invitation to a local orchard and selected a large tree bough to be cut and brought back to the pub.

'Cider House' (artist unknown) a lino cut which was hanging in the bar of the Barton Inn, Barton St David, nr Somerton, Somerset (below)

During the day the bough was placed in the middle of the pub and securely attached all round the room before being decorated profusely with streamers. In the evening ceremony, wassail songs were sung, mainly written by the pub based on old Wurzels hits. Liberal amounts of cider were passed around in the pub's Wassail Bowl. Toast was placed in the tree bough and cider poured on the tree 'roots', by the Wassail Queen, usually a buxom Somerset maiden, but one year a bloke who just happened to get the bean in the cake.

Where be that app'l tree I know where he be
He be in yon app'l orchud and I be after he
Now I sees he and likes the look, bugger'd if I don't get 'en
With my chainsaw I'll cut 'en down App'l tree I'll have 'ee
La la la la la la la
La la la la la la la

(Wassail King / Queen) 'Ows the timber?

(Everyone) All right!

Barton St David Wassail song (based on traditional / Wurzels)

Damon showed us the pub's considerable scrapbook; wassails stretching back over several years.

The ceremony ends with everyone firing masses of party poppers at the tree, scaring away any evil spirits who might not already have been frightened out into the cold January air. Afterwards, some entertainment, the Langport Mummers perhaps! Damon showed us the pub's considerable scrapbook; wassails stretching back over several years and we got the chance to talk to some of his regulars, all of whom couldn't wait for wassail time to come round again.

Another singular wassail takes place at Tolpuddle, deep in the Dorset countryside, first time in 2012. It shouldn't be surprising that the wassail party is based around the Martyrs Inn, as the sentencing of six men from Tolpuddle to be transported to Australia in 1834, for swearing oaths to each other as part of their membership of the Friendly Society for Agricultural Labourers (an early trade union) is a significant historical event. They became known as the Tolpuddle Martyrs: a petition of 80,000 signatures was collected, so that they could be released and they were returned to England in 1836.

From the Inn, the wassailers go to Orchard Meadow where more than sixty people form a circle around the oldest apple tree - the guardian tree to represent all the apple trees of the village. Armed with accordians and instruments, pots and pans there's great hollering and screaming to wake the trees – in 2012 they even had a banshee! The youngest member of the party and the eldest place toast in the tree and the Wassail Queen pours cider on the tree roots. Everyone then went to the far end of the meadow where four young trees had been recently planted. Here the toast ritual was performed by the four eldest people present. After that there was dancing from Festus Derriman Morris before everyone went back to the pub for a meal. As well as the Morris, a local Dorset song group, the Muddlecombe Men were there to help the evening along. The Tolpuddle Martyrs Cider Circle took some cider to the pub to be tasted and it was voted very drinkable. A couple of new members for the circle were recruited to help the following year. When the singing started, there were such choice hits as 'My Ol' Man's a Dustman', and 'Ernie, the Fastest Milkman in the West', but as the local website jokes "The piece de resistance was the '12 days of Wassailing', with memo boards (which were usually upside down) ... using the tune of 12 days of Christmas, we were split into 4 groups and each had to sing 4 verses, of such classic prose such as: A Robin in an apple tree; 3 pickers picking; 4 scrumpers scrumping; 5 baskets full etc etc. Each time these verses were sung, the noise got louder as each group tried to outdo the other, it was great fun, and in the end everyone was laughing, and joining in, stamping their feet, clapping and whistling".

Evenings like this end in the blink of an eye, though a lot of money was raised for charity, not least from the sales of cider. Like everyone at the Barton Inn, the people of Tolpuddle know what wassailing is: blessing, renewal, spirit and enormous fun; but they do it their way using the strength of the countryside that has served them through good times and bad for centuries.

Several of the pub events and events that place high value on history described above are unique. They are wassails in a true sense of that word but they could probably not be replicated anywhere else. Individual people make them as they are but only in the context of the community where they take place. The community shapes the wassail, yet the wassail also shapes both the community and the Place.

Nowhere is wassailing more synonymous with place that at Carhampton, Somerset, whose Butcher's Arms pub has seen wassails continuously for over a hundred and fifty years. All the ingredients of a Devon or Somerset orchard wassail are here: perhaps they are the time honoured ingredients because they are here, as elements of the Carhampton ceremony have definitely been copied many times. The centrepiece at Carhampton is the local wassail song, the 'Carhampton Song and Chant' It's anybody's guess how old the 'Carhampton Chant' really is. Certainly well over two hundred years as it was printed in the Gentleman's Magazine (1788), and probably on several other occasions in the years that followed. Its tune seems to be a major key version of the Miller of Dee and is also associated with a Harvest Toast, long defunct, from Suffolk printed by both Dixon (1846) and Bell (1857).

The Butchers Arms, Carhampton, Somerset; nowhere is wassailing more synonymous with place.

The survival of Carhampton wassail is testament to its resilience and the love people hold for it. Recent Landlord Kevin Nicholls has commented "It's good for the village, especially in changing times when so many people move into an area and don't know its traditions.". More than this, it's good for the region, probably for the whole country. Without Carhampton the wassail might have been consigned to the museum rather than be experiencing a glorious and vibrant reawakening. Wassailing is the spirit of the place: the place is the spirit of the Wassail.

Chapter 8

Community Orchards
Wassailing into the Future

In 2006, Sue Clifford and Angela King, from the environmental charity Common Ground, published England in Particular, which had till that time been the name of their website, drawing together aspects of English history, mystical heritage, horticulture, topography, locality and customs. The book, intended primarily for the environmental movement, included an outline description of wassailing as guidance to anyone setting up a wassail event:

"The word 'Wassail' comes from the Anglo-Saxon waes-hael - to be healthy, so wassailing apple trees was a way of encouraging a good crop in the following season....Often farm workers and villagers carrying lanterns, a pail and pitcher full of cider, shotguns and horns, walk to their local orchard, which is sometimes lit by bonfires, and gather around the largest or most prolific tree. This tree is known as the Apple Tree Man and is fêted as the guardian of the orchard. Cider or beer is poured on its roots and pieces of soaked toast or cake put in branches for the robins - guardians of the spirits of the trees".

Not only was the Wassail Reawakening well under way, with much knowledge passing by word of mouth from Morris Dancers etc., but also by the time England in Particular was published, the Community Orchards movement was also gathering strength. Much information in this book had previously been available on the England in Particular website, but the book opened up a second communication channel of an arguably more concrete nature and can be credited with a major contribution towards bringing wassailing and community orchards together. This was followed up by The Apple Source Book (2007) and the Community Orchards Handbook (2008). Many Community Orchard enthusiasts were not folkies or cider bibbers, i.e. they represented a new market, people with a passionate interest in apples, seasonal food, sustainability, good taste in all its meanings, who might take up Wassailing because it fitted nicely into an annual programme of tree management. These might be, indeed were, people happy to take up the customs of the past, alongside local English apple varieties and hands on methods of cultivation. Looking at the fifty five events used as sources in this chapter, it is remarkable how frequently the England in Particular formulation has been followed.

Yet it isn't that simple. Of the fifty five events reviewed here, just over half take place in urban environments: London, Bristol, Birmingham etc. Many of the sponsoring Community Orchards are relatively small, constantly looking for new volunteers to work and get involved. These orchards represent the tip of a potentially large iceberg both for their own movement and for wassailing. It must be asked how well rural customs might sit in an urban setting. Many people who are not folkies are happy to come to folk events on an occasional basis (having a good time at a barn dance or watching Morris Dancing) before returning to their normal life pattern. Might they enjoy an annual Wassail? Alternatively, could it be that because orchards are looking for a bit more commitment, wassailing in its folk / country form might take a bit of adjusting to, or even have to be adjusted itself? Some orchard enthusiasts may have looked at the

Of the wassails in this chapter, half take place in urban environments.

transformational and spiritual nature of wassailing and seen this as being more important than the mere mechanics of the ceremonies. Another alternative just values a good winter party! In this closing chapter assumptions will be made about the ceremonies where they appear similar to those organised by Morris Dancers, cider orchards and village hall committees. Instead focus will be placed on what makes community orchard wassails singular and how some urban wassail organisers are approaching the task of turning wassailing into an urban custom as well as one celebrated in the countryside.

Reclaiming the Land

Community Orchard wassails differ from most others in the interest which active orchard group members have in reclaiming derelict or unused land and in their practical involvement with cultivation (with fruit tree varieties or learning horticultural

skills in order to tend their orchard effectively). While a few medium sized businesses are included here, most community orchard groups rely on a small nucleus of volunteers. This is not to say that they are not interested in or have not acquired business skills – for many getting organically produced sustainable and seasonal food to market is a major part of their raison d'être. Reclaiming the land itself may be their primary or initial task; lands that had once been orchards, before changes in ownership and patterns of use had led to trees being grubbed up; lands that had recently been allotments, Lands where industrial uses have ceased, allowing them to be returned to

Community orchard groups may reclaim derelict land that had recently been allotments.

horticulture. Where many other sponsors may see an annual wassail as a one off event, for community orchard groups wassailing is an integral part of their annual event programme – they believe it is effective in increasing yields, but it's also fun, and offers the chance for publicity and to recruit new members. As these are people with a personal relationship with the trees they tend, it might be argued that this resembles the position of farmers and farm workers in C18-19 (see Ch 3)

The Conference Pear, developed in 1888 at Rivers Orchard, Sawbridgeworth, Hertfordshire

One of the longest running community orchard wassails has taken place at Rivers Orchard, Sawbridgeworth, in Hertfordshire since 1998, with a bonfire, verse saying, songs and ceremonial. The land had been in the Rivers family, prominent horticulturalists, since the early C18, and the orchard is probably best known for the development of the Conference Pear (1888) and for paintings by Mary Rivers used widely in fruit classification. However, in 1990 the family decided to sell the land to the local Community Hospitals Group. Almost immediately, efforts to salvage as much of the old orchard as possible began: with the support of East Hertfordshire District Council, the Rivers Nursery Site was established as a Community Orchard. The first Apple Day event took place in 1992. By 2008, Rivers Laxton Superb Apple Juice was available for sale; honey from newly colonised beehives available to taste and considerable collaborative work on lost Hertfordshire fruit varieties undertaken with the historic orchard at St Elizabeth's Much Hadham. After fifteen years the Wassail is a significant part both of the Orchard's annual calendar and of its rejuvenation.

A similar background surrounds Shenley Park, also in Hertfordshire, with the orchard first planted in the early 1900's as part of Porters Mansion. In 1935 the estate was acquired by Shenley Hospital and twenty two acres of orchards were planted to provide fruit for the Hospital kitchen and local markets. Patients were actively involved picking and storing fruit until the 1970's when this became frowned upon and the Orchards fell into disuse. Now only one orchard remains, restored by Shenley Park Trust Staff and volunteers, but with over 450 apple trees and 120 varieties planted, many of which are unusual, including the Seabrook Pearl that originated in Essex. On Wassail day, after the procession, noisy ceremony and fireworks, everyone retires to the Orchard Tea Room for soup and bread, mulled wine and cider. Donations from people contribute to the work but the real satisfaction arises out of the success of the wassail in generating a wonderful supply of apples over many years.

Long term success is also evident at Frieze Hill Community Orchard, Taunton in Somerset. The original gift of land was made just after World War I, but since the Community orchard opened in 2004 over one hundred trees have been planted, including dessert apples like Blenheim Orange and Devonshire Quarrenden (early C18), and Somerset Cider varieties like Kingston Black, Stoke Red and Yarlington Mill. The orchard is also a designated nature reserve supported by Taunton Deane

Shenley Park orchard, where once fruit was grown to feed hospital patients, is now a community orchard of 450 trees and 120 varieties.

Borough Council and Natural England. Their wassail takes place around a bonfire led by a Wassail King aided by the Lord of Misrule. The 'King Tree' is wassailed with toast in its branches, cider poured on its roots and the celebrated Carhampton Chant declaimed.

At Forty Hall, Enfield, Middlesex, developments are at a much earlier stage with an initial wassail in 2012, when the first trees to be planted for over a century were blessed. From the original orchard, which dates back to at least 1656, only one tree survives, but the group has won around £1,000 from the Mayor of London, to grow all kinds of fruit and become a community farm. At Highbury Community Partnerships, Birmingham, the former home of leading C19 Birmingham politician Joseph Chamberlain, work is also at an early stage, bringing volunteers together to work the land including planting an orchard with apple and pear cuttings from trees of the Chamberlain era, together with some bee hives. Their wassail was timed to take place so that real keenies could afterwards go on to a second wassail at nearby Kings Heath Community Garden with Morris Dancing, storytelling and a tree pruning demonstration.

After a long campaign, the Daisy Field, Shirehampton was granted Town Green status and became a community orchard with members sharing the fruit and vegetables produced there.

At Horfield Organic Community Orchard, Bristol the wassail is held on the nearest Saturday to Old Twelfth Night. The orchard was set up on the site of very overgrown allotment plots in 1998 since when volunteers have cleared the ground, composted like crazy, and planted 100 different fruiting trees, bushes and vines. Now, locally grown fruit is eaten all year round, with soft fruit, plums and cherries in early summer, as well as polytunnel-grown apricots, peaches and nectarines. Early apples and pears ripen in July. Later varieties are harvested until November and with good storage these fruits ripen and keep throughout the winter. Wassail day sees a good crowd, Morris Dancers and instruments of all sorts. Tree branches are dressed with ribbons, clouties, and shining things while everyone toasts the New Year with mulled orchard juice and homemade cakes. Not too far away at Shirehampton, on 15th January 2012, a new orchard was blessed, with Morris Dancing, food, mulled wine, wellie throwing and a bonfire. This followed a long campaign to safeguard the Daisy Field in Shirehampton following attempts by Bristol City Council to sell off the land, (which had once been a refuse tip and after that allotments) for development. Campaigners applied for Town Green status for the Daisy Field to set up the community orchard as a farm project, with each member paying a fee against the cost of renting the land, depending on how big a share they wanted of fruit and vegetables produced.

The production of local apple varieties, some specifically suited to cider making, was encouraged by organisations supporting the new community orchards.

As a complete antithesis to Shirehampton and indeed most Community Orchards, Warfield Walk 'n' Wassail took place at Jeallott's Hill Community Landshare in Berkshire for the first time in 2013, led by experienced Wassailers, OBJ Morris (for fuller details of OBJ Wassail – see Ch 5). This project follows the lease donation by world-leading agriculture research and technology company Syngenta of a six acre piece of land at Jeallotts Hill for the local community. It includes a 250 tree orchard and half acre vineyard for the community to grow produce but also to become as mentors to other groups coming to the site to gain skills, knowledge etc., including those seeking employment and people with disabilities. After a gentle walk around Warfield, OBJ led everyone in a ceremony involving toast, ribbons, and a wren to signify the turn of the year, the crowning of a Wassail King and Queen and lots of noise. Smaller community orchards who have fought battles to secure land on which to develop might well cast an envious eye towards Jeallott's Hill and be excused any cynical thoughts. If in years to come the local community of Warfield is able to develop and market its own produce without their success leaching into Syngenta's marketing and image development, then Syngenta's gift will have been truly altruistic, comparable with other gifts of land referred to in this section

Support Groups

Though reclaiming land, planting, grafting, pruning and all the tasks relating to tree management are vital, for sustainability to fully work, planting and harvesting must lead to manufacture and marketing of products such as juice, cider or fruit to generate revenue for reinvestment. Community orchards are enterprises: expertise comes at a premium creating a need for sharing and pooling resources wherever possible. Over the years many have drawn on support from Common Ground and other organizations. The name 'Transition' has cropped up repeatedly during the project. With an objective of solving global problems of food production through local initiatives, Transition is a worldwide network, with independent groups all over the USA and Canada, in Europe and with approximately seven hundred separate groups in the UK, most operating within a limited geographical area. In Dorset the Transition Town Dorchester community orchard group organized the purchase of land from Network Rail in 2011 to create the Railway Orchard. Work days have cleared the overgrown area ready for planting and the

launch wassail held in 2012. The first East Greenwich Pleasaunce Memorial Orchard Wassail took place on 6 January 2013, with performers May Birds, Morrigan, and storyteller Rich Sylvetser, The Holly Man. Trees were planted by an orchard group grown out of Transition Westcombe, but the whole venture was a collaboration also involving the Friends of the Pleasaunce and Greenwich Council. In the two years since the planting, apple, pear and plum trees are thriving, so the wassail was preceded by a work session to mulch the trees. The orchard at Hilly Fields, Lewisham has been greatly assisted by Transition Brockley, and this year, for the first time the wassail included music and singing traditional and improvised wassail songs. Other Transition initiatives have helped orchard development in Nailsea, Somerset; Penarth, South Wales; Edinburgh; Willesden and Redditch, and probably many other places as well.

In some places local council involvement has been invaluable, notably Sawbridgeworth; Frieze Hill (Taunton); Kenninghall in Norfolk; and Lichfield, Staffordshire. Elsewhere other support organizations provide assistance (sometimes including wassailing) both establishing new projects and marketing. At Stowe Landscape Gardens, Bucks, (NT), orchard management is undertaken by Midshires Orchard Group, who also manage the wassail, which includes children's craft activities, singing and a firework display. Horfield Community Orchard, Bristol, was originally set up by Avon Organic Group but had grown sufficiently by 2011 for a member-led group to manage the orchard as an independent community food enterprise. Abundance London, which seeks to harvest as much as possible from apple trees in people's back gardens, also organizes the Wassail at Chiswick House, where two hundred newly planted trees surround one ancient mulberry that is the focus of the celebration. The London Orchards Project is involved with at least four projects including Bethlem Royal Hospital, Bromley and Horton Country Park. Two of the projects involve wassails: at Claybury Park woods, where the orchard dates back to the

1920s and 30s when the grounds were associated with a psychiatric hospital, and at Camley Street, Kings Cross, in the heart of an industrial estate behind Kings Cross Station, where there is also a strong link with organic food production and distribution through Alara Foods – for a full description of this wassail please see Page 190.

Remodelling the Ceremonies

While wassails' core ceremonial has many almost universal features, event structure varies considerably, influenced by size and provision needed for numbers attending, and by organisers' choices in key areas. At Painswick in Gloucestershire, (first wassail 2013) the MC is a Green Man. This also happens at Nailsea, where the Green Man is described as 'taking the role of Butler'. At Claybury Park, Ilford, Essex, (first wassail also 2013) the Green Man is present but as a large decorated wooden sculpture. As the spirit of fertility the Green Man seems a logical choice as MC, protecting the trees from anything that might threaten them or their crop. At Fairfield Millennium Orchard Lancaster the Oak King and the Apple Queen preside, chosen by drawing lots at the event from among young and old people who come dressed as Oak King or Apple Queen. At Willsbridge Mill, near Bristol, home of Avon Wildlife Trust the event starts with the crowning of the Wassail Queen and Holly Boy. At Frieze Hill, Taunton, Somerset, and at Kenninghall, Norfolk the Lord of Misrule presides, scaring away the 'nasty frost giants'.

In some places there is reluctance to make use of guns. The Claybury Park wassail happens near a residential area. Even though organisers recognise that sharp crack of gunfire could have a practical purpose dislodging insects like the woolly aphid from crevices in the tree bark, they have decided to avoid using shotguns as a mark of respect to the neighbourhood. Amongst community orchard wassails it seems that the link with folk music is less strong than elsewhere. While Morris Dancers and folk musicians feature quite widely, there are fewer Mummers Plays, but conversely more events have storytellers and local choirs have been booked to assist with singing, with organisers perhaps concerned that audiences might be reluctant to sing songs they didn't already know. Some of the Morris teams seem not long established with members sometimes also orchard volunteers. In two places, Hook and Cleethorpes, the whole Wassail has been created around the local Morris team (respectively Hook Eagle and Grimsby), enabling both of these small orchards to celebrate and attract new recruits. Morris Dancing also features widely in community orchard wassails in Bristol.

Grimsby Morris

When we went to Headless Cross Wassail, Redditch, in early February 2013, it was clear that organisers had given considerable thought both to past wassail traditions and also to how to create a wassail that was appropriate for a newly planted orchard in an urban, once industrial, space. The previous year they'd had a Morris team as entertainment – this year they couldn't come so as an alternative the Wassail included a local brass band with a Town Crier as MC. The ceremony was thoughtful incorporating elements from (local) Herefordshire Wassails. But the piece de resistance was the song, written by someone living twenty or so miles away. 'Juice-alem', wonderful for the brass band and the crowd had absolutely no trouble at all singing it straight off the sheet. We have yet to find out who the author, William Bloke, really is but we'll keep looking.

And did those teeth in ancient times crunch upon England's apples green
And was the Bramley apple pie on England's dining tables seen
And did the cider pure and strong pour forth in pints and quarts and gills
And did the apple bring good health to folks in dark satanic mills

Bring me my Cox of burnished gold; bring me my Worcester firm and sweet
Bring me my Pippins new or old; bring me some English fruit to eat
I shall not eat that tasteless Pomme, nor shall a French fruit soil my hand
Till English apples rule again in England's green and pleasant land

(Reproduced by kind permission of Vaughn Hully of Shakespeare Mummers)

Headless Cross Wassail,
Headless Cross Green, Redditch
2nd February 2013

Proving that the Wassail season now extends for at least a month, we had journeyed in early February, to Redditch in the urban Midlands, its prosperity founded on needle making and motorbikes but now a 'New Town', a dormitory for Birmingham. Headless Cross is in the old part of Redditch. Its Green, where the wassail took place was completely built up until the 1970s and housing foundations have been found beneath the present surface. In the middle of the Green is a small group of mature trees, including an Apple Tree used as the focus for the Wassail, the 'Old Apple Man'. Around the Green is a young Community Orchard, with 20 or so trees planted in 2010, apple and plum, mainly Worcestershire varieties with names like the Doddin, native to Redditch and once very widespread, Pershore Purple and Rushcock Pearmain as well as King Coffee. Redditch is a Transition Town with residents and local schools combining to turn the Green into a wildflower meadow as they share the mission of reducing global problems with local solutions. Through Transition Redditch an apple press has been bought for residents. The organisers of the Community Orchard are also very active, with a 'May Fayre' and an 'Apple Day' in October as well as the Wassail

We arrived in the very nick of time. Karen drove our van into the car park in the manner of a well practiced hooligan and we scrambled on to the Green to hear a large handbell rung lustily by the Town Crier leading a procession from the local social club where just by chance a beer festival was going on. As they crossed the road, the Arrow Brass Band struck up with a version of 'Here we come a Wassailing' that I hadn't heard before. Then the Town Crier called everyone to order and led us through the ceremony. Somewhat surprisingly he first threatened the tree with an axe. The 2012 wassail had not succeeded in overcoming the magic of an impending hosepipe ban and the wettest summer on record. In common with everyone else Redditch's apples had suffered terribly. This should not happen again, the tree was warned else a dire fate might overtake it. Then a change of mood into a Wassail chant / incantation "old apple tree we wassail thee and pray that thou might bear .....little heaps under the stairs, and in my pockets too" Wassail. The atmosphere vibrated to the noise of shouting, drums and saucepans and anything people could lay hands on.

As the handbell sounded again we were called to order and the Town Crier summoned the Wassail Queen to place toast into the tree which she did slowly and deliberately before we all shouted 'Wassail' and the racket broke out again. Then the bell sounded and the Town Crier himself now ceremonially poured cider on to the tree and its roots leading everyone in the Herefordshire dirge chant "Auld ci-der, auld ci-der, auld ci-der" — more noise and then another bell before everyone was asked to join in the recently written local song "Juice-alem" to its well known tune with full brass band. How woolly aphids, let alone evil spirits could survive this is anyone's guess!

All too soon though the ceremony was over, the crowd broke up into smaller groups and we set about asking some of the organisers about Redditch's wassail and its community orchard. We had some mulled cider from a stand just by the brass band and gave a donation to the Community orchard in return. Most of the Wassail script had been researched from the Internet but it was based on Wassails from times past and hung together very effectively. We'd not expected to find Wassails in an urban setting, but they work as well as in the countryside. Most of the participants were young and enjoyed themselves thoroughly, without being hampered by any thought as to whether or not things were being done 'properly'. We retired to the beer festival happy in the knowledge that beer on top of cider would be less intoxicating than the opposite way round, and this year there shouldn't be the threat of a hosepipe ban, so the Wassail magic will certainly work!

Colin Cater

Preparatory Events before the Wassail

One of the most distinctive features of Community Orchard Wassails is the events that take place before the wassail starts. Many of these have to do with tree planting and management. At Highbury Community Partnerships, Birmingham a preparatory work session included clearing brush, laying brick footpaths, building a new tarpaulin canopy, and preparing for the wassail itself. Bridport Community Orchard, Dorset combined tree planting with their first wassail in 2009, bringing tradition, celebration and positive community action together. Bridport people rose to the occasion and on the day the response was overwhelming. A similar preparatory planting event takes place at Enmore Green, Shaftesbury, Dorset, whilst before the wassail at both Comrie's Community Orchard, Cultybraggan Camp, Perthshire and Broadlands Orchardshare, Bathford, Somerset, pruning and tidying up sessions were planned. A new hedgerow was planted as part of one Willsbridge Mill, Bristol event. At Varnycrooks Orchard in Threapland, Cumbria, the wassail was preceded by a 'working bee' - volunteers working to build top bar beehives as well as making torches and lanterns, and the bonfire in the next field. The Varnycrooks group was seeking skilled and self taught

Workshops may provide pre-wassail activity for children who may be able to parade their creations during a procession.

woodworkers using downloadable plans available free from a named website.

Because many Community Orchard Wassails are urban, careful thought is needed to make events attractive to town and city people. Often events take place in the daytime rather than the evening to be children and family friendly. Willsbridge Mill, Bitton, near Bristol, HQ of Avon Wildlife Trust worked in collaboration with a local school organising a workshop nearly two weeks prior to the Wassail to create an orchestra of sculptural sound pieces to make noise at the event. On the day itself children from a local primary school met to make "Wassail orchard ladders from recent Hazel tree prunings, which became frameworks for music making at the event". Wassail activities also included fruit and nut trails, orchard games and homemade apple cakes using local recipes. The event at St Werburgh's City Farm, Bristol has included craft workshops for children, whilst at Occombe Farm, Paignton in South Devon there were workshops to make toffee apples and glass lanterns. At Trumpington, Cambridge and at Donkeyfield Community Orchard, Portobello, Edinburgh, the emphasis was more towards learning wassail songs, including newly written ones, to prepare the audience for singing during the ceremony itself

How much might urban wassail ceremonies need to be remodelled?

If wassailing is to be widely accepted in towns and cities, the question remains, will it be sufficient to gradually alter the rural character of most current events, or will more fundamental change be needed to translate a country ceremony into an urban setting. Survey evidence suggests near general acceptance of the spiritual aspects of wassailing in most urban celebrations: noise drives out evil spirits; toast feeds the Robins – the guardian spirits of the orchards, and the 'Old Apple Man' or 'King Tree' personifies the orchard, and wassailing this tree will secure increased yield for all the trees. Transformational Magic rules.

Wherein then might lie the difficulty?

In part its cause is to do with uncertainty amongst wassail organisers, which could be part of a learning experience. Wording on the Highbury Community Partnerships website says "Wassail seems to come from an old salute to someone's health: Waes hál, be whole! It is similar to words meaning hale and healthy. So wassailing is somewhat like blessing ..... Lucky us, we had a hale and healthy turnout of more than 25 people, in addition to our dozen volunteers, who sipped hot apple juice and chanted at the trees in very good cheer". At nearby Cottridge Park, things are less sure "For centuries – and probably longer – there has been a tradition of having a party in orchards ..... All very pagan and probably just another excuse for a mid-winter party" At Hengrove and Stockwood Neighbourhood Orchard, Bristol wassailers are advised to bring cider, a pot and a stick, a lantern or torch and as many friends as possible. But what will happen? "That said, I suppose we should try to do a few Wassailing type things, but I don't know that much about it. Perhaps we could agree on some sort of wording to read 'to the trees' without having to actually sing it. We need a master/mistress of ceremonies to lead us along a line of trees maybe. Any volunteers, I'm not too sure about lifting anyone up into a tree"

A partial solution may exist at Cosmeston Lakes, Penarth in South Wales, where wassailers are encouraged "Don't worry if you've never Wassailed before, there's a first time for everything ... ; it's a tradition in apple growing areas such as the West Country and Herefordshire and ... a good reason for a get together. As part of the event we'll be writing our own Wassailing poem to encourage the trees". Elsewhere, people are taken on sometimes quite lengthy walks. At Cotteridge Park, publicity asks people to "Join us for a free taster walk as part of the annual wassailing .... Every walker will get a free cup of spiced apple juice. This fantastic walk will explore Cotteridge Park and its surroundings and finish at the Wassail in the Park". Walking is also an integral part of the wassail at Hackney, about two and a half miles. Song sheets are provided to reduce people's unease. Organisers know what wassailing used to be about but now "apple wassailing today is largely a cheerful frolic, vaguely associated with good luck". Better if people bring food and drink to share, itself a regular feature of wassails in smaller community orchards.

So the question needs to be posed "What's needed for something to be a wassail?" Is a spiritual purpose really necessary if the real intention is just to have a jolly? Why not call anything a Wassail? Well, some people do, but unless there is a blessing, 'Waes Hael – Be of good health', whether in that form or as 'Old Apple Tree, we wassail thee' or 'Stand fast root, bear well top...' or any equivalent expression of wellbeing towards an object other

Apple themed food and drink provides a feast for the wassailers.

than yourself, use of the word Wassail is probably nothing more than a corruption of language. There are plenty of other synonyms for party in the English language.

Much more significant is a different question. If wassailing is about blessing and wishing good health, how important is the manner in which it's done? Amongst wassails in the survey it's often possible for cider to read apple juice: sometimes for shotguns read party poppers. For the farmer as Master of Ceremonies, read The Butler, or Green Man or Lord of Misrule; for old songs read new ones or no songs at all, or maybe poetry. Who needs Morris Dancers? Lots of wassail organisers book them, but you can get away without any, with a brass band or storytellers, or contemporary urban music. Stripped down to its bare bones Wassailing is blessing, wishing good health and waking the trees up to kill off the evil spirits or the bugs. Everything else is embellishment, justifiable in terms of archive from centuries past and recent Reawakening practice, because it works, but ultimately a matter of choice for a Wassail organiser – to include or not to include.

"Stand fast root, Bear well top!"

Together with careful pruning, Wassailing will encourage an abundant crop of apples.

At Willesden Green in North West London, they've been wassailing for four years, blessing the apple trees in midwinter - in a manner re-appropriated to an urban setting. There are no orchards left in Willesden Green - there isn't even a Green, but every year wassailers process from the Underground station to Willesden Library where apple trees have been planted. Supported by Transition Town Willesden and led and founded by storyteller Rachel Rose Reid, this is a truly multi-cultural event reflecting Willesden itself. Wassailers will be celebrating the local businesses with an adaptation of an ancient wassail song chanted along the procession route. After the ceremony outside the Library everyone retires inside for apple cake washed down by a generous glug of spicy cider. A Performance artist, Chris Lewis-Jones, of Nu Urban Gardeners, is central to the wassailing ceremony at St Ann's Community Orchard, Nottingham. The apple trees are serenaded and their roots blessed with cider or ale and every year there are more wassailers "The first year we had just a handful of orchard volunteers and their friends. Last year we had about thirty and this year we are anticipating at least double that."

Two or three years ago The Ethicurean Restaurant took over the café at the listed Victorian walled gardens at Barley Wood, Wrington near Bristol, once an orangery built for the Wills tobacco family. Described in 'The Guardian' as "outrageously jolly", most of the food served in the restaurant is grown in the Walled Gardens, its watchword sustainability. The orchards hold seventy varieties of unsprayed dessert and cider apples, and they're wassailed with a traditional and modern ceremonial mixture. In 2012 they held a full day of poetry, storytelling and art workshops with three confirmed acts in the evening. The 2013 wassail had to be a serious business as with the atrocious spring and summer weather, 2012 had been the toughest year for apple growers in recent history. Everything started with a flaming torchlight procession. Cider was poured on the roots of these Victorian trees by a Wassail King & Queen chosen by the hidden bean in the Wassail cake fed to everyone. Mummers performed their play in a circle of fire, and that before they'd had any cider to drink! Even the Robin has a name, 'Scamp' the guardian of the orchard. Later, there would be a singer and a DJ. The Wassail includes a blessing using the Carhampton Song and Chant, and they describe it as "a synergism of numerous cultural traditions and we can trace its evolution across our entire apple producing counties" It's not a cheap night either, though the food comes highly recommended by The Guardian. Is it worth trying to disentangle the serious purposes from the marketing hype? Does it matter? Washed down with Janet's Jungle Juice it sounds like an evening to remember and takes Wassailing to places and people who might not otherwise encounter it.

Equally passionate about food and sustainability are the London Orchard Project, the Slow Food Organization and Alara Wholefoods. So it was that our very last wassail of what seemed an extended season took us to the unlikely setting of an industrial estate behind Kings Cross Station on the final Friday in February 2013. Here a community orchard has been planted, not in serried ranks on a green field but in what might otherwise have been unused land between industrial buildings – there was no shortage of trees either as we would find out in the procession later on. As dusk fell a drab mechanical setting was transformed

Hot spiced cider or apple juice and apple and cinnamon fritters fried on the fire, a blues band and a bonfire of pallettes to warm the wassailers on a cold February evening.

Wassailing at Alara Foods in the heart of London, while trains rattled in and out of Kings Cross station; a truly modern urban Wassail!

into an arena of light, from the bonfire of pallets, the windows of the moving trains going in and out of Kings Cross and St Pancras, and dare one say it, the London lume. The wassail was all about waking the trees, blessing them and bidding them be about their work – see Karen's extended description, p190.

Afterwards the talk was all about power, ley lines, spiritual force, St Pancras Old Church, England's ancient history and the possibility that Joseph of Arimathea may even have once sailed up the River Fleet in ancient times. A five piece blues band and a considerable supply of mulled cider and apple juice lubricated the sociabilities of people from all over London and the whole world. There was no toast, no Robins, no Wassail songs, no Wassail King or Queen, no Green Man, Morris Dancers or Mummers. Yet this was a Wassail with as strong a spiritual purpose as I have ever encountered. It was also entirely appropriate for the built up setting in which it took place and the culturally diverse city people who shared its power. When the time came to leave, both Karen and I had a spring in our step – we were uplifted, feeling the warm rosy glow we've often experienced taking part in traditional ceremonies, not least because this event proved beyond any doubt that trees can be wassailed anywhere and with any configuration of ceremony, provided that the spirit is willing.

King's Cross Orchard, Alara wholefoods, Camley Street, London

22nd February 2013, 5pm

Having allowed extra time to get through London traffic we arrived early at the headquarters of Alara Wholefoods in Camley Street, just behind Kings Cross and St Pancras Stations. Camley Street is strangely isolated, accessible from one direction only and part of an enclave of at least two wholefood businesses, factories, warehouses and green spaces, including Camley Street Natural Park, a wooded nature reserve on the site of a former coal yard. We parked in a large concrete forecourt where stood several piles of wooden pallets, some of which were set out as a cooking and serving area festooned with bunting, and with hot mulled cider, apple fritters and porridge being prepared. Another pile would soon be lit as a bonfire which would be replenished throughout the evening from the rest of the palettes nearby, which doubled as seating until then. During the next hour or so, as darkness fell, this scene was transformed. People arrived gradually, from all over the world to judge by their accents and appearances. A five piece blues band set up in the loading bay of the factory building, their music creating a very relaxed atmosphere. Mulled cider or apple juice was circulated freely by volunteers and a sense close to unreality was created by the moving lights of trains going in and out of Kings Cross station.

It was about 6.30pm and fully dark when Alex, from Alara, called the company up to the loading bay to begin the wassailing. First he told us to concentrate on the land on which we were standing. The land is the spirit of the place he said; close by flows the Fleet, the ancient sacred river of London, and the oldest place of worship in London, St Pancras Old Church, is just across the road. The spirit of the land together with the power of the sky, with its source of life, the sun, would cause the sap to rise in the trees, but to help this to happen we would now take metal baking trays (used in the factory) and bang them with spoons to wake the trees from their winter slumbers and shout the wassailing chant "Rise up sap! Bear forth fruit!" as we walked around the orchard.

The 'orchard' consisted of strips of land around and between the different buildings, which had been planted with a variety of fruit trees intended to provide some of the ingredients for the factory's products. This seemed to me such a practical use of ground that would otherwise be waste-land in this urban setting. Everyone gathered with spoon and tray and Alex led us down a passageway, so narrow that we were obliged to go in single file, between two buildings to begin the circumambulation. As I walked I felt a certain apprehension as if we were passing into a different realm, which in a way we were, as when we reached the end of the passage, far from the somewhat scruffy industrial environment we had so recently left, there we found a well tended garden with herbs and shrubs, gravel paths and fruit trees barely seen in the dark and shifting light. Clamorous clanging of spoon and tray accompanied the procession, but people were concentrating on keeping their footing in the gloom and most forgot to chant, except Alex, who knew the paths well and called out clearly "Rise up sap! Bear forth fruit!" from the front. I endeavoured to sustain the chant, but when we arrived at a sharp turn in the path, with a drop of almost three feet, it took all my concentration to step down onto the gravel-filled tyre that served as a step, then down to the next level, where we found ourselves doubling back along the bottom of this strip of orchard and returning to close to where we had begun. Then across the forecourt, past the entrance to the next-door warehouse where a fenced area at the front, adjoining the road, formed another part of the orchard.

The Wassailing completed, we made our way back to the bonfire, returning the trays and cutlery en route. The band was still playing, the hot cider was still flowing and little knots of people had reformed to continue their conversation, while a group of children threw more planks onto the fire. We were interested that this particular event was very late in the wassailing season, but when we found Alex to ask him about the timing of the event, he explained the formula as the nearest Friday to the second full moon of the year. It is said that the full moon has a strong effect on the rising of sap, just as it does on the tides, and as this is approaching the very beginning of the trees' growing season, it made perfect sense.

This was the third year a wassail had been held at Alara wholefoods, and judging by the size of most of the trees, they may well only be three or four years old, so clearly the event is still evolving. There was no elaborate symbolic ritualised ceremonial involving shotguns, toast or singing, in fact the impression formed was of a no nonsense ceremony designed to say "come on, trees, wake up, it's time to be about your business". This seemed to me eminently appropriate in this urban industrial location, amongst a cosmopolitan population, giving the event a practical character, contemporary and unfettered by slavery to the 'proper' way of doing things, but without losing its spiritual significance or sense of tradition.

Karen Cater

Apple Tree Plate by Ark Pottery, S. Devon
from our own collection.

Epilogue and post script

It's frequently said that the only certainties in the world are death and taxes: well we regularly hear of individuals that manage to avoid paying taxes! but if life and death are both part of an ongoing continuum of change, perhaps the saying should read '...death and change'. This study has followed the fortunes of a series of customs once very widely established that fell into decline almost to the point of vanishing, before experiencing a miraculous comeback. Setting our study up, we took the view that full understanding of folk tradition required the observer to be comfortable with change, believing that culture adjusts in response to the conditions in which people live. During C20 and C21, the population of the UK has both continued to grow and become more urbanized. Much of the turbulence of the early and mid C20 has subsided. People's average life span continues to increase and whilst the religious base has broadened becoming increasingly multicultural, some parts of society have become more secular. Amongst the many other changes, communication has become more open, both through travel and by social interaction through the internet and social networking. Against this background is a paradox: whilst authority systems seem ever more powerful, the ability to circumvent these has also increased.

Both the decline of wassailing and the early stages of its reawakening have been slow processes. Decline happened because the social groups involved had themselves declined or because of changes in fashion: reawakening has happened because new social groups have emerged to take the custom up, or in some cases because former sponsors have resumed. In all but a few cases new sponsoring organizations have been small –

efdss

english folk dance and song society

small farms, individual pubs, Morris dance clubs, schools, community orchards, village hall committees. The major exceptions to this pattern are commercial cider producers. Support has come from intermediate bodies providing information and expertise rather than tangible resource. These include the environmental charity Common Ground, the Transition Network, English Folk Dance and Song Society and other folk organisations. Latterly as both information and images have circulated more freely on the internet increasing numbers of people have been encouraged to set up new Wassails. There has been some input from mass media – new recordings by Blur and Kate Rusby; TV programmes about customs, mainly on BBC4, but the bulk of initiatives have come from the grass roots – it's been a real bottom up process.

Reawakened wassails are not direct copies of their precursors. House visiting collecting ceremonies prior to Christmas Day have in the main not come back. The notion of travelling bands of wassailers is also much reduced but includes several wassails surviving from earlier times. Some reawakened ceremonies involve visits to several orchards and / or pub tours. Dates have shifted in many places (some to 17th January) and are continuing so to do, right up to the end of February. Though Wassails always were self made entertainment, sometimes with more than one part and lasting several hours, they are now more open as people travel long distances to attend and the entertainment as well as the ceremony is a major part of the attraction. However, as wassailing grows in the community orchards, so too will wassailers increasingly become stakeholders in apple growing, often organically produced sustainable food.

As a postscript to this study, we decided to carry out a second internet search of Wassails, this time those taking place in 2013. Expecting an increase in numbers, we were not disappointed: from 170 ceremonies found in 2012, the number had risen to 226 in 2013, although sixteen events did not show up a second time round. However finding a further fifty events in a single year is rapid growth. Care is needed in interpreting internet searches: although the web can provide much information it is also very adept at recycling fashionable disinformation, particularly on the origins of wassailing and to some extent on the most suitable dates for ceremonies to happen. The total number of celebrations is always under reported: some don't report every year; many wassailers do it privately and would not think of publicizing their events on the web so that it's almost certain that the actual number of wassails in 2013 is greater than 226, probably by some distance.

Morris Dancers and the Community Orchards movement remain the principal drivers of the Wassail Reawakening, although an increasing number of village communities now hold

Wassails and two medium sized towns, Marlborough, Wiltshire and Bewdley, Worcestershire held their first wassails in 2013, each with strong support from the Town Mayor, perhaps recognizing the chance to combine a winter celebration with a public commitment to the environment and to local

Bewdley Wassail with Wytchwood Morris, 2013 supported by the Mayor

English produce and horticulture. It's too soon to call this a trend, but wassailing offers opportunities for winter celebrations in communities all over Britain. In other ways the custom is spreading too – 2013 sees the first report of wassails in Derbyshire, Leicestershire and Cheshire; several new events took place in Wiltshire and Berkshire, also in both Scotland and Wales. In other places, numbers of events have grown sufficiently to talk about clusters – this was already the case in Somerset and around Bristol, both sides of the Avon gorge, but it's now also true in Gloucestershire, particularly around Stroud, in the West Midlands, particularly south west of Birmingham and in London. Perhaps this is why the wassail season is also gradually extending. Although many organizers recognize the significance of both Twelfth Night and Old Twelvey Night only a minority of events happen on those dates: practicalities of organizing public entertainment almost demand a weekend date. While some events (Bankside, Chanctonbury Ring) have developed permanent calendar slots, others move between weekends for local reasons, so that an accurate Calendar of wassails is almost impossible to predict. In 2013, matters were complicated by the snow on January 19th which led to some events being cancelled but also to beautiful pictures of others. Overall in 2013 though, thirty three wassail events took place between January 25th and the end of February.

Looking at ceremonies, the extent of diversity is mind boggling. In every aspect of Wassailing, several alternative ways of doing things are possible. More will surely be developed in years to come, indeed this must happen if the old country custom is to continue its spread into towns and cities. At its heart, wassailing has a very deep seated core. It is about pledging good health to other people as they pledge to us, to people immediately around us, to buildings and perhaps above all to trees in the hope that they will prosper and bear fruit. If nasty things, evil spirits can be driven out and if good things, birds and bees can be nurtured this is more likely to happen. This process is spiritual, magical and transformational. There is no absolute guarantee though as the disastrous 2012 harvest has proved, but the act of Wassailing protects the spirit of those blessed – trees, birds and people – and uplifts the spirit of those making the blessings. Long may it continue and grow!

Wassail! (23rd May 2013)

January snow causes some wassails to be cancelled, but may result in beautiful photos of others

Headless Cross Wassail

photo - Headless Cross Wassail

P.S.

Last night while I was out with my Morris team, I was asked if I was going to be playing for Good Easter Molly Gang when they dance at the very first Wassailing of a newly planted (April 2013) community orchard of 65 trees in the parishes of Chignal & Mashbury (immediately north-west of Chelmsford) at about 5pm on Saturday 4th January 2014.

It is to be a family friendly event; apple juice rather than cider, but for those who prefer their refreshment a little stronger, afterwards repairing to The Three Elms at Chignal St James. Knowing the Molly Gang, there will probably be a bit of a song and tune session there.

So you see, there are new wassails springing up all over the place, all the time!

Good Easter Molly Gang at the Plough, Little Downham January 2012 (Colin Cater melodeon middle musician)

In The Three Horseshoes, Duton Hill later that night. (bottom left, concertina)

Appendix 1

Wassail Songs

A brief collection of 18 songs is included here reflecting musical traditions supporting wassailing in different times and places during the last four centuries. The older songs (at the end) come from printed sources and are both elaborate and flowery, celebrating the Twelve Days of Christmas. Most are visiting songs requesting entry to a large house and offering exchange of blessings in return for food, and drink from the Wassail Bowl. Different parts of the estate (fields, orchards, animals) are blessed but above all the master and mistress to whom long life and prosperity are invariably wished.

Of more recent origin are the 'collected' folk songs, recovered from different parts of England. Folk song collectors nearly always altered songs from the way in which they had been sung by their informants; sometimes substantially but usually just by annotating and publishing them, defining them in the process, rather than allowing them to continue to evolve naturally. Folk song collection goes back at least to 1843 (Sussex Sugar Wassail). Much recovery took place between 1900 – 1914, though some songs were not found until the 1950s. Many collected songs reflect established wassailing traditions: visiting songs, blessing great houses offering largess. Songs about visiting local neighbourhood houses were by 1900 also popular, particularly 'Here we come a-Wassailing' found all over England. Many visiting parties were exclusively girls and young women, particularly in the North. Very few of this group of songs are specifically about apple tree wassailing or cider.

The third group is of recently made songs, and would have benefited from being much larger. Other songs, fragments and poems are included in the main text. New creativity is bound to be an essential part of the Reawakening and spread of wassailing, so that it's likely that much has been missed in preparing this book. If it goes to a second edition we would hope to put this right, so we'd welcome anything sent to us.

Collected folk songs

CARHAMPTON WASSAIL SONG

& CHANT (Somerset)

Origins of this song and chant probably date back to the eighteenth century, and it has been used in both Gloucestershire and Somerset. Its tune is a major key version of the 'Miller of Dee', and was once used for a Suffolk Harvest Toast. It is one of the few songs associated solely with apple wassailing and has been widely adopted in the West of England and elsewhere.

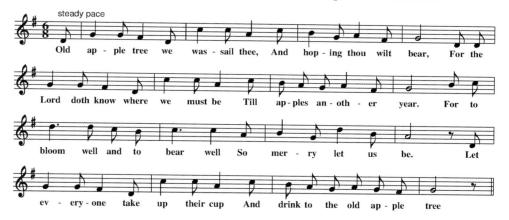

Old apple tree we wassail thee and hoping thou wilt bear
For the Lord doth know where we may be 'til apples another year
For to bloom well and to bear well so merry let us be
Let everyone take up their cup and drink to the old apple tree

The sung part is followed by the spoken verse;

"Old apple we wassail thee and hope that thou wilt bear
Hats full, Caps full, three bushel bags full,
And a little heap, under the stairs.
Hip, hip hooray!"

WHIMPLE WASSAIL SONG (Devon)

This song is from the singing of Jim Causley on his CD 'Fruits of the Earth'. Jim has led the music at Whimple Wassail on Old Twelvey Night (Jan 17th) for many years, starting from the New Fountain Inn to the three orchards visited each year. The words and guidance show that different verses of the song are intended to be sung at different venues during the evening.

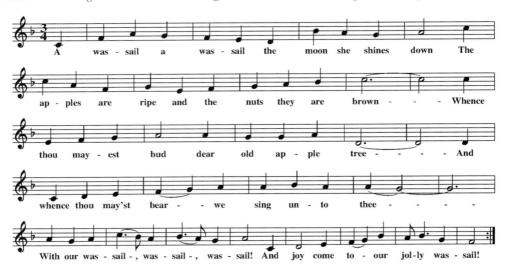

Verses sung around the apple tree

A-wassail, a-wassail! The Moon she shines down;
The apples are ripe and the nuts they are brown.
Whence thou mayest bud, dear old apple tree,
And whence thou mayest bear, we sing unto thee.

Chorus:
With our wassail, wassail, wassail!
And joy come to our jolly wassail!

Apple tree prosper, bud, bloom and bear,
That we may have plenty of cider next year.
And where there's a barrel, we hope there are ten,
That we may have cider when we come again.

Chorus

Verses sung at each home visited

Oh Mistress and Master, our wassail begin,
Please open your door and let us come in;
Besides all on earth you'll have apples in store;
Pray let us come in for 'tis cold at the door.

Chorus

Come fill up our wassail bowl full to the brim,
See, harnessed and garnished so neat and so trim,
Sometimes with laurel and sometimes with bays,
According to custom, to keep the old ways.

Chorus

Now for this gold liquor, to us, that you bring,
We lift up our voices and merrily sing,
That all good householders, long may they remain,
And long to continue the same to maintain.

Chorus

GLOUCESTERSHIRE WASSAIL

This song was published in Observations on Popular Antiquities (John Brand, 1813) with commentary suggesting links back to the court of Henry VII (1485 – 1509). It was included in the Oxford Book of Carols (1928) using a text collated from two different singers. It was still then sung in Gloucestershire with many villages having their own version of the song. Although a visiting song, animals are blessed and the role of Butler as MC in many modern wassails probably owes much to this song.

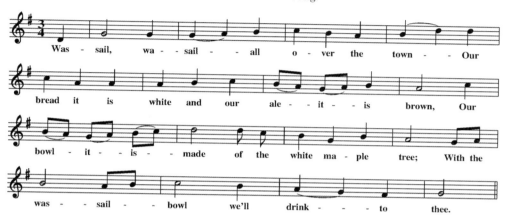

Wassail, wassail all over the town
Our toast it is white and our ale it is brown
Our bowl it is made of the white maple tree
With the wassailing bowl, we'll drink to thee

So here is to Cherry and to his right cheek
Pray God send our master a good piece of beef
And a good piece of beef that may we all see
With the wassailing bowl, we'll drink to thee

And here is to Dobbin and to his right eye
Pray God send our master a good Christmas pie
A good Christmas pie that may we all see
With the wassailing bowl, we'll drink to thee

So here is to Broad Mary and to her broad horn
May God send our master a good crop of corn
And a good crop of corn that may we all see
With the wassailing bowl, we'll drink to thee

Further published verses blessing different farm beasts

Come butler, come fill us a bowl of the best
Then we hope that your soul in heaven may rest
But if you do draw us a bowl of the small
Then down shall go butler, bowl and all

Then here's to the maid in the lily white smock
Who tripped to the door and slipped back the lock
Who tripped to the door and pulled back the pin
For to let these jolly wassailers in.

TRURO WASSAIL (Cornwall)

From the singing of Mary Humphreys and Anahata, this song was collected by Peter Kennedy in the 1950s from both Charlie Bate of Padstow and the Truro Wassail Boys, a group of three singers going out every Christmas. The song bears marked similarity to the nearby Malpas Wassail, but also to nineteenth century Cornish Wassail Songs which place the ceremony at different times between early November and Twelfth Night.

Now Christmas is over and the New Year begin
Pray open your doors and let us come in.

Chorus:
With our wassail, wassail,
Wassail, wassail,
And joy come with our jolly wassail.

O Master and Mistress sitting down by the fire
While we poor wassail boys are travelling the mire.

Chorus

This ancient house we will kindly salute
It is an old custom you need not dispute.

Chorus

We are here in this place, we orderly stand
We're the jolly wassail boys with a bowl in our hands.

Chorus

We hope that your apple trees prosper and bear
And bring forth good cider when we come next year.

Chorus

We hope that your barley will prosper and grow
That you may have plenty and more to bestow.

Chorus

Good Mistress and Master, how can you forbear
Come fill up our bowl with cider or beer.

Chorus

Good Mistress and Master, sitting down at your ease
Put your hands in your pockets and give what you please.

Chorus

I wish you a blessing and a long time to live
Since you've been so free and so willing to give.

Chorus

SUSSEX SUGAR WASSAIL

Probably the earliest collected Wassail song (by John Broadwood, father of Lucy Broadwood 1843), this visiting song has many of the best known floating verses, but also some that are not often found elsewhere, and the delightful verse about 'bees and apple trees' that doesn't appear anywhere else. Sussex was one of the traditional Wassailing areas.

A wassail, a wassail, a wassail we begin
With sugar, plum and cinnamon, and other spices in

Chorus: With a wassail, a wassail, a jolly wassail
And may joy come to you, and to our wassail

Good master and good mistress as you sit beside the fire,
Consider us poor wassailers who travel through the mire.

Good master and good mistress if you would be willing,
Come send us out your eldest son, with a sixpence or a shilling

Good master and good mistress if thus it should you please,
Come send us out your white loaf, likewise your Christmas cheese

Good master and good mistress if you will so incline
Come send us out your roast beef, likewise your Christmas chine

If you've any maids within your house, as I suppose you've none
They wouldn't let us stand a-wassailing so long on this cold stone

For we've wassail'd all this day long and nothing could we find
Except an owl in an ivy bush and her we left behind

We'll cut a toast all round the loaf and sit it by the fire
We'll wassail bees and apple trees until your heart's desire

Our purses they are empty. Our purses they are thin
They lack a little silver to line them well within.

Hang out your silver tankard upon your silver spear
We'll come no more a wassailing until another year

CROWCOMBE WASSAIL (Somerset)

A number of Somerset Wassail songs refer to the 'Great Dog of Langport', supposedly the defeat of the Danes by Alfred the Great in the eighth century. Collected by Cecil Sharp in 1908, what characterises this song is the grinding poverty it describes, in sharp contrast to the opulence of wassailing in 'great' houses. Parts of this song were used to construct the wonderful 'Apple Tree Wassailing Song' on the Watersons LP "For Pence and Spicy Ale"

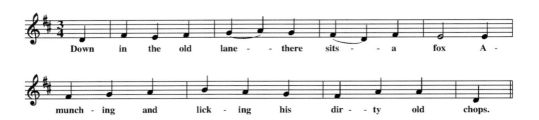

Down in the old lane there sits an old fox
A-munching and licking his dirty old chops

Shall we go catch him my boys if we can
Ten thousand to one if we catch him or none

Catch him or none, catch him or none
Ten thousand to one if we catch him or none

Wassail, wassail all round the town
Our cup it is white and our ale is brown

The great dog of Langport burnt off his tail
And this is the night we go singing wassail

I will go home to Old Mother Joan
And tell her to put on a big marrow bone

Boil it and boil it and skim off the scum
And we will have porridge when we do go home

Home my boys home, home my boys home
And we will have porridge when we do go home

Wassail, wassail all round the town
Our cup it is white and our ale is brown

Spoken:
Bud, blossom, bloom and bear
Ready to tear
So that we shall have apples and cider next year
Hat fulls cap fulls, three bushel bags full
And little heaps under the stairs
Cider running out gutter holes
Hip hip hurrah

CURRY RIVEL WASSAIL SONG (Somerset)

Collected by Cecil Sharp from Henry Richards (69) of Curry Rivel in 1909, the characteristic three line stanza is also found in wassail songs from Drayton and Langport. The Curry Rivel ceremony takes place on Twelfth Night (Wassail Eve), and members of the Richards family have been part of it for over 150 years, in current times Bill Richards – See Ch 7. The song has changed a bit since 1909, as the Curry Rivel Community website shows.

Wassail, wassail, all over the town,
The cup it is white and the ale it is brown,
The cup it is made from the good old ashen tree,
And so's the beer from our best barley.

To you our wassail.
Aye and joy come to our jolly wassail.

O maid, O maid with the silver headed pin
Pray open the door and let us all in
All for to fill our wassail bowl and sail away again

O maid, O maid with your glove and your mask
Pray come to the door and shown your pretty face
For we are truly weary of standing in this place

Oh Master and Mistress if you are so well please
To set all on your table your white loaf and your cheese
With your roast beef, your porrops* and your peas

Oh Master and Mistress, we done you any harm,
Pray pull fast this door, and let us pass along,
And give us hearty thanks for the singing of our song,

One voice speaks:
God bless Master and Missus and all the family,
hoping they've had a Merry Christmas and wish
them a Happy New Year and many.
Thank you Missus, thank you very much. [Applause]
Thank you very much.

*young leeks or onions

HERE WE COME A-WASSAILING 1

Here we come a-wassailing is the most widespread of all the English Wassailing songs, with twenty seven different collected versions and more than one song group structure. This one has been chosen as representative of the 'Wassail bough' or 'Wassel Boo' grouping

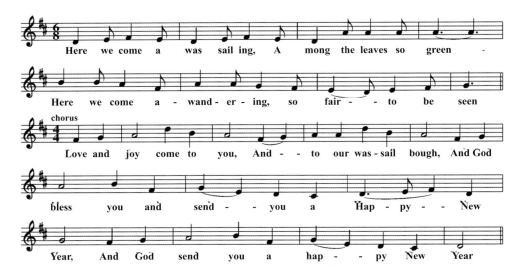

Here we come a-wassailing among the leaves so green,
Here we come a-wand'ring so fair to be seen.

Chorus:
Love and joy come to you, and to our wassail bough,
And God bless you, and send you a Happy New Year,
And God send you a Happy New Year

We are not daily beggars that beg from door to door,
But we are neighbours' children whom you have seen before

Good master and good mistress as you sit beside the fire,
Pray think of us poor children who wander in the mire.

We have a little purse made of stretching leather skin;
We want some of your small change to line it well within.

Bring us out a table and spread it with a cloth;
Bring us out a cheese, and of your Christmas loaf.

God bless the master of this house, likewise the mistress too;
And all the little children that round the table go.

HERE WE COME A-WASSAILING 2

The Watersons sang Here We Come A-Wassailing in 1965 on their first album, Frost and Fire, contributing to early wassail reawakenings. Unlike the other version of this song on the previous page, there are references to apples and cider, though it is still a visiting, cadging song, rather than one seeking to bless the givers or trees. There are also echoes of the penury of the Crowcombe song.

Here we come a - was - sail - ing a - mong the leaves so green

Here we come a - wan - der - ing so fair - ly to be seen

Now is win -ter time strangers travel far and nearAnd we wish you; send you a   Hap - py New Year

Here we come a-wassailing among the leaves so green,,
Here we come a-wandering so fairly to be seen
Now is winter time strangers travel far and near,
And we wish you; send you a happy new year.

Bud and blossom, bud and blossom, bud and bloom and bear,
So we may have plenty of cider all next year,
Apples are in capfuls, are in bushel bags and all,
And there's cider running out of every gutter hole.

Down here in the muddy lane there sits an old red fox,
Starving and a-shivering and licking his old chops,
Bring us out your table and spread it if you please,
And give us hungry wassailers a bit of bread and cheese.

I've got a little purse and it's made of leather skin,
A little silver sixpence would line it well within,
Now is winter time strangers travel far and near,
And we wish you; send you a happy new year.

GOWER WASSAIL (South Wales)

Sung by Phil Tanner, the Gower Nightingale, to Peter Kennedy in the 1950s, this song was included by The Watersons on 'Frost and Fire' a decade later. Phil Tanner's recording only has these four verses, though other printed versions are longer. Many Welsh visiting customs including the Mari Lwyd and Hunting the Wren were often described as wassailing, although the reference to apples in this Welsh song is slightly more surprising.

A wassail, a wassail throughout all this town,
Our cup it is white and our ale it is brown,
Our wassail is made of good ale and true,
Some nutmeg and ginger, the best we could brew

Chorus:
Fol the dol, fol the doldy dol,
fol the doldy dol, fol the doldy dee,
Fol the dairol, fol the daddy, sing tooral-aye-do!

Our wassail is made with an elderberry bough,
And so my good neighbour we'll drink unto thou.
Besides all on earth, you'll have apples in store,
Pray let us come in for it's cold by the door.

Chorus

We know by the moon that we are not too soon
We know by the sky that we are not too high
We know by the stars that we are not too far
And we know by the ground that we are within sound

Chorus

Now master and mistress – thanks to you we'll give
And for our jolly wassail as long as we live
And if we should live till another new year
Perhaps we may call and see who do live here

Chorus

Recently made songs

COCK ROBIN (traditional)

This is both a song and a nursery rhyme, collected by Cecil Sharp at Littleport, Cambridgeshire, and also included in Traditional Games of England, Scotland and Ireland by Alice Gomme. So why include it with recently made up songs? Because it was sung as 'Oliver Cromwell is buried and dead' at Claybury Park orchard Wassail in Redbridge, East London, Saturday 5th Jan 2013

Cock Ro-bin is dead and gone to his grave gone to his grave gone to his grave,

Cock Ro-bin is dead and gone to his grave Ee I gone to his grave.

Trad) Cock Robin is dead and gone to his grave
Gone to his grave, gone to his grave
Cock Robin is dead and gone to his grave
Ee, Aye, gone to his grave

There grew an old apple tree over his head....

The apples are ripe and ready to fall....

There came and old woman to gather them all....

Cock Robin he rose and gave her a thump
Gave her a thump, gave her a thump
Which made the old woman go hippity hump
Ee, Aye, Hippity hump

The saddle and bridle they lie on the shelf
lie on the shelf, lie on the shelf
If you want any more you can sing it yourself
Ee, Aye, Sing it yourself

New) Oliver Cromwell is buried and dead
buried and dead, buried and dead
Oliver Cromwell is buried and dead
Ee, Aye, buried and dead

There grew an old apple tree over his head....

The apples are ripe and ready to fall....

There came and old woman to gather them all....

Oliver Cromwell rose and gave her a drop
Gave her a drop, gave her a drop
Which made the old woman go hippity hop
Ee, Aye, Hippity hop

The saddle and bridle they lie on the shelf
lie on the shelf, lie on the shelf
If you want any more you can sing it yourself
Ee, Aye, Sing it yourself

DUTON HILL WASSAIL SONG (Essex)

words & music by Colin Cater

Written in 2008 to celebrate Wassailing in a contemporary folk context of wassailing parties touring pubs and large houses, either before or during the Christmas holiday, celebrating the turn of the year and performing to raise money for charity. We have used it at each of the three Duton Hill wassails held so far. Wassailing parties might have included anyone who could do a turn, and in time honoured tradition would include a blessing for the host and the entire company.

This song appears on CD 'A Penny for the Ploughboys' by Colin Cater available from Hedingham Fair, see p249

We've been travel-ling this count-ry by the light of the moon And we
hope you are re - ady that we hav-ent come too soon. We've brought
fid - dlers and dan - cers and a great ma - ny more. Please
let us come in for it's cold at your door.
Chorus
It's Your Wass ail Our Wass ail Joy come to you and a Jol - ly Wass
- - ail Come fill up our bowls now with ci - der and beer and we
wish you ma - ny bles - sings till we come a - gain next year - - -

We've been travelling this country by the light of the moon
And we hope you are ready, that we haven't come too soon
We've brought fiddlers and dancers and a great many more
Please let us come in for its cold at your door
Chorus:
It's your wassail, our wassail
Joy come to you and a jolly wassail
Come fill up our bowls now with cider and beer
And we wish you many blessings till we come again next year

The Quack Doctor is here with a top hat on his head
Prince Paradine will fight again though he was dead
With King George, Lord Nelson, the Wild Horse and Old Tosspot
And Old Father Christmas who will never be forgot

When our play it is over we will end with a song
And dance with our rapiers that are hard, sharp and long
When the swords are raised high all the company will cheer
It's a mark of our unity over hundreds of years

For the year it is turning and the new Sun is born
To return soon to ripen our apples and corn
With beer bread and cider, we'll bless orchard and field
That a plentiful harvest in time they will yield

We wish health and prosperity and long life to give
To this great house and everyone that in it does live
And to all this fine company that dwell far and near
Bright Yule, Merry Christmas and a Happy New Year.

THE PRESSES ARE RUNNING WITH GOLD

words & music by Colin Cater

Written to celebrate apples in all their varieties (even plums and pears), sustainability,
the passage of the year for growers and above all, wassailing.

Not long ago the food we eat
came from farms not far away
Apples you bought in the greengrocer's shop
were fresh from the market that day
There was nowt so pernicious as golden delicious,
created to ravage your gut (There was)
Sweet Coppin for cider, Bramleys for cooking
and Pippins were sweet as a nut

CHORUS
And the presses are running with gold,
the presses are running with gold
Fine yellow nectar for young and for old;
the presses are running with gold

An apple a day keeps the doctor away,
he won't have to cure any ills
They're good for colitis, the gout and arthritis;
you won't need any potions or pills
They'll strengthen your heart and drive away flatulence,
give you great vigour and pep
Drown melancholy and make you feel jolly,
you'll walk with a spring in your step

So we planted a tree in seventy three;
there's a fine orchard growing there now
We wassail in January, prune 'em in March,
then the blossom comes out on the bough
If there's not too much wet, the fruity it will set
and you won't have to say any prayers
For when Apple Day comes there'll be hatfuls and capfuls
and little heaps under the stairs

There's Devonshire Quarrenden, Somerset Dabinett,
the Doddin and Worcester Pearmain
Warwickshire Drooper that makes the Plum Jerkum,
wow we're going to be legless again
And Riverses Orchard in Sawbridgeworth
developed the Conference Pear
There isn't a county in all of the land
but there's local apple varieties there

So when the apples have fallen and the vats are all full
and the snow lies thick on the ground
Break out the apple juice, mulled cider and wine
and pass the Wassail Cake round
With rough music and shotguns, maybe a horn,
we're certain to make a great din
We'll pledge to the robins, the trees and each other;
then the season starts over again

BRANSCOMBE WASSAIL SONG (Devon)

This song was made by the children of Branscombe Primary School, East Devon with assistance from Folk South West and the National Trust. It captures the spirit of many modern wassails, blessing the trees for their own sake, as well as what they might produce; driving out things that harm the trees whether bugs or bad spirits.

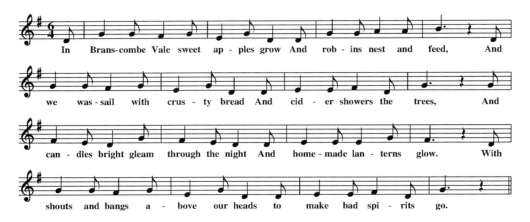

In Branscombe Vale sweet apples grow And robins nest and feed, And we was-sail with crusty bread And cider showers the trees, And candles bright gleam through the night And home-made lanterns glow. With shouts and bangs above our heads to make bad spirits go.

SING:

In Branscombe Vale sweet apples grow,
and robins nest and feed
And we wassail with crusty bread,
and cider showers the trees
And candles bright gleam through the night,
and home-made lanterns glow
With shouts and bangs above our heads,
to make bad spirits go.

SHOUT:

Make the trees grow
Plenty of cider, plenty of juice
And plenty of apples to eat
Lots for us, lots for the birds
Go away bad things
Wake up good things, make the trees grow
Wassailing we go, make the trees grow

SING:

We've Ironsides and Golly Knapp,
and Thomas Legg and Putt
There's Old Pig's Nose and Neverblight,
next to our King's Fav'rite
With Buttery Door which we adore,
and Devonshire Quarrenden
With Slack mi Girdle last not least,
and now our Wassail's done

SHOUT:

Make the trees grow
Plenty of cider, plenty of juice
And plenty of apples to eat
Lots for us, lots for the birds
Go away bad things
Wake up good things, make the trees grow
Wassailing we go, make the trees grow

Early Wassail songs

GIVE WAY, GIVE WAY, YE GATES AND WIN

One of a number of Wassail poems by Robert Herrick (1591-1674), this is set to a traditional English Melody and printed by W. H. Husk in the nineteenth century. *A manchet is a small loaf of fine wheaten bread. The founder of the Hospital of St. Cross, near Winchester, directed that every stranger should receive a manchet of bread and a cup of ale.

Give, way, give way, ye gates, and win
An easie blessing to your kin
And basket by our entering in

May both with manchet* stand repleat,
Your larders, too, so hung with meat,
That there of them many folk may eat

Yet ere twelve moones shall swirl about
Their silv'rie spheres, there's none may doubt
But more's sent in then was served out.

Next, may your dairies prosper so,
As that your pans no ebbe may know;
But if they do, the more to flow

Like to a solemne sober stream
Bankt all with lilies and the cream
Of sweetest cowslips filling them

Then may your plants be presst with fruit,
Nor bee or hive you have be mute,
But sweetly sounding like a lute.

Next, may your duck and teeming hen
Both to the cocks-tread say, Amen;
And for their two eggs render ten,

Last, may your harrows, shares and ploughes,
Your stacks, your stocks, your sweetest mowes,
All prosper by your virgin vowes.

A JOLLY WASSEL-BOWL

A Carrol for a Wassel-Bowl - to be sung upon Twelfth-Day at Night, to the tune of "Gallants, come away". It was found in a manuscript of the antiquarian Anthony Wood (1662-1695) in the Ashmolean Museum, Oxford. Another example with a series of persuading verses was recorded by Mr Rann of Dudley in 1819 and published in Hone, 1825. This carol was said to be popular in Staffordshire and Warwickshire. The participants were female, a form of social inversion or 'The World Turned Upside Down'

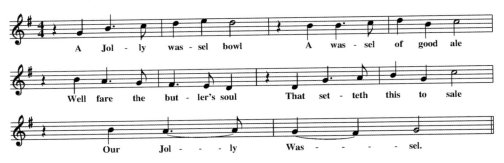

A jolly Wassel-Bowl, a Wassel of good ale,
Well fare the butler's soule, that setteth this to sale
Our jolly Wassel

Good Dame, here at your door our Wassel we begin
We are all maidens pure, we pray now let us in
With our good Wassel

Our Wassel we do fill with apples and with spice
They kindly will agree, to take a good carouse
Of our Wassel

If any maidens be here dwelling in this house
Them grant us your good will to taste here once or twice
Of our Wassel

But here they let us stand all freezing in the cold
Good Master give command To enter and be bold
With our Wassel

Much joy into this hall with us is entered in
Our master first of all we hope will now begin
Of our Wassel

And after his good wife our spiced bowl will try
The Lord prolong your life, good fortune we espy
For our Wassel

Some bounty from your hands our wassel to maintain
We'll buy no house or lands with that which we do gain
With our Wassel

This is our merry night of choosing King and Queen
Then be it your delight that something may be seen
In our Wassel

It is a noble part to bear a liberal mind
God bless our Master's heart for here we comfort find
With our Wassel

And now we must be gone to seek out more good cheer
Where bounty will be shown as we have found it here
With our Wassel

Much joy betide them all our prayers shall be still
We hope and ever shall for this our great good will
To our Wassel

CAROL FOR TWELFTH DAY

From a MS of Cornish Carols compiled by John Hutchens about 1826. The carols were copied from an old book, so were considered "ancient" in the early 19th century. 'Nappy ale' is old slang for strong ale that is brown and stale, so called because it makes one sleepy. Louis Killen sang the Carol for Twelfth Day in 1978 on his Front Hall album 'Old Songs, Old Friends'

Sweet master of this habitation with our mistress be so kind,
As to grant an invitation that we may this favour find;
To be now invited in and in joy and mirth begin,
Happy, sweet and pleasant songs which unto this time belong.

Refrain line at the end of every verse;
Let every loyal, honest soul contribute to our wassail bowl.

So now may you enjoy the blessings of a loving, virtuous wife,
Riches, honour now possessing and a long and happy life;
Living in prosperity, endless generosity
Always be maintained, I pray, don't forget the good old way.

So now before the season is departed in your presence
we appear,
Therefore then be noble-hearted and afford some dainty cheer;
Pray let us have it now what the season doth allow,
What the house may now afford should be placed
upon the board.
Whether it be roast-beef or fowl and liquor well
our wassail bowl.

For now it is the season of leisure then to those
who kindness show,
May they have wealth and peace and pleasure and
the spring of bounty flow,
To enrich them while they live that they may afford to give,
To maintain the good old way, many a long and happy day.

Therefore you are to be commended if in this you will not fail,
Now our song is almost ended fill our bowl with nappy ale;
And we'll drink a full carouse to the master of this house,
Aye and to our mistress dear, wishing both a happy year
With peace and love without control
who liquored well our wassail bowl.

GRAMPOUND WASSAIL SONG (Cornwall)

They obviously like 'em long in Cornwall – another wassail song for the Christmas period up to the end of the Twelve Days. The song was recovered in the nineteenth century from more than one singer and was already considered old. The first three verses are usually sung outside the house. The singers carry a bowl into which all liquor given is poured, and when they leave they usually carry some away in case they should meet anyone on their way to the next house. Should they do so the ninth verse is sung. Verses 10 and 11 are only sung on Twelfth Day

1. Now here at this house we first shall begin
To drink the King's health which a custom has been
Now unto the Master we'll drink his good health
We hope he may prosper in virtue and wealth

Chorus
With our wassail! Wassail! Wassail
Wassail and joy come to our jolly wassail

2. Now here at your door we do orderly stand
Our jolly wassail and our hats in our hand
We do wish a good health to the master and dame
To the children and servants we wish it the same

3. In the friendliest manner this house we salute
That it is an old custom we need not dispute
O ask not the reason from hence it did spring
For we very well know 'tis an ancient old thing

4. Now for this good liquor to us that you bring
We lift up our voices we merrily sing
That all good householders may continue still
To provide the brown liquor our bowl for to fill

5. We hope that your barley will prosper and grow
That you may have barley and beer to bestow
And where you have one bushel we hope you'll have ten
That you may have beer against we come again

6. We hope that your orchards may blossom and bear
That you may have cider against the next year
That where you've one hogshead we hope you'll have ten
That you may have cider when we come again

7. We wish you great plenty and long may you live
Because you are willing and free for to give
To our wassail so cheerful, our wassail so bold
Long may you live happy, be lusty and old

8. Now neighbours and strangers you ever shall find
The wassailers courteous, obliging and kind
We hope our civility you will approve
With a piece of small silver in token of love

9. A welcome kind Sir as we merrily meet
With our jolly wassail as we pass up the street
O welcome kind Sir, if it please you to stop
A piece of small silver in our bowl for to drop

10. Now jolly old Christmas is passing away
He's posting off from us, and this the last day
That we shall enjoy long 'oy you to abide
So farewell, Old Christmas, a merry good tide

11. Now jolly old Christmas, thou welcomest guest
Thou from us are parting which makes us look wisht
For all the twelve days are now come to their end
And this the last day of the season we spend

12. Now for this good liquor, your cider, your beer
And for the fair kindness that we have had here
We return you our thanks and shall still bear in mind
How you have been bountiful, loving and kind

13. Now for the great kindness that we did receive
We return you our thanks, and we now take our leave
From this present evening we bid you adieu
Until the next year and same season ensue

'Next crown the bowl full
With gentle lamb's wool
Add sugar, nutmeg and ginger,
With store of ale too;
And thus ye must do
To make a wassail a swinger'

- Robert Herrick; 'Twelfth Night' (c1648).

And sometimes lurk I in a gossip's bowl,
In very likeness of a roasted crab,
And when she drinks, against her lips I bob.'

– Shakespeare; Puck, in 'A Midsummer Night's Dream'.

Appendix 2
Wassail Recipes - Drinks

Lambswool

In the earliest accounts, the drink provided in a Wassail Bowl was usually 'Lambswool'. Lambswool is made from hot sweetened spiced ale, sometimes mixed with a fortified wine, and occasionally with cider. It may be transformed by the addition of eggs and cream into a very rich drink. Roasted apples (older recipes insist on the use of crab apples) float on the surface. It will become apparent as you read these recipes that just about any mixture of ale, wine, cider etc that takes your fancy may be heated with your favourite combination of sugar and spices, then perhaps mixed with eggs and/or cream and served with roasted apples – experiment and enjoy!

Native British Crab Apples; tiny sour apples, small rounder smoother leaves, quite unlike apples from cultivated stock.

There are two quite separate accounts of the origin of the name 'Lambswool'. It has been said that it derives from "La Mas Ubhal", pronounced 'lamasool', which means "the day of the apple fruit"; the first day of November, dedicated to the angel presiding over fruits and seeds – this would be Pomona, the Roman nymph or goddess who tends and protects fruit trees.

A more down to earth explanation is that 'Lambswool' describes the appearance of the pulp bursting from the roasted crab apples floating on the surface of the drink.

LAMBSWOOL *Recipe 1*

A very rich drink including eggs and cream, with the fat balanced by the addition of a dash of whisky.

1lb crab apples roasted till bursting

4pts strong dark ale

A few cloves

2 sticks cinnamon

1inch cube root ginger, finely sliced.

4 allspice berries

Brown sugar to taste

2 eggs

¼ pt / 150ml single cream

Dash of whisky

⬤ Heat the Ale and spices together in a large pan. Keep it hot for 45mins to 1 hour to develop the flavour of the spices. Do not allow the liquid to boil as this will evaporate the alcohol and spoil the flavour.

⬤ Strain and add sugar to taste.

⬤ Whip eggs, cream and whisky together, mix into spiced ale.

⬤ Pour into serving bowl.

⬤ Spoon crab apples carefully onto the surface of the drink, ensuring they float.

A Yorkshire Dales sheep-farmers toast; 'to wool and mutton'

LAMBSWOOL *Recipe 2*

Drunk with a wassail toast 'to wool and mutton', wishing prosperity on Yorkshire Dales sheep-farmers.

4-5 cooking apples (studded with a few cloves if you like a
spicier flavour)

5pts brown ale

1 bottle sweet white wine

½ nutmeg, grated

1 inch cube root ginger, finely sliced.

2 sticks cinnamon

Brown sugar to taste

Stand the apples in a tray with a little water, bake at 200C, 400F Gas6 until soft.

Meanwhile heat the Ale, wine and spices together in a large pan. Keep it hot until the apples are done (about 45mins) to develop the flavour of the spices.

Do not allow the liquid to boil as this will evaporate the alcohol and spoil the flavour

Skin apples and mash to a pulp.

Remove the cinnamon and ginger and pour the hot drink over the apple pulp, mix together.

Add sugar to taste.

Strain through a sieve into the wassail bowl.

Spoon remaining apple pulp carefully onto the surface of the drink, ensuring it floats.

LAMBSWOOL *Recipe 3*

A C19 nutritious wine-based recipe.

4 bottles Port, Sherry, or Madeira wine

The following whole spices;

3g mace

12g cloves

10g cardamom seeds

7g cinnamon

3g nutmeg

13g ginger

13g coriander seeds

1 ½ lbs. sugar

12 egg yolks

6 egg whites

12 apples roasted till soft

In a large stainless steel pan, simmer the spices in just enough water to cover.

When done, add the port, sherry, or Madeira wine.

Add sugar to taste

Warm over a low heat

Meanwhile, whisk the eggs till frothy and trebled in size.

Then, when the wine is warm, add the whisked eggs a little at a time, stirring briskly.

Float the 12 roasted apples in the liquid, and turn the heat right up. The apple skins will burst as the wine gets hot. When almost, but not quite boiling, dip tankards or cups into the Lambswool and enjoy!

LAMBSWOOL *Recipe 4*

Wassail Cup from C17. A simpler version of Lambswool, using a mixture of ale and cider.

4 apples

4 oz. of sugar or clear honey

½ pint of brown ale

½ pint of cider

2 or 3 cinnamon sticks

3 blades of mace

4 cloves

1 teaspoon of freshly grated nutmeg

1 ginger root, crushed or sliced

 Core the apples and sprinkle with sugar and water. Bake at 375 F or 190 C for 30 minutes, or until tender.

Mix ale, cider and spices together. Heat for 30 minutes but do not allow to boil.

Strain and pour over roasted apples.

Serve in a punch bowl.

MULLED ALE

'Oh good ale, thou art my darling,
Thou art my joy both night and morning'
-traditional song

Hot spiced ale, or 'Mulled Ale', which forms the basis of many Lambswool and Wassail recipes, was originally made by mixing a combination of the usual spices with a little sugar into a pewter mug filled with ale, which was then 'mulled' in the following way: A poker would be pushed deep into a blazing fire and left there to become red-hot, when it would be extracted, any embers sticking to it knocked off on the fender. The poker would immediately be plunged into the tankard, making the ale boil and bubble, hissing and spitting and sending up a cloud of steam, and releasing the flavours of the spices into the hot drink. It must have seemed very like a blacksmith quenching a horseshoe in cold water once the shaping of the hot metal was completed. A toper's alchemy!

A very pleasant evening may be passed sitting by a cosy inglenook fire with a big jug of ale, a tankard and a poker, perhaps with a dog dozing at your feet whilst outside the wind howls and the sleet dashes at the windows.

WASSAIL

'Pass the bowl around and let the toast run free'
-traditional song

A hot spiced cider, drunk from a three-handled Wassail bowl – the idea is that as you drink, you hold two handles, that way people can see both your hands and it is clear that you are not planning to stab anyone with a concealed dagger! As you pass the bowl to the next person, they take the free handle, ensuring the bowl is not dropped accidentally, and as you let go, they then take another handle, which has the effect of rotating the bowl as it is passed from one drinker to another.

When travelling bands of Wassailers visited big houses, they might have had toasted bread floating on top of the wassail drink, giving rise to the origin of 'toasting' good health.

Karen Cater's Simple Wassail Recipe

For a simple, fail-safe Wassail drink that works every time. This is the one I always use, and my friends love it! Use cheap supermarket cider – it works fine, but try experimenting with different artisan ciders for a richer, stronger flavour.

This recipe makes enough to fill a large wassail bowl.

1ltr Dry Cider

2-3 tablespoons brown sugar to taste

2 sticks cinnamon

12 cloves

A little freshly grated nutmeg

A few slices fresh ginger

Slices of apple

Place all ingredients in a saucepan and heat gently, do not boil as this will evaporate the alcohol. Keep the wassail on a low heat for 30 minutes or so to develop the flavour before serving.

Pour through a sieve to remove spices.

If you plan to serve the wassail all evening, you may top up the mixture with more cider, adding spices and sugar as required.

For a non-alcoholic version use apple juice instead of cider, but do not add much sugar unless you want a very sweet drink.

Wassail Cakes

No self-respecting Wassail party would be complete without a Wassail cake to share. Either as a centre-piece to the table at a private house, or handed around on a big platter among a crowd in the orchard. Here are a few ideas for Wassail cakes - or try adding spices, honey and chopped apples to a basic cake recipe.

SOMERSET CIDER APPLE CAKE

This is a substantial, not-too-sweet, very tasty cake for sharing – best hot from the oven. I made it with strong, oak seasoned vintage Cider for a lovely boozy flavor! As this is a SOMERSET Cider Apple cake, it is imperative that you use a Somerset cider!!!

100g /3oz soft brown sugar

125g /4oz softened butter

2 eggs beaten

250g /8oz plain flour

half a teaspoon grated nutmeg

1 teaspoon bicarbonate of soda

200ml /7fl oz dry cider

1 med Cooking apple chopped

Demarara sugar for sprinkling

Put butter, sugar and eggs into a food processor/ mixer and wiz till fully mixed

Sift the flour, bicarbonate of soda and nutmeg together; add in 2 batches and wiz again after adding each batch

Add cider a bit at a time, whizzing between each splosh, continue whizzing till the mixture is thick and creamy

Fold in apple chunks, ensuring they are evenly distributed throughout the mixture.

Pour into a greased and base lined, deep 7 inch tin and

sprinkle the top with demarara sugar to form a crunchy topping

🎃 Bake at 190 C, 375F, Gas 5 for 1 - 1½ hours.

OR, *if you are not using a food processor;*

🎃 In a large basin cream together sugar and butter until the mixture is light and fluffy.

🎃 Mix in the beaten eggs, beat until fully combined.

🎃 Sift the flour, bicarbonate of soda and nutmeg together and fold in.

🎃 Stir in the cider, a bit at a time. Beat till thick and creamy.

🎃 Continue as before

This is a SOMERSET Cider Apple cake, so it is imperative that you use a Somerset cider!!!

Gluten Free APPLE CAKE

A moist gluten free cake that keeps well
(being coeliac myself, this one's a must! - Karen)

2 crisp eating apples (Granny Smith works well)

Splash of lemon juice

175g / 6oz golden caster sugar

175g / 6oz unsalted butter softened

3 eggs, separated

175g / 6oz ground almonds

1 teaspoon baking powder

Icing sugar for dusting

Peel and slice the apples fairly thinly. Toss them in a little lemon juice. Sprinkle 1 tablespoon of the sugar over them and set aside.

Cream butter and remaining sugar together until light and fluffy.

Add egg yolks and beat to combine.

Sift the ground almonds and baking powder together, and stir in.

In a separate bowl, whisk egg whites till stiff, then fold into the cake mixture carefully in two batches, to maintain as much air in the mixture as possible.

Take half the apples and pat dry on kitchen paper, then add them to the mixture together with any juice left in their bowl, mix gently to combine.

Transfer to a greased and base-lined 20cm cake tin with a removable base.

Smooth the top of the mixture and arrange the remaining apple slices on top.

Bake at 160C, 350F, Gas4 for 1hr 15mins or until golden and a skewer inserted comes out clean.

Run a knife around the edge of the cake and leave in the tin until cold.

Remove from the tin and dust with icing sugar.

Serve sliced cold, or reheat and serve with whipped cream or vanilla ice cream as a dessert.

"I like it cold, 'cos it's quicker to eat isn't it?"

Mary Humphreys

WASSAIL PUDDING

For a really interesting pudding at a Wassail dinner;

LITTLE WASSAIL CAKES

(Makes 24 fairy-cakes)

250g / 8oz unsalted butter or margarine

250g / 8oz sugar

1 medium egg

150ml / 4fl oz Advocaat

250g / 8oz self-raising flour

2 tsp baking powder

125g / 4oz mixed dried fruit

½ teaspoon ground mixed spice

½ teaspoon ground nutmeg

½ teaspoon ground cinnamon

½ teaspoon ground ginger

24 paper cake-cases

Put all Ingredients except the dried fruit into a food processor and whizz until thick and smooth.

Stir in dried fruit

OR, *if you are not using a food processor*

Cream the butter and sugar together,

Add the egg and advocaat, mix well

Sift together the flour, baking powder and the spices, fold into the mixture.

Stir in the dried fruit.

Line two cake trays with 24 paper cases and spoon in the mixture.

Bake at 200C, 400F, Gas6 for 20 minutes.

In a casserole dish, alternate layers of these little wassail cakes with sliced apples, sprinkling brown sugar between layers. Pour 1pint of your favourite spiced wassail drink over the whole lot and bake at 200C, 400F, Gas 6 for 30mins. Serve with Whipped cream, Vanilla ice cream or Brandy Butter.

HEREFORDSHIRE WASSAIL CAKE

In Herefordshire, Worcestershire and Gloucestershire a cake made with Caraway seeds would be soaked in cider and eaten at the wassail supper after the tree blessing was over.

175g /6oz butter, softened

175g /6oz golden castor sugar

3 eggs

175g /6oz self raising flour

1 tablespoon caraway seeds

Demarara sugar for sprinkling

175ml /½ pt good strong cider

Cream together the butter and sugar till light and fluffy

Beat the eggs and add, mix in

Sift flour into the bowl and mix well

Stir in the caraway seeds

Pour into a greased and base lined 7 inch tin and sprinkle the top with demarara sugar to form a crunchy topping

Bake at 160C, 350F, Gas4 for an hour or until risen and golden, and a skewer inserted into the middle comes out clean.

Stand the hot cake in a large deep bowl, pierce the top all over with a skewer and pour cider over, allowing the cake to soak up the cider for half an hour. Serve with whipped cream.

Herefordshire Wassail Cake, a buttery caraway seed cake, soaked in cider and served with whipped cream and or vanilla ice cream.

232

TWELFTH CAKE

At Lewes Saturday
Folk Club, because
we can't go outside
and wassail a tree in
the course of the
evening, for some
years I have been
bringing in some
branches of an apple
tree from my garden
and Bryan Creer has
fired his home-made
comedy shotgun,
which fires party
poppers, through
them while we chant
a wassail rhyme.
Last year I had the
bright idea of inviting
other people to bring
in branches of their
own trees to add to it
so that they can
share any blessing the
ceremony conveys.
It's a way of applying
magical thinking to
changing
circumstances.

Valmai Goodyear

Thanks to Valmai Goodyear (Committee member, Lewes Saturday Folk Club)
for this recipe, she says;

"This is my version of a traditional recipe, based on descriptions of a
rich cake containing ginger and honey. It's also traditional to bake a
dried bean until hard and add it to the mixture; whoever gets the bean
in their slice is chosen as the Lord of Misrule and is supposed to decide
what games will be played on Twelfth Night, but I haven't tried doing
that yet myself.

This cake should be made well in advance in order to allow time to
add the rum or brandy and for maturing."

900 g crystallised ginger
900 g good crystallised peel
375 g plain flour
375 g butter
350 g dark brown sugar
generous tablespoon runny honey
6 eggs
heaped teaspoon ground nutmeg
heaped teaspoon ground cinnamon
grated rind of one lemon & one orange

After baking

rum or brandy
2 tablespoons marmalade & the juice of half a lemon
1 packet marzipan & 500 g royal icing sugar

⬤ Grease a 9-inch, 23 cm cake tin and double-line with
greaseproof paper.

⬤ Rinse crystallised ginger in plenty of hot water to remove
surface sugar, then pat it dry.

⬤ Dice ginger and peel; mix and sprinkle thoroughly with flour
from the measured amount.

🌰 Cream butter, sugar, honey & grated rind.

🌰 Beat eggs together thoroughly with fork and beat into creamed mixture a little at a time.

🌰 Sift flour with spices, beat into mixture; add ginger & peel. If you're using an electric mixer you may need to transfer the mixture to a larger bowl and use a wooden spoon to add the ginger & peel.

🌰 Spoon mixture into prepared tin and bake at 150C, 300F, Gas2. for 3 hours just below the middle of the oven.

🌰 Test to check that it's done. A skewer stuck deep into the cake will come out clean.

🌰 When cool, turn out of tin and wrap loosely in fresh greaseproof paper and store in an airtight plastic box rather than a metal tin which may rust.

🌰 Pierce the cake with a skewer here and there and sprinkle with a couple of tablespoons of rum once a fortnight or so. The aim is to soften the cake rather than dissolve it.

🌰 About four days before you need the cake, put marmalade and lemon juice together in a cup in the microwave for half a minute. Stand the cake on more greaseproof paper; brush its top and sides with the mixture, leaving any large lumps of orange peel behind in the cup.

🌰 Measure the height of the cake and its diameter: dust work surface with ordinary icing sugar and roll out the marzipan to a circle an inch wider than the diameter plus twice the circumference. Apply the rolled marzipan to the cake - you'll have to make a few tucks or trim it here and there along the sides. Its main function is to prevent the body fluids of the cake leaking into the icing. Leave it 24-48 hours to dry, then make up the royal icing following the instructions on the packet and leave it at least a day to dry before cutting the cake. It looks less like a geographical feature if you pin a broad decorative ribbon round its sides.

Appendix 3

Wassails Reported 2012 - 2013

This list draws together all wassails reported as happening either in 2012 or 2013, by county. No attempt to indicate date has been made. Our researches suggest that many wassails are arranged at quite short notice, often at weekends as this offers the best chance of drawing a crowd. A number of events change weekends each year, to best relate to either 5th or 17th January, or to enable organisers to book preferred performers. A small number of wassails take place in the run up to Christmas or during the Christmas period, and the 'Wassail Season' is also gradually extending into early and mid February. Wherever possible postcodes are provided for SatNav reference together with contact telephone numbers. Please check the internet or contact organisers before attending.

Where wassails appear in the text of this book, Chapter no.s are shown in brackets after listings e.g.(2,6) = Chapters 2 & 6; In = introduction; Ep = epilogue.

BEDFORDSHIRE
Dunton, Nr Biggleswade, SG18 8RR: Church Farm, 7.00pm 01767 316124

BERKSHIRE
Bracknell, RG12 2RX: Lily Hill Park, 5.30pm 01344 354000
Bracknell, RG12 2LU: OBJ Wassail, The Boot, Park Road, 12 noon 01344 454532 (5)
Cold Ash, RG18: Community Orchard , afternoon 01635 200907
Bracknell Forest, RG42: Jealott's Hill, Warfield Walk 'n' Wassail 1.30 pm 01344 457777 (5 & 8)

BIRMINGHAM
Cotteridge Park, B30 2HG: Franklin Rd, Cotteridge, 2.30pm 07876 757018 (8)
Highbury Orchard, B13 8QG: Yew Tree Road, Moseley, 3.30pm 0121 242 1845 (8)
King's Heath, B14 7DB: Community Garden, Heathfield Road, 1.00pm 0121 464 6717

BRISTOL
Hengrove and Stockwood Neighbourhood Orchard, (8)
Horfield, BS7 8JP: Horfield Organic Community Orchard, King's Drive, Bishopston, 2pm (8)
Kingswood, BS15 9SE: Grimsbury Farm. Grimsbury Road, nr Baden Road, 4.15pm 0117 960 5140
Shirehampton, BS11: Tynings Field, Woodwell Road 1.00pm (8)
Bristol, Avon BS2 9YJ: St Werburgh's City Farm, Watercress Road, 12 noon 0117 9 42 8241 (8)
Thornbury BS35 2AB, The Barrel, St Mary St, 01454 413592
Bitton, BS30 6EX: Willsbridge Mill, 2.00pm 0117 932 6885 (8)

BUCKINGHAMSHIRE

Chesham, HP5: Lowndes Park Community Orchard, 10.30 a.m.

Stowe MK18 5EQ: Landscape Gardens, New Inn Farm, 2.00pm, 01280 817156 (6& 8)

CAMBRIDGESHIRE

Great Gidding , PE28 5NT Wassailing and Cider 7.00pm (7)

Trumpington, CB2 9JP: Community Orchard, Foster Road. 2:30 pm
trumpingtonorchard@yahoo.co.uk (8)

CHESHIRE

Stretton, nr Malpas, SY14 7JA: Stretton Watermill, Mill Lane 4pm 01606 271640

CORNWALL

Bodelva, PL24 2SG: Eden Project Wassail, Private ceremony for gardeners 01726 811911 (6)

Bodmin, PL31 2DB: Traditional house visiting wassail, Mount Folly, 12 noon 01208 76373 (In,2,4,7)

Rillaton, Callington, PL17. Evening (7)

Penzance, TR20 8TE: Polgoon Winery, Rosehill, 6.00pm 01736 333946

Saltash, PL12 6TA: Cotehele orchards, St Dominick, 11.30am 01579 351346 (6)

Truro, TR3 6QL: Trelissick Gardens, Feock, 5.00pm, 01872 862090 (6)

CUMBRIA

Kendal, LA8 8DB: Crook Morris Wassail, Lyth Valley Hotel, Lyth, 1.00pm 01539 568233 (5)

Threapland, CA7: Varnycrooks Orchard, afternoon, info@riversmeet.org

DERBYSHIRE

Bonsall, DE4: afternoon

Chesterfield, S40 4BP: Inkerman Park, Ashgate Rd, 2.30 p.m. 01246 345735

Ripley, DE5 9TE: Waingroves Community Centre, 2.00pm 01773 749064

DEVON

Barnstaple, EX32 7NF: Ostler's Cider Mill, Goodleigh, evening 01271 321241

Bere Ferrers, PL20: Church Hall, 6.30 pm, 01752 299700 (7)

Blackdown Hills, EX15 3RJ: Hemyock Castle, evening, admin3@hemyockcastle.co.uk

Bovey Tracey, TQ13: Dartmoor National Park, B3387 Eve 01364 661520 (5)

Branscombe, EX12 3DA: Primary School, 6.00pm. 01297 680339 (7)

Crediton, EX17 4LW: The Lamb Inn, The Square, Sandford, 7.00 p.m. 01363 773676

Dunkeswell, EX14: House visiting ceremony followed by midnight visit to orchard, evening (In,2,4,7)

Exeter, EX4 7JU: Mincinglake Orchard, Calthorpe Road, Beacon Heath, 3 p.m. 01392 205800

Exeter, EX4 4EP: The Old Firehouse 50 New North Rd, Exeter, 7.30 p.m. 01392 277279

Lympstone, EX8 5BE: Sowden House, 7.00pm (7)

Paignton, TQ3 1RN: Occombe Farm, Preston Down Road. 4.45pm 01803 (8)

Plymouth, PL7 1UH: Saltram House, 6.00pm 01752 333503

Princetown, PL16 0JL: Roadford Outdoor Centre Broadwoodwidger, Lifton, 6.30pm 01566 771930

Stoke Gabriel, TQ9 6SE: Village Orchard, Paignton Road, 4.30pm 01803 782394 (4)

Tiverton, EX16 8RE: Bickleigh-on-Exe Primary School Bell Meadow, Bickleigh, 01884 855357 (7)

Topsham, EX3 0HR: The Globe, Fore Street, 7.00pm 01392 873471

Torbryan, TQ12 5UR: Old Church House Inn, 8.00pm, 01803 812372 (4,5)

Torrington, EX38 8QA: Yarde Orchard: 6.30pm 01805 624007
Whimple, EX5 2TA: New Fountain Inn Church Road 6.30pm 01404 822350 (2,4,7)
Yelverton, PL20 6EY: Buckland Abbey, 3 pm 01822 853607

DORSET

Bridport, DT6: Community Orchard, South Street, (behind St Mary's Hall) 10.00am 01308 458480 (8)
Buckland Newton, Dorchester, DT2 7BY: 9.30am 01300 345393
Dorchester, DT1: Railway Orchard off Monmouth Road, 2.00pm 07760 313305
Enmore Green, Shaftesbury SP7: Donkey Field Community Orchard (8)
Lyme Regis, DT7 3QA: Lyme Regis Museum, Bridge Street, at 3.00pm 01297 443370 (5)
Piddle Valley First School Piddletrenthide, DT2 7QL: Daytime 01300 348219
Tolpuddle, DT2 7ES: Martyr's Inn, Main Road, 7.00pm, 01305 848249 (7)

ESSEX

Duton Hill, nr Thaxted, CM6 2DX: The Three Horseshoes, 8.00 pm 01787 462731 (5)

GLOUCESTERSHIRE

Arlingham, GL2 7JJ: Wick Court. Overton Lane, 7.00pm 01452 741023 (6)
English Bicknor, Coleford, GL16: Community Orchard, evening.
Hartpury, GL19 3DB: Perry Pear Orchard Centre, Blackwell's End, 7.00pm 01531 828330
Lydbrook, GL17 9PA: Ragmans Lane Farm, Bishopwood, 4-6.00pm 01594 860244
Newland, Forest of Dean, GL16 8NP: Ostrich Inn, 8.00pm 01594 833260 (5)
Painswick, GL6: Orchard Group Wassail, 5pm, 01452 812879 (6)
Stroud, GL5 5NG: The Lawn, Selsley Rd, North Woodchester, 6pm 01453 756955
Stroud, GL6 0PE: Horsley Orchard Project, Tickmorend House, Horsley, 4.00pm, 01453 833699
Thrupp, GL5: 5pm thrupporchard@googlemail.com
Winchcombe, GL54 5PB: Hayles Fruit Farm, Broadway Road, Hailes, 3.00pm, 01242 602123
Woodchester, GL5 5EQ: Orchard Pastures at 4.00pm then the Ram Inn, Station Road, 01453 873329
Wotton-under-Edge, GL11 6DL: Eley's Orchard, Dursley 1.30pm 07970 637 449
Wotton-under-Edge, GL12 8UG: Townsend Orchard, Tytherington, 2.30pm 01454 411739 (6)

HAMPSHIRE

Bursledon, SO31 1BH: Manor Farm Country Park, 01489 787055 (6)
Durley, SO32 2BT: Wickham Morris,. Farmers Home, Heathen Street, 7.00 pm 01489 860 457 (5)
Hartley Wintney, RG27 8NY: Waggon & Horses, High St, Hook. 7.00pm 01252 845152 (5,7)
Hook, RG27 9NN: Allotments, afternoon 01252 642444

HEREFORDSHIRE

Bromyard, HR7 4QS: Queen Elizabeth Humanities College, Ashfields 7.00pm 01885 482230 (7)
Ledbury, HR8 2RG: evening, different venue each year 01531 670263
Leominster Morris Wassail: different orchard each year, evening 01568 720426 (4,5)
Ludlow, SY8 4LW: The Cliffs, Little Hereford 3.00pm, 01584 819030
Much Marcle, HR8 2NQ: Weston's Cider, 7.00pm, 01531 660233(4,6)
Preston on Wye, HR2 9JT: The Yew Tree Inn, 6:30pm 0871 951 1000
Ross-on-Wye HR9 6QG: Broome Farm, Peterstow, 6.30pm 01989 567232 (4,6)

HERTFORDSHIRE

Bishops Stortford, CM23 2NG: Beerfordbury pub tours, British Legion, Windhill 01279 653284 (2,5)
Croxley Green, Rickmansworth, WD3 3HN: 6.30 p.m. 01923 778677
Sawbridgeworth, CM21 9AH: Rivers Nursery Orchard, 6.30 pm 07887 763258 (8)
Shenley, WD7 9DW: Shenley Park, Radlett Lane, at 6.30 pm 01923 852629 (8)
St Albans, AL1 1SQ: Watercress Wildlife Association, Riverside Road 2.00pm

ISLE OF WIGHT

Freshwater, PO40 9XR: The Apple Farm Orchard, Afton Park, 4.00 pm 01983 755774 (6)

KENT

Faversham: Kent Cider Co, Wassail or Yowling (invitation only), 07738 573818 (6)
Keston, BR2 6BQ: The Fox. Heathfield Road Keston, 8pm 01689 852053 (5)
Marshside, Canterbury, CT3 4EB: Gate Inn, evening 01227 860498
New Ash Green, Longfield, DA3 8JB: New Ash Green, 4.45pm 07810 503995
Woodchurch, nr Tenterden TN36: late morning / afternoon 01233 860861

LANCASHIRE

Lancaster, LA1 5ED: Fairfield Millennium Orchard, Sunnyside Lane, 3.00pm
Ramsbottom, BL8 4HS: Incredible Edible, Hollymount School, Bury 1.30 p.m. 07564 991071

LEICESTERSHIRE

Donisthorpe, DE12: Engine PH Church Street 6.30 pm 01530 271038
Ratby, LE6 0JR: The Railway Inn, 191 Station Road, 7.30 p.m. 0116 239 5808

LINCOLNSHIRE

Cleethorpes, DN35 9ND: Crow's Nest, Balmoral Road, 3.30 pm 01469 540378
Louth, LN11 7DH: Skidbrooke Cider Company, The Grange, 11.00am. 01507 339368 (5)
Stamford, PE9 1HS: Community Orchard, Christ Church Close, off Green Lane, eve, 01780 484180

LONDON

Bankside, SE1: 12.45pm arrival of The Holly Man & 12th Night celebration 0780 325 1936 (4,7,Ep)
Brockley, SE4: Hilly Fields Community Orchard 4.00pm (8)
Claybury Park, Redbridge, IG6 2GQ: off Stalham Way jamie@thelondonorchardproject.org. (8)
Eltham SE9 4QF: Eltham College Grove Park Road, 7.30pm 020 8857 1455 (7)
Enfield, Middlesex EN2 9HA: Forty Hall Community Orchard, Forty Hill, 3.30pm. 07912 327936
Ferry Lane, N17 9NG: Ferry Boat Inn 5.30 pm 020 8808 4980
Greenwich, SE10 0LB: Pleasaunce, Chevening Road, 11.30 a.m. 07833 538143 (8)
Hackney, E8: Community Orchard, Hackney Downs, 12 noon, 07970 573870
King's Cross, NW1 0PF: 110 Camley Street, 5.00pm 020 7833 2311 (8)
Rotherhithe, SE16 4LF: Brunel Museum, Railway Avenue, 6.30 p.m.
Walthamstow, E17 9NH: The Vestry House Museum, Vestry Road 2.30pm 020 8496 4391 (7)
Willesden, NW10 2SF: Tube Station, Walm Lane, 2.30pm 020 8937 3400 (8)

MONMOUTHSHIRE

Chepstow, NP16 5EY: Wassail and Mari Lwyd. Three Tuns, Bridge St, 3.30pm 07870 611979 (4,5)
Llanarth, Usk, NP15 2LU: Raglan Cider Mill, Tynewydd Farm, 5.30 pm 01600 780253

NORFOLK

Kenninghall, NR16: Kenninghall Lands Trust, Kenninghall Wood. 4.30pm 01953 887424 (4)

Norwich, NR3 3AQ: The White Lion, 73 Oak Street, evening 01603 632333

NORTHAMPTONSHIRE

Daventry, NN11 2JB: Daventry Country Park, Northern Way, 12 noon

Northampton NN1:Wilson's Orchard, Magnolia Close, off Billing Road East, 4.30pm 01604 630719 (6)

Sulgrave, OX17 2SD: Sulgrave Manor, nr Banbury, 11.00am 01295 760205 (6)

NOTTINGHAMSHIRE

Nottingham, NG3 5FW: St Ann's Community Orchard. Ransom Road, 2.00pm 0115 911 0207 (8)

OXFORDSHIRE

Bloxham, OX15: Pig Pen Pottery, Old Bridge Road 4.00 pm 01295 721630

Chipping Norton. OX7 5XS: Elmsfield Paddock, Worcester Road 11.00am, 01608 659750

SOMERSET

Bath, BA1 7LR: Broadlands Orchardshare, Box Road, 3.00pm 07532 472256 (8)

Bath, BA2 0QF: Radford Mill Farm, Timsbury, from 4.00pm 01761 479391

Bath, BA1: The Orchard, Broadmoor Lane, Weston at 7.00pm

Blagdon: BS40 7SB: New Inn Park Lane, then Eldred's Orchard, 12 noon, 01761 462475 (4)

Carhampton, TA24 6LP: Butcher's Arms, Main Road, 7.15pm 01643 821333 (In,3,4,6,7)

Chew Magna, BS40 8SZ: Woodbarn Farm, Denny Lane, 2.00 p.m. 0845 617 1174

Clevedon BS21: Community Orchard, off Brookfield Walk 3.00pm, then to Old Inn

Compton Dando, BS39 4JZ: Parish Hall, Court Hill Road, 6.00pm 01761 490955

Curry Rivel, TA10 0EZ: House visiting & Burning the Ashen Faggot, King William IV, High St,
      01458 259200 (In,2,4,7)

Drayton: Traditional house visiting wassail (private village event) (In,2,4,7)

Dunster, TA24 6SD: Buttercross Community Orchard 7.45pm 01643 822315 (7)

Frome, BA11 1JA: 4 Gentle Street, 1 p.m. 01373 474532

Glastonbury, BA6 9EL Abbey Wassail Magdalene Street, 01458 832267 (members only)

Glastonbury, BA6 8DB: Rural Life Museum, Abbey Farm, Chilkwell Street. 7.30pm 01458 831197 (6)

Highbridge: Rich's Farmhouse Cider, Mill Farm, Watchfield, 7.00pm 01278 783651

Highbridge, TA9 4BE: West Croft Cider, at the foot of Brent Knoll. 6.30pm 01278 760762 (4,6)

Hutton, BS24 9SE: Wood View orchard, Moorcroft Road, 6.00pm, 01934 814409

Ilminster, TA19 0NQ: Barrington Court, 5.30pm 01460 241938

Ilminster, TA9: Shepton Cider Mill, Stewley Orchard (invitation only) 8.00pm 0844 875 1513 (4,6)

Keinton Mandeville, TA11 7pm Keinton Mandeville Village Hall 07889 130495

Kingston Seymour, BS21: Village Hall 7pm

Nailsea, BS48 2PF: The Old Farmhouse Pub, East End, 7.00pm 01275 851889

North Wootton, BA4: Mid Somerset Show Wassail Evening, 7.00 pm, Village green orchard

Pill, BA4: Candle-Lit Wassail, Orchard, Watchhouse Hill, Ham Green 5 pm

Porlock,TA24 8QB: Dovery Manor Museum 6.30pm. Village event touring orchards 01643 863150 (2,7)

Portishead, BS20 6:30pm-7:30pm Community Wassail Weston Moor Orchard, Weston-in-Gordano

Priston, near Bath BA2: 2.45pm 01761 453 565

Radstock, BA3 5TD: Kilmersdon Village Hall, 12.30pm 01761 436767

Rooksbridge BS26 2TG: Orchard Barns 7.00 pm 01934 750255

Sandford, BS25 5RA: Thatcher's Cider (private), Station Road, 7.00 pm 01934 822862 (6)

Somerton, TA11 6BZ: Barton Inn, Barton St David 8.00pm 01458 850451 (7)

Taunton, TA1: Frieze Hill Community Orchard, path from Staplegrove Road 5.30pm, 01823 352512 (8)

Tintinhull, Nr Yeovil, BA22 8PZ: Crown and Victoria, 14 Farm St, 01935 823341

Wedmore, BS28 4TE: Bagley Community Orchard, Snake Lane, 4.00pm 01934 713660

Wedmore BS28 4TU: Wilkins' Cider Wassail, Mudgley, 7.00pm 01934 712385 (6)

Westbury-sub-Mendip, BA5: Old Ditch Farm, Stoke Road, 7.30pm

Wincanton, BA9 8DG: The Stags Head Inn, Pound Lane, Yarlington, 7.00pm 01963 440393 (7)

Wrington, BS40 5SA: Barley Wood Walled Gardens, Long Lane, 7.00pm 01934 863713 (8)

Yeovil, TA15 6XP: Montacute House 6.00pm 01935 823289

STAFFORDSHIRE

Stoke-on-Trent, ST12 9AA: Duke of York Inn, Longton Rd, Barlaston, 9.30pm 01782 373316 (7)

Whittington, WS14: Community Orchard, Jubilee Park, Vicarage Lane at 4pm 01543 432238

Wolseley Bridge near Rugeley, ST17 0WT: Staffordshire Wildlife Trust at, 3.00 pm

SURREY

Carshalton, SM5: Carshalton Jack Frost, Wassail tour of pubs admin@strawjack.co.uk (7)

Haslemere, GU27 2HU: Swan Barn Farm, Collards Lane, 6pm 01428 652359

Leatherhead, KT22 8BZ: The Running Horse, 38 Bridge Street 8.00 p.m.
        bagman@ewellmorris.co.uk

Limpsfield, RH8: Community Orchard. 7.00 p.m. 01883 712312

Redhill, RH1 5PW: Outwood Post Mill, Gayhouse Lane, 7.00pm (7)

SUSSEX

Bolney, RH17 5SE: Old Mill Farm, Cowfold Road, 6.00pm 01444 881356 (In,4,5,8)

Hastings, TN34 3BJ: The Stag Inn 14 All Saints' St, 01424 425734 final stop on visiting tour (2,5)

Pevensey, BN24 5ET: Stone Cross Nurseries Dittons Road, 5: 30pm

Rudgwick, RH12 3JJ: Sports and Community Centre, Rudgwick Howl info@rudgwickcider.com

Rye, TN31 7SY: The Royal Oak, Rye Foreign, Peasmarsh. 7.00pm 01797 230494 (7)

Sompting, BN14 7NJ: The Vine, Tarring High Street, 5.00pm 07779 722809

Waldron, TN21 0RA: Long Man Morris Wassail, Star Inn 8.00pm 0871 951 1000 (4)

West Sussex RH20: Different orchard each year with Broadwood Morris Men,
        bagman@broadwoodmorris.info

WARWICKSHIRE

Alcester, B49 5JA: Coughton Court (NT) 4.30pm and 7.30pm 01789 400777

Coventry, CV3 3GW: Brandon Marsh Nature Reserve, 3.30pm 024 7632 8785

Coventry, CV8 3LG: Ryton Gardens, Wolston Lane, 11:00am 02476 303517 (7)

Long Itchingdon, CV47 9QJ: The Duck on the Pond, The Green, 11.00am 01926 815876 (In, 2, 5)

WILTSHIRE

Bradford-on-Avon, BA15 1AQ: Woolley Grange Orchard, 5 pm 01225
Lacock, SN15 2LG: Lacock Abbey, 7pm – 8.30 pm 01844 249895
Marlborough, SN8: 3.30 pm (Ep)
Wroughton, SN4: Moat Pond, then Bowls Club, 6.00 pm 01793 813766

WORCESTERSHIRE

Alvechurch, B48 7SQ: Weighbridge Inn, Scarfield Wharf. 7pm 0121 445 5111
Bewdley, DY12 2EL: Gardeners Meadow daytime 01299 405516 (Ep)
Colwall Green, WR13 6ED: Yew Tree Inn, Walwyn Road, at 6.00pm 01684 540498 (4,7)
Cookley nr Kidderminster, DY11 5YL: Fox's Morris, The Anchor, Caunsall 7.15pm 01562 850254 (5)
Evesham, WR11 7JE: The Fleece, Bretforton, 6.30 pm. 01386 831173 (5)
Redditch, B97 4LB: Headless Cross, Rocklands Social Club, Birchfield Road, 7.00pm, 01527 544356 (8)
Stourbridge, B60: Tardebigge Cider in Tutnall.
Upton on Severn, WR8 OSA: Clive's Fruit Farm, Upper Hook Road, 12 noon, 01684 592664

YORKSHIRE

Hull, HU4: Pickering Road Community Orchard Cranberry Way, Hull. 2.00pm 01482 503577
Leeds, LS4: All Hallows in Burley 7.00 p.m. 07858 129 331.

WALES

Cardiff CF11 9JP: Riverside Community Gardens, Pontcanna Fields, 12.00, 0845 122 1176
Holywell, Flintshire CH8 7: Basingwerk Abbey, Greenfield Valley Heritage Park, 01352 714172
Llantwit Major, South Glamorgan CF61: 2.00 pm 07804 624795
Penarth, S. Glamorgan CF64 5UY: Cosmeston Lakes Park, Lavernock Road 2.00 pm, 029 2070 1678 (8)

SCOTLAND

Comrie, Perthshire PH6: Community Orchard, Cultybraggan Camp, 3.00pm
emargrett@comrie.org.uk (8)
Edinburgh, Midlothian EH10: Rudolf Steiner School, Spylaw Road, 4.00pm 0131 337 3410
Edinburgh, Midlothian EH15 1NA: Donkeyfield Orchard, Bailleyfield Road, Portobello
        12 noon, 0131 258 4483 (7)
Megginch Castle, Perthshire: 2pm – 5pm 01738 787278

Bibliography

Alford, Violet (1978): The Hobby Horse and other Animal Masks

Anonymous (1859) The Christmas Book: Christmas in the Olden Time: Its Customs and their Origin

Arthur, Dave (2012): Bert – the Life and Times of A. L. Lloyd

Baring Gould, Sabine (1908): Devon Characters and Strange Events

Beamont, W. O. (1920): the Apple Tree Wassail - A Survival of a Tree Cult

Bere, Charles (1861): A Garland of Songs

Bell, Robert (1857) Ballads and Songs of the Peasantry of England

Boase, Wendy (1976): The Folklore of Hampshire

Bourne, Henry (1775): Antiquitates Vulgares

Bord, Janet and Stuart (1982): Earth Rites: Fertility Practices in Pre-Industrial Britain

Bradtke, Elaine (1999): Truculent Rustics: Molly Dancing in East Anglia before 1940

Brand, John (1813): Observations on Popular Antiquities

Briggs, Katharine (1974): Folklore of the Cotswolds

Broadwood, John (1843) Old English Songs

Broadwood, Lucy and Fuller-Maitland J. A. (1890), English County Songs

Bourne, Henry (1725): Antiquitates Vulgares or the Antiquities of the Common People

Bullen A. H (1885): A Christmas Garland.

Bushaway, Bob (1982): By Rite: Custom, Ceremony and Community, 1700 -1880

Cater, Colin (2009): A Penny for the Ploughboys

Cater, Karen (2007): Ogham Sketchbook

Chambers, Robert, (1864): The Book of Days

Chappell, William (1838): English National Airs

Clifford, Sue and King, Angela (2007): The Apple Source Book

Clifford, Sue and King, Angela (2006): England in Particular

Clifford, Sue and King, Angela (2008): Community Orchards Handbook

Courtney, M. A., (1890): Cornish Feasts and Folklore

Davies, Gwilym (2011) www.gloschristmas.com

Dearmer, Percy, Shaw Martin and Vaughan Williams, Ralph (1928): Oxford Book of Carols

Devonshire Association (1876): Report & Transactions of Vol 8

Dixon J. H (1846): Ancient Poems, Ballads and Songs

Doel, Fran & Geoff (1992): Mumming, Howling & Hoodening - Midwinter rituals in
                    Sussex, Kent & Surrey

Fletcher H.L.V. (1968): Portrait of the Wye Valley

Forrest, John (1999): The History of Morris Dancing 1458 - 1750

Fosbrooke T. D. (1807): Abstract of Records respecting the County of Gloucester, formed into a History

Frazer, James G. (1890): The Golden Bough

Geoffery of Monmouth (1140): History of the Kings of Britain

Goddard, Sean (2001): We'll wassail bees and apple trees: Apple Howling in Sussex, EDS Vol 63, No 1

Green, Marian (1980): A Harvest of Festivals

Green, Miranda (1995): Celtic Goddesses. British Museum Press

Greig, Rauridh (1988): Seasonal house visiting in South Yorkshire, University of Sheffield

Halliwell, James Orchard (1849): Popular Rhymes and Nursery Tales

Hasted, Edward (1797): The History and Topographical Survey of the County of Kent, Vol. 2

Herrick, Robert (1591-1674): Ceremonies of Christmas Eve

Henderson, William (1879): Notes on the folk-lore of the northern counties of England and the borders

Hole, Christina (1976): Dictionary of British Folk Customs. Hutchinson

Hone, William (1825 and 1827): The Every Day Book,

Hone, William (1832): Ancient Mysteries Described

Hone, William (1832): The Year Book of Daily Recreation and Information

Horsfield, T. W. (1827): The History and Antiquities of Lewes and its Vicinity, Sussex Press

Hutton, Ronald (1991): The Pagan Religions of the Ancient British Isles

Hutton, Ronald (1994): The Rise and Fall of Merry England

Hutton, Ronald (1996): The Stations of the Sun, Oxford University Press

Irving, Washington (5th Ed.1886): Old Christmas – From the Sketch Book of Washington Irving pp.132-5

Judge, Roy (1979): The Jack in the Green

Karpeles, Maud (1973, revised 1987): An Introduction to English Folk Song

Kennedy, Peter (1975): Folksongs of Britain and Ireland

King, Gregory (1696): Natural & Political Observations & Conclusions upon the State & Condition of England

Latham, Charlotte (1878): Some West Sussex Superstitions lingering in 1868, Folk Lore Record 1

Leather, Mrs Ella Mary (1912): Folklore of Herefordshire

Lloyd, A.L. (1967): Folk Song in England

Malcolmson, Robert (1973): Popular Recreations in English Society 1700 - 1850

Northall, G. F. (1892): English folk-rhymes, a collection of traditional verses relating to
            places and persons, customs, superstitions, etc

Owen, Trefor M. (1991): Customs and Traditions of Wales

Palmer, K. and Patten, R. W. (1971): Some Notes on Wassailing and Ashen Faggots in South and
            West Somerset, Folklore Vol. 82, No. 4 pp. 281-291

Palmer, Kingley (1976): Folklore of Somerset.

Palmer, Roy (1994): Folklore of Gloucestershire,

Pegg, Bob (1981): Rites and Riots: Folk Customs of Britain and Europe.

Polwhele, Richard (1816): History of Cornwall

Radford Edwin and Radford, Mona (1949): Encyclopedia of Superstitions

Rickert, Edith (1914) Ancient English Christmas Carols, 1400-1700 p. 243

Roud, Steve (2006): The English Year

Roud, Steve (April 2012): verbal communication, Bures, Suffolk

Russell, James (2011): Wassail for beginners, internet blog

Sandys, William (1847): Festive Songs and Carols

Sandys, William (1852): Christmas-tide

Sawyer F. E. (1883): Sussex Fiolklore and Customs connected with the Seasons

Sharp, Cecil and Marson, Charles (1904): Folk Songs form Somerset:

Sharp, Cecil (1909): Folk Songs form Somerset, Vol 5

Sharp Cecil (1907): English Folk Songs – Some Conclusions

Sharp Cecil (1920): English Folk Songs, with pianoforte accompaniment

Simpson, Jacqueline (1976, revised 2003): Folklore of the Welsh Borders

Stewart, R. J. (1990): The Underworld Initiation

Stone, Benjamin (1905): Sir Benjamin Stone's Pictures: Festivals, Ceremonies and Customs

Stubbes, Philip (1583): Anatomie of Abuses

Taylor, Ellen (2003): An investigation into the Custom and Practices of Wassail

Thiselton Dyer T F ((1876): British Popular Customs Present and Past

Thiselton Dyer T F (1889: Facsimilie reprint 1994) The Folk-Lore of Plants

Train, J. (1845): Historical and Statistical Account of the Isle of Man

Tylor, E. B. (1871): Primitive Culture

Wales, Tony (1968): Field and Furrow

Wallis, Kathy (2013): Private communication dated 19.02.13

Whiteway, E. V. M. (1990): Whiteway's Cyder: A Company History

Willey G. R. (1978): The wassail Tradition at Curry Rivel, Folklore Vol. 89, No. 1 pp. 60-65

Wooders, Jameson (2013): Private communication dated 14.05.13

Index

Colin Cater was born in Stourbridge, West Midlands in 1943. Most of his youth was spent in Bristol, in Penarth, South Wales and in Harrogate, North Yorkshire. He trained as an historian in the 1960s, later immersing himself in Sociology researching an earlier published work. A lifelong folk enthusiast he is a singer, event organiser, Morris Dance musician, ceilidh band player, author, songwriter and regular participant in traditional ceremonies in Essex; with Good Easter Molly Gang on Plough Monday; at Thaxted Morris Weekend, and the Duton Hill Wassail; also at 'Hunting the Earl of Rone', Combe Martin, North Devon. In 1997 he formed the design and giftware company Hedingham Fair with his artist wife Karen, to illuminate and illustrate all things 'folklore' particularly as they happen in current time. As the editor of the Hedingham Fair Calendar of Traditional Customs (annually since 2001), Colin has researched traditional customs widely; balancing customs with long provenance with movements and events originating in contemporary times. Much research has been active, going to; Abbots Bromley Horn Dance, Olney Pancake Race, Allendale Tar Barrels, Marshfield Paperboys, Whimple Wassail, Eastbourne Lammas Fair and many others. Selling cards, T-shirts and gifts takes him to folk festivals including Sidmouth, Whitby, Chippenham, Towersey, Bromyard etc. Talking to everyone he rubs shoulders with gives him a

feel of what 'doing it' is really like for them, personally.

In 'Wassailing – Reawakening an ancient Folk Custom' Colin has combined this first hand knowledge with his history and sociology background, to examine the development, decline and reawakening of wassailing customs through an extended period of several centuries and amongst an ever changing background of social events and people participating in the ceremonies. Colin now lives in Essex with Karen, where, apart from running Hedingham Fair and writing, he organises Duton Hill Folk Club, sings and plays melodeon and concertina for Blackmore Morris and at music sessions around East Anglia.

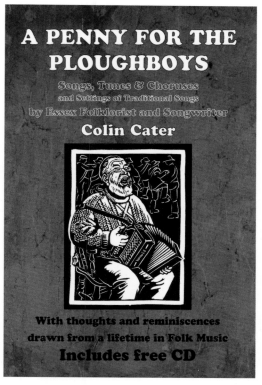

also by the same author
A Penny for the Ploughboys
Book & CD

This book contains a fascinating account of Colin's experience as a singer around the folk song club scene from the early days of the 1960s revival ; how the thinking of folkies developed about the meaning of 'tradition' and the problems faced by later folk fans as the theories did not always match up with what people saw happening around them.

Colin examines the reality of the folk process and offers an alternative view of how tradition could be reinterpreted and made more relevant in the 21st century.

The CD contains 15 tracks including the 'Duton Hill Wassail Song' and 'A Penny for the Ploughboys', Colin's song about Molly Dancing and the turn of the year, popularised by Pete Coe and recently described as 'a classic', now rapidly becoming included into 'traditional' repertoir.
All the songs are either written by Colin Cater or are traditional songs that he has re-visited and updated.

The recording also features Mary Humphreys & Anahata, Dave Holland and Karen Cater.

Available from www.hedinghamfair.co.uk

ISBN 978-0-9556475-1-2

Hedingham Fair's annual
Calendar of Traditional Customs

including

Calendar customs, public and religious holidays,
folk music festivals, folklore, commentary on featured
events, contact details for event organisers,
and much more!

Available from

www.hedinghamfair.co.uk